BERLITZ®

DISCOVER
ROME

Edited and Designed by
D & N Publishing,
Lambourn, Berkshire.

Cartography by
Hardlines, Charlbury, Oxfordshire.

Phototypeset by Wyvern Typesetting, Bristol.

Printed in the USA by Ringier America, New York.

Although we have made every effort to ensure the accuracy of all the information in this book, changes occur incessantly. We cannot therefore take responsibility for facts, addresses and circumstances in general that are constantly subject to alteration.

Acknowledgements

The author would like to thank the following for their help and support during the writing of this book: Roberto d'Onorio and Giuseppina Zampetti, Luigi Coppé and the staff of the Rome Tourist Board, Isabella Faraoni, Alessia Fontana, Michael Gilmartin, Linda Glenn, Janet Roberton and Sally O'Shaughnessy.

Front cover photograph: Trajan's Column (Berlitz Publishing Co Ltd)
Back Cover Photograph: St Peter's Basilica (Jason Best)

Photographic Acknowledgements

All photographs by the author except the following which are courtesy of: The Bridgeman Art Library, p224; The Hulton Picture Company, pp57, 58, 60,125; Intra-Film, p43; The Italian State Tourist Office (ENIT), London, pp70, 93, 213 (top and bottom), 221, 225. The following photographs © Berlitz Publishing Co. Ltd: pp9, 11, 50, 55, 62, 106, 122, 136, 158, 171, 231, 240;

 The Berlitz tick is used to indicate places or events of particular interest.

BERLITZ®

DISCOVER
ROME

Jason Best

Contents

ROME: FACTS AND FIGURES

A Fleeting Glimpse of the Eternal City

"Seductive beyond resistance", is how the American author Henry Adams found Rome. It's easy to agree. The city's sights and sounds, even its smells, all conspire to intoxicate the senses, while contemplation of all those centuries of history and art can make the visitor positively giddy. So don't resist: let yourself succumb to the Eternal City's everlasting charm.

Rome, the Eternal City, has been attracting foreign visitors for centuries. They've come as slaves and as traders, for plunder or for pilgrimage: for over 2,000 years the self-styled *caput mundi*, head or centre of the world, has been exerting its own form of gravitational pull.

People have been writing guidebooks about the place for almost as long. As early as the 6th century AD pilgrims had specially written books to

*P*agan and Christian merge in the Forum. The ancient Sacred Way points to the church of Santa Maria Nova, while behind looms the ruined hulk of the Colosseum.

direct them to the sites of the city's holy relics and shrines. Medieval tourists flocked to see the pieces of the True Cross that St Helena had brought back from the Holy Land or the arrows which had pierced the body of St Sebastian.

What should the visitor head for today? There are the obvious destinations: the great ancient monuments, the Pantheon and the Colosseum; the great churches, St Peter's and the other patriarchal basilicas; the famous public spaces, like the Spanish Steps and Piazza Navona; the great art treasures, from the Sistine Chapel ceiling in the Vatican to the classical sculptures on the Capitoline. There's the extravagant Baroque genius of Bernini to revel in, and the earthy realism and dramatic

*H*igh culture at
street level.

chiaroscuro of Caravaggio. There's the
High Renaissance purity of the Raphael Stanze to appreciate, or the Rococo
exuberance of the Trevi Fountain.

Then there are the more out-of-the
way places and pleasures to explore,
like the old working-class district of
Testaccio, where a man-made hill
formed by centuries of discarded amphorae rises above the shell of Rome's
disused slaughterhouse. After a visit
there, go and hear Brazilian music in
a club across the Tiber in Trastevere,
or sample French cuisine in a restaurant run by French nuns that's housed
in a 16th-century papal palace.

Pagan and Christian, classical and
medieval, Renaissance and Baroque,
all Rome's different eras merge together—in the words of the Italian film
director Federico Fellini—like "a giant
plate of fettucini". Enjoy!

Passports and Visas

Passports are required by citizens of
the EC, USA, Canada, Australia and
the Republic of Ireland wishing to enter Italy. (British citizens may also enter on a Visitor's Card.) No visas are
required for visits of under three
months. Those wishing to stay longer
must arrange for a *permesso di sog-
giorno* (permission to stay), obtainable
from a local police station (*Questura*).

By law visitors are obliged to register with the police within three days of
entering the country. If you are stay-
ing at an hotel this procedure is taken
care of for you, if not you are supposed to register yourself. In Rome
there is a special Police Information
Office which gives assistance to tourists
and has interpreters available (Tel.
4686 ext. 2858 or 2987). You are
legally obliged to carry your passport
with you at all times in Italy.

*T*he Emperor Trajan marked his victories in Dacia with this giant column, designed by the great architect Apollodorus and decorated with spiralling reliefs illustrating the campaign.

When To Go

Rome's main tourist season runs from Easter to the end of September and the city's climate is at its most agreeable in spring and autumn. At Easter the city is packed with pilgrims, as it has been for hundreds of years; accommodation is hard to find, and tourist sites and restaurants are crowded. In July and August the temperature can go as high as 35–36°C (95–97°F), making it foolhardy to toil around the sites in the midday sun, but the balmy evenings can be extremely pleasant. If you do go in high summer, take refuge in the middle of the day (most sites and churches will be closed anyway), take a siesta and emerge refreshed later on. In August Rome becomes something of a ghost town, particularly after **Ferragosto** (15 August), as Romans desert the city for the beach en masse. Most shops, bars, restaurants and cinemas are then closed but the city's summer arts festival, **l'estate Romana**, which runs from June to September, ensures that there are some things to do and see for those who remain behind. October can be a good time to visit the city, with mild days and cool evenings, not to mention fewer tourists, but it's also Rome's rainiest month. The Roman winter is relatively mild but it can be wet and in January and February the temperature may drop to 0°C (32°F).

Average Monthly Temperatures in °C (°F)	
January	7.4 (44)
February	8.0 (46)
March	11.5 (52)
April	14.4 (57)
May	18.4 (64)
June	22.9 (73)
July	25.7 (78)
August	25.5 (78)
September	22.4 (72)
October	17.7 (63)
November	13.4 (56)
December	8.9 (48)

Average Monthly Rainfall in Millimetres (Inches)	
January	74 (3)
February	87 (3½)
March	79 (3)
April	62 (2½)
May	57 (2)
June	38 (1½)
July	6 (½)
August	23 (1)
September	66 (2½)
October	123 (5)
November	121 (5)
December	92 (3½)

Public Holidays

New Year's Day—*Capodanno*
6 January (Epiphany)—*La Befana*
Easter Monday—*Lunedi di Pasqua*
25 April—Liberation Day
1 May (May Day)—*Primo Maggio*
15 August (Assumption)—
  Ferragosto
1 November (All Saints')—*Ognisanti*
8 December—Immaculate
  Conception
25th December (Christmas Day)—
  Natale
26 December (Boxing Day)—*Santo Stefano*

In addition, Rome has a local holiday on 29 June, the Feast of Saints Peter and Paul, the city's patron saints. (For additional feasts and festivals *see* A YEAR IN ROME.)

Time
Italy is one hour ahead of Greenwich Mean Time. Italian Summer Time runs from the last weekend of March to the last weekend of September.

Getting There

By Air
Travellers on scheduled flights arrive at Leonardo da Vinci Aiport, more commonly known as Fiumicino, 32 km (20 miles) south-west of the centre of Rome. Charter flights arrive at Ciampino, a military airport, 18 km (11 miles) south-east of the city.

From Fiumicino Airport to the City
Trains operate between Fiumicino airport and Roma Ostiense railway station at frequent intervals (varying from 15 to 30 minutes). Services from Fiumicino to Roma Ostiense run from 6.25 a.m.–1.00 a.m.; and from Roma Ostiense to Fiumicino from 5.30 a.m to 11.30 p.m. The journey takes 22 minutes and currently costs 1,800 lire. Roma Ostiense station connects with the Piramide stop on Metro line B, which takes you into the city centre.

Buses: there is no longer a bus service from the airport to the city.

Taxis: there is a taxi rank outside the airport's arrivals hall. Only use the official yellow taxis and be wary of the unofficial taxi drivers who solicit foreigners and comprehensively overcharge their passengers (official taxi drivers do not solicit fares). Standard fares are comparable to those in London but the metered price is misleading—there are always extras. Expect to pay supplements for each piece of luggage, night service (10 p.m to 7 a.m.), Sundays and public holidays. There is also a fixed supplement for the trip to and from the airport (note that the journey from the city to the airport is more expensive).

The journey from airport to city takes around 30–40 minutes. Radio Taxis: Tel. 3570/3875/4994/88177.

From Ciampino Airport to the City

ACOTRAL run a bus service from the airport to the Anagnina stop on Metro line A, which takes you into the centre of the city (note that the Metro closes at around 11.30 p.m.). A taxi journey into the city should take 20 minutes.

By Train

Eurotrain offers discounts of up to 40 per cent on fares in Europe to travellers under 26. Tickets are valid for two months and allow unlimited stopovers *en route*. Another possibility is a Rome Explorer ticket, which allows stopovers on a round trip that passes through half a dozen countries. For information contact Eurotrain Italy, Via Nazionale 66, Rome: Tel. 06-46791.

For those under 26 whose travel plans are more ambitious, an Inter-Rail card is valid for a month and gives unrestricted travel in 24 countries in Europe and the Mediterranean. A similar Inter-Rail Senior card is available for the over-60s. In the UK the card is only available for those who have been resident in the country for at least six months. Those resident outside Europe and North Africa can obtain a EurRail pass which gives unrestricted first-class travel for periods of

The evocative ruins of Ostia Antica, Rome's ancient seaport, are easily reached by train.

between 15 days and 3 months. Note that the pass must be purchased before travelling to Europe. (For information on reductions on Italian Railways *see* GETTING AROUND—BY TRAIN.)

By Car

If you are driving to Italy you must have a valid national driving licence, your vehicle's registration certificate and a translation of your driving licence (available from British motoring organizations or at ACI frontier offices). A translation is not needed if you hold a pink EC-type driving licence. If the car you are driving is not your own, you must have the owner's written permission to drive the vehicle. Third-party insurance is compulsory. Green Card insurance is not compulsory for EC citizens but is strongly recommended.

*T*wo friends put their heads together on top of the Dome of St Peter's.

Routes

All roads may lead to Rome but the main one is the Autostrade del Sole, which runs the length of Italy, thigh to toe, from Milan to Reggio Calabria (north of Rome it is the A1, south of Rome, the A2). On the outskirts of Rome it joins the GRA (*Grande Raccordo Annulare*—the city's ring road). From the GRA follow the signs into the city. Alternatively, if you are driving down the coast, the A16 follows the Tyrrhenian shore from Civatavecchia (72 km [45 miles] N) to Rome. The AA provides a computerized routes service to its members and can tailor a route to your requirements, whether you want to get there fast or go the scenic way.

Currency

The Italian monetary unit is the *lira* (plural *lire*, often abbreviated to L, placed before the amount). Notes are issued for 500, 1,000, 2,000, 5,000,

10,000, 20,000, 50,000 and 100,000 lire. Coins are 5, 10, 20, 50, 100, 200 and 500 lire. The first three coins are practically worthless and you may find yourself given sweets in place of very small change, particularly in supermarkets.

Credit Cards

The major credit cards (American Express, Visa, Access, Diner's Club, Eurocard, Mastercard) are accepted in most shops, restaurants and hotels, but not at petrol stations.

Exchange

You can change foreign currency and traveller's cheques at most banks. Hotels will change currency but at a significantly less favourable rate. There are two Bureaux de Change (*Cambio*) offices in the Stazione Termini which stay open until late, one in front of the platform entrances, the other in the underground halls.

The American Express offices in Piazza di Spagna also has an exchange facility but be prepared for long queues at the weekend.

Getting Around

By Bus

Strap-hanging on a crowded bus that is crawling through rush-hour traffic, glumly watching pedestrians casually outstripping you, this is not one of Rome's most rewarding experiences.

On Foot Around Rome
The best way of getting to know the city intimately is to go about on foot. As capital cities go, Rome is fairly compact. Many of the major sites occupy a comparatively small area and in some cases, now that large areas of the centre have been made traffic-free zones, on foot is the only way to reach them.

That said, remember that Rome was built on seven hills and has since embraced several more. Distances can sometimes be deceptive, particularly when you are walking beside the Tiber, and the Roman sun can sap the most ardent of walkers.

Take care of the traffic: Roman drivers have little respect for the highway code and even less for those on foot. (Not for nothing is the Italian word for "pedestrian", *pedone,* the same as that for "pawn".) Don't automatically assume that cars will stop at traffic lights or pedestrian crossings. On some of Rome's wide boulevards you may have to cross the road lane by lane with Rome's hectic traffic hurtling past you on either side.

Good areas to explore on foot, well away from the traffic, include the Medieval Quarter, around Piazza Navona and the Pantheon; the Renaissance Quarter, around Palazzo Farnese and the Campo dei Fiori; the nearby Ghetto; Trastevere; and the Aventine Hill; not to mention Rome's many beautiful parks and gardens, like the Villa Borghese, Villa Celimontana and Rome's largest green space, the Villa Doria Pamphili.

But, used intelligently, Rome's ATAC bus system can open up the city, take you to places off the beaten track and save on shoe leather.

The best bet is to buy an ATAC bus network map and one of the weekly season tickets for tourists (*abbonamenti settimanali per turisti*). This is valid for the entire day and night bus network (except line 110—the sightseeing bus) and the Metro for seven days, including the date of issue. The tickets currently cost L.10,000, the maps L. 1,000; both are available from the ATAC kiosk in Piazza dei Cinquecento (outside Stazione Termini).

Alternatively, you may buy tickets for each single journey (*corso semplice*) or, slightly cheaper, in blocks of ten. Another type of ticket is valid for half the day on the entire ATAC network (either 6.00 a.m to 2.00 p.m. or 2.00 p.m. to 12.00 a.m.). A *biglietto integrato* (BIG) lets you travel all day on buses and the Metro, plus urban trains and some out-of-city ACOTRAL buses. All tickets are available from tobacconists, bars and newspaper kiosks.

A ticket must be bought before you board the bus—there are no conductors. Get on at the rear of the bus and punch (*convalidare*) your ticket in the machine near the door. When you want to get off, alight by the central doors. The door by the driver is for those with passes (*tessere*). Watch out for pickpockets on crowded buses, particularly on the tourist routes, and be prepared for sudden strikes that may only last a few hours but can leave you stranded in some remote location for the duration.

ACOTRAL buses are bright orange and services run from 5.30 in the morning to around midnight, with a regular night service (*Servizio Notturno*) on many routes (indicated on the bus stop signs). *Capolinea*, incidentally, means the end, or head, of the line.

> **Rome's Romantic Trams**
> Rome still has a handful of trams, including the delightful Route 30 tram, which circles around the city and takes in many of the main tourist sites on the way, including two museums, the Zoo, three of Rome's pilgrimage churches, the Colosseum, the Circus Maximus and the cemetery where Keats is buried.
>
> The trams may look rickety and romantic but they are built like tanks and woe betide any car which gets in their way. Traffic lights with right-hand turns have white lines to indicate where it is safe to pull up. Not so long ago, a sleek BMW unwisely overhung the line. The coming tram didn't stop but sheared off the front part of the car. Only then did the tram driver stop. He got out, went back to the wreck, paused thoughtfully and then laconically remarked, "*Quella era una bella macchina*" ("That was a beautiful car").

By Metro

Rome's Metro system, the Metropolitana, has two lines. Line A, opened in 1980, runs from Anagnina, in the south-eastern suburbs of the city, to Ottaviano, just north of the Vatican. The older Line B runs from Rebibbia in the north-east of the city through Stazione Termini to EUR in the south-west (last stop Laurentina). Some trains branch off at Magliana and go on to the coast, reaching Ostia Antica and Lido di Ostia. Stations are identified by a large red sign containing a white letter "M". Trains run from 5.30 a.m. to 11.30 p.m.

The Metro can be just as crowded as the buses but it's a much quicker way of getting about, if the site you wish to visit is on one of the routes. Buy your tickets (same cost as for the

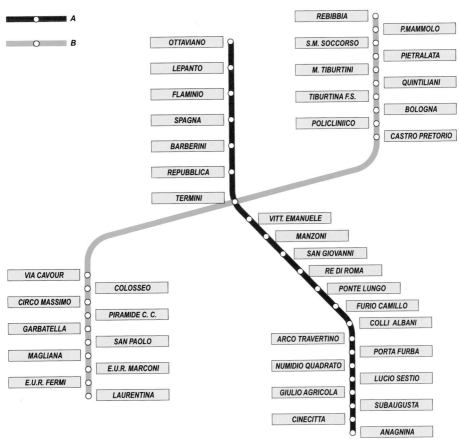

A

B

OTTAVIANO	REBIBBIA
LEPANTO	P.MAMMOLO
FLAMINIO	S.M. SOCCORSO
SPAGNA	PIETRALATA
BARBERINI	M. TIBURTINI
REPUBBLICA	QUINTILIANI
TERMINI	TIBURTINA F.S.

REBIBBIA
P.MAMMOLO
S.M. SOCCORSO
PIETRALATA
M. TIBURTINI
QUINTILIANI
TIBURTINA F.S.
BOLOGNA
POLICLINIICO
CASTRO PRETORIO

OTTAVIANO
LEPANTO
FLAMINIO
SPAGNA
BARBERINI
REPUBBLICA
TERMINI

VITT. EMANUELE
MANZONI
SAN GIOVANNI
RE DI ROMA
PONTE LUNGO
FURIO CAMILLO
COLLI ALBANI

VIA CAVOUR
COLOSSEO
CIRCO MASSIMO
PIRAMIDE C. C.
GARBATELLA
SAN PAOLO
MAGLIANA
E.U.R. MARCONI
E.U.R. FERMI
LAURENTINA

ARCO TRAVERTINO
PORTA FURBA
NUMIDIO QUADRATO
LUCIO SESTIO
GIULIO AGRICOLA
SUBAUGUSTA
CINECITTA
ANAGNINA

*R*ome's Metro system, the Metropolitana.

buses) beforehand from tobacconists or newspaper kiosks; inside the stations they are only available from machines (which take 50, 100, 200 and 500 lire coins). The weekly season tickets and the daily **BIG** ones described above for the buses are also valid on the Metro.

By Taxi
Only use the licensed bright yellow taxis (beware of cowboy drivers who tend to pounce on unwary foreigners at the airports and main railway station—official taxi drivers do not solicit fares). Expect to pay supplements for luggage, night service (10 p.m. to 7 a.m.), Sundays and public holidays.

Radio Taxis: Tel. 3570/3875/4994/88177.

By Bicycle and Scooter
Bicycles can be hired by the hour, day or week from Collati, Via del Pellegrino 82 (near Piazza Campo dei

15

Fiori), Tel. 6541084; I Bike Roma, Villa Borghese Car Park (lower level, third sector), Tel. 3605240, open every day, including holidays, 9 a.m. to 8 p.m. Scooters and bicycles can be hired from Motonoleggio, Via delle Purificazione 84 (near Piazza Barberini), Tel. 465485, open all week 9 a.m. to 7.30 p.m. Scooters can also be hired from Scoot-a-long, Via Cavour 302, Tel. 6780206, open all week 9 a.m. to 7 p.m.

By Carriage

Carrozzelle, horse-drawn open carriages, can be found at many of the major tourist sites across the city, including Piazza San Pietro (St Peter's), the Colosseum, Piazza Venezia, Piazza Navona, Piazza di Spagna, Trevi Fountain, Via Veneto and Villa Borghese. Rides can be taken for a half-hour, one hour, half-day or whole day. Prices are expensive and should be agreed with the driver in advance.

*B*ike Roma!
Freewheeling through the Villa Borghese.

Boat Trips

For information on boat trips on the Tiber contact EPT, Via Parigi 5, Tel. 463748.

By Train

The cost of train travel in Italy has been rising in recent years but still represents a bargain when compared with prices in many other countries. If you are planning to do a good deal of travelling within Italy you should consider buying one of the reduced-rate travel passes available from Italy's state railway, the FS (*Ferrovie dello Stato*).

Tourists are eligible to buy special Travel-at-Will tickets (*Biglietto turistico libera circolazione*, or BTLC). These tickets are valid for periods of 8, 15, 21, and 30 days and allow unlimited

travel on the entire Italian state rail network, including the fast *Rapido* trains, which normally require the payment of a supplement. The tickets are available in 1st and 2nd class, with half price for children under 12.

The Flexi Card is similar to the Travel-at-Will tickets but, as its name suggests, more flexible and a good deal cheaper. It allows unlimited travel up to a certain number of days within a set period: 9 days (4 days travel); 21 days (8 days travel) and 30 days (12 days travel). Another option is the *Chilometrico* ticket, which can be used by up to five people at a time but requires the payment of supplements on some trains.

In Britain these passes are available from CIT, Marco Polo House, 3–5 Lansdowne Road, Croydon, Surrey (Tel. 081-686 067) and Wasteels Travel, 121 Wilton Road, London SW1 (Tel. 071-834 7066). In the US contact Italian State Railways, 66 Fifth

A restful moment for the drivers of Rome's carrozzelle—and their horses.

Ave, New York, NY 10103, Tel. 212-397 2667. In Rome itself they are obtainable from the Termini Station.

A word is required on Italy's bewildering categories of trains. In declining order of speed and luxury they are: *Super Rapido Inter City*, including EC (*Eurocity*) and TEE (*Trans-Europe Express*)—fast and luxurious air-conditioned trains running between the major cities, 1st class only, seat reservation obligatory and supplement payable. *Rapido*—fast trains running between main towns, supplement payable, sometimes 1st class only and compulsory seat reservation. *Espresso*—long-distance express trains stopping at main stations, usually extremely crowded. *Diretto*—slow trains stopping at most stations. *Locale—*

even slower, stops at every local station, right down to the proverbial three-chickens-and-a-dog railway halt.

Take care of which category of train you catch, particularly if making a long journey. The TEE/Eurocity train between Rome and Milan takes 4 hours, the Espresso gets there in 8 hours.

Italy's trains are a great way to see the country and provide a chance to meet a fascinating cross-section of Italian society: sleek businessmen on the *Rapidi*; whole families travelling the length of the country on *Espressi*, filling entire compartments and armed with provisions to feed an army, while nuns and soldiers sit side by side in the corridors without; sun-tanned teenagers going to the beach on *Locali* and *Diretti*.

At the Station

Long-distance journeys start at Rome's Termini Station, where the queues are truly interminable. The ticket-issuing system is hopelessly inefficient and the ticket clerks often rude and unhelpful when, after perhaps waiting for half an hour or more, you find yourself at the head of the queue. If you are going to pay by credit card (Visa is accepted) make sure you inform the clerk before he or she issues the ticket.

To avoid the queues and bother, get your tickets in advance from an authorized travel agency (one displaying the FS—*Ferrovie dello Stato*—logo).

Guided Tours

Guided sightseeing tours and out-of-town excursions are provided by American Express (Piazza di Spagna 38, Tel. 67641), Appian Line (Via Veneto

---

Caesar ad sum Traffic Jam
In 45 BC Julius Caesar banned all chariots, carts and other wheeled vehicles from the city centre during daylight hours in an effort to cure ancient Rome's chronic traffic congestion. Rome's traffic problems haven't changed, the city is still choked to the point of suffocation. The Roman authorities today haven't gone quite as far as Caesar yet, but since 1988 large areas of the historic centre have been made no-go zones for private cars.

Rome's traffic jams don't just affect the present-day city, they are having a catastrophic impact on the past. The exhaust fumes of cars have caused more damage to ancient monuments in the last 25 years than all the air pollution of the previous 2,000. The faces of statues have been eaten away, reliefs dissolved and marble turned into limestone by the fumes. According to the Commune di Roma Health Department, levels of sulphur dioxide, nitrogen dioxide and carbon monoxide are all ten times the maximum limit. Hence the scaffolding and protective green netting on many monuments.

84, Tel. 464151) and CIT (offices at Termini Station, Tel. 4740923; head office Piazza della Repubblica 68, Tel. 47941).

Rome's bus company, ATAC, provides an inexpensive sightseeing tour which takes in many of the major tourist sights. ATAC bus 110 leaves the Piazza dei Cinquecento every day at 3.30 p.m. (in winter, only on Saturdays, Sundays and holidays, at 2.30 p.m.). The trip takes approximately 3 hours and costs around a quarter of the more up-market tours. Tickets from the ATAC office in Piazza dei Cinquecento.

By Car

Driving in Rome should only be contemplated by the cool of nerve and the even of temper. Roman traffic is chaotic and Roman drivers reckless. They are also quick-witted but prone to break every rule in the highway code, from jumping traffic lights to overtaking on the hard shoulder of the autostrada. Given these habits and the crowded driving conditions, it comes as no surprise to note that almost every car with ROMA licence plates has its share of dents and scratches.

Roman drivers have sharp reflexes and, as everyone is behaving the same way, the system seems to work, give or take the odd bump and scrape. But it only takes the introduction of a faint-hearted non-Italian driver obeying a different set of driving rules to throw the system out completely.

Car Hire

Hiring a car in Italy is expensive compared with other countries. It may be easier and more economical to arrange car hire in advance, as part of a fly-drive package like the Alitalia-Avis Jetdrive scheme, for example. The major international hire firms have branches at Rome's two main airports, at Termini Station and throughout the city. To hire a car, drivers must be at least 21 years old and have held a driving licence for at least a year.

Avis
Piazza Esquilino 1
Tel. 4701216
Via Sardegna 38/a
Tel. 4701228
Fiumicino
Tel. 601579/601531

Ciampino
Tel. 7240195
Stazione Termini
Tel. 4701219.

Hertz: offices at Fiumicino, Ciampino, Termini, Central Booking Tel. 547991.

Maggiore: Italy's leading car-hire firm, offices at Fiumicino, Ciampino, Termini, Central Booking Tel. 8541620.

Crime and Police

Follow the usual precautions you would expect to take in any big city.

Beware of pickpockets in busy street markets and on crowded buses and the Metro. Be particularly careful of gangs of very young gypsy children, who will often crowd around you begging for money and surreptitiously relieve you of your wallet or purse. A favourite technique is for one child to thrust a piece of cardboard at you while a companion ducks beneath to rifle your pockets. Be warned, these artful dodgers have very nimble fingers. Shoo them away at the first opportunity.

Unaccompanied women may find themselves pestered by Italian men. Their attentions are mostly for show: an annoyance rather than a genuine threat. At night, however, women should avoid walking alone outside the well-lit and populous centre. As a rough guide, the further away from the city centre you are, the more care you should take. Particular areas to avoid at night are around Stazione Termini and the Baths of Caracalla (the haunt

A couple of carabinieri *pose in a side street between the Corso and Piazza di Spagna, Rome's fashion district. Effortlessly stylish, they even had Giorgio Armani design their summer uniforms.*

of prostitutes, as is testified by the scorched marks in the pavement left by the bonfires they light at night to keep warm).

Heroin addiction is a serious social problem in Italy and you may notice spent needles on the ground in the more out-of-the-way parks. Provided you are not going about barefoot this should not present any problems.

Terrorism (of the left- and right-wing varieties) was a grave problem during the 1970s and early 80s, the so-called *anni di piombo*—the "years of lead". It has now, to all intents and purposes, disappeared and is no longer a serious consideration: largely thanks to the successes of a prolonged and vigorous police campaign.

Serious crimes like terrorism are handled by the *Carabinieri*, who are technically a part of the Italian army. Their uniform is dark blue with a red stripe. General crime is dealt with by *La Polizia* (uniform: navy blue jacket, light blue trousers; headquarters: *La Questura*). Traffic problems in the city are handled by the *Vigili Urbani* (white jackets, navy blue trousers and white helmets). Policemen and women speaking a foreign language wear badges on their left arms indicating the languages spoken.

Hotels

Rome has been playing host to travellers for centuries—from footsore medieval pilgrims to 18th-century aristocrats on the Grand Tour—and this experience is reflected in the wide range of hotels on offer today. At the top end are the opulent and palatial Luxury 5-star hotels on the Via Veneto patronized by jet-setting celebrities; at the bottom are the humble *pensioni* around the station favoured by the backpack crowd. In between, there is something for just about everyone else.

When choosing a hotel decide whether your prime consideration is close proximity to the major sites or guaranteed peace and tranquility. Early-morning traffic noise is somewhat less of a problem now that daytime traffic has been banned from large areas of the historic centre, but pick a room with a view and you may find a gang of Roman youths furiously revving their motor bikes and mopeds beneath your window at one in the morning.

The Italian State Tourist offices abroad (ENIT) will supply on request a copy of the annually updated brochure listing all the hotels in Rome and its surroundings (*Alberghi di Roma e Provincia*). In Rome itself, the city's EPT information offices in Via Parigi, at Fiumicino airport and at the main rail station provide assistance with details of hotel accommodation but are generally very hard pressed in the summer. The EPT also has information offices at the (Roma-Nord) Salaria service area on the A1 autostrada and at the (Roma-Sud) Frascati service area on the A2 autostrada.

Opening Hours

Banks: 8.30 a.m. to 1.30 p.m. 3–4 p.m. (Afternoon hour may vary from bank to bank.) Closed Saturdays, Sundays.

Exchange Offices: 9 a.m. to 1.30 p.m., 4.30–8 p.m. Closed Sundays.

Churches: generally open 7 a.m. to 12 noon, 4–7 p.m. The larger basilicas, such as St Peter's, stay open all day.

Museums: Most museums are only open in the mornings, typical hours 9 a.m. to 1 p.m., sometimes 2 p.m., with shorter hours on Sundays and holidays. Usually closed Mondays.

Open-air sites: 9 a.m. to 1 hour before sunset. When you plan your sightseeing, try to take advantage of the few museums with longer opening hours, such as the Capitoline Museums, which are also open on Tuesdays from 5–8 p.m., and on Saturdays 5–8 p.m. and 8.30–11 p.m.)

Petrol Stations: 7 a.m. to 12.30 p.m., 3–7/7.30 p.m.

Chemists: 8.30 a.m. to 1 p.m., 4.30–8.00 p.m. Closed Saturday afternoon and Sunday. To find chemists open at night and on holidays, phone 1921 or check the notices displayed by all chemists. Late-night chemists in central Rome: Farmacia della Stazione, Piazza dei Cinquecento 49/51; Farmacia Internazionale, Piazza Barberini 49; Farmacia Doricchi Valori, Via XX Settembre 47; Farmacia Piram, Via Nazionale 228.

Post Offices: 8.a.m. to 2 p.m., Saturdays 8.30 a.m. to 12 noon. (*See* POST AND TELEPHONE SERVICES.)

Restaurants: usually 12 noon/1–3 p.m., 7.30–11 p.m. Some stay open later, particularly in summer. Closed one day a week.

Shops: 9 a.m. to 1 p.m., 4–7.30 p.m. Closed Sundays and Monday mornings (Saturday afternoons in summer).

Food shops 8 a.m. to 1.30 p.m., 5–7.30 p.m. Closed Thursday afternoons in winter and Saturday afternoons in summer.

Street Markets: generally open Mondays–Saturdays 6 a.m. to 2 p.m.

News stands: Rome has a number of all-night news stands dotted about the city, where half an hour after midnight you can buy the first edition of the next day's Italian morning papers.

In the Summer, after *Ferragosto* (15 August), Romans perform a mass exodus from the city and most shops, restaurants and cinemas close for the rest of the month. Rome's daily newspapers, such as *La Repubblica*, publish up-to-date lists of those chemists and petrol stations which remain open.

Spoilt for choice. Magazines galore in a news stand in Piazza della Rotonda.

Post and Telephone Services

Central Post Office: Palazzo delle Poste, Piazza San Silvestro, Tel. 6771. Open 8.30 a.m. to 9 p.m. Saturdays 8.30 a.m. to 12 noon. The Telegraph Office is open 24 hours a day (Tel. 6795530).

Branch offices are open 8.30 a.m. to 2 p.m. Saturdays 8.30 a.m. to 12 noon. Postage stamps can be bought from tobacconists (*tabacchi*: look out for the sign of a white "T" in a black rectangle). Italy's postal service is notoriously slow but an alternative exists in the shape of the Vatican's postal service, which is admirably efficient and puts the State system to shame. There are offices in St Peter's Square and in the Vatican Museums (open until 7 p.m., Saturday 6 p.m.). In summer you will find a blue-and-white Vatican post-office van in the square. The Vatican's post boxes are blue; ordinary pillar boxes are red.

Telephones

Telephone boxes are still somewhat thin on the ground but you can make calls from many bars (look out for the telephone symbol—feel free to make calls inside a bar without the obligation to buy a drink). Some bars will have phones you can use that register the cost of the call on a counter by the cash register where you should pay after having made your call.

New style telephone boxes accept 500, 200 and 100 lire coins, and phone cards (5,000 and 10,000 lire—available from newspaper kiosks and bars, and from vending machines). The minimum cost of a local call is 200 lire.

Some of the old-fashioned telephones—particularly those you may encounter in bars—only accept telephone tokens, called *gettoni* (worth 200 lire each). *Gettoni* are obtainable from bars, newspaper kiosks, etc., and are also valid as ordinary coinage.

International dialling codes: Great Britain 00 44; Canada 00 1; USA 00 1; Australia 00 61; New Zealand 00 64. Phoning Italy from the UK: 010 39; from USA/Canada: 01139. Rome code 06. (Remember to omit the first 0 of the city code if phoning Rome from abroad.)

Telephones with the word "*teleselezione*" allow you to make direct international calls to the UK, USA and most western European countries. If you make a long-distance call in a hotel expect to be heavily surcharged.

You can make long-distance and international calls (as well as receive calls by appointment) from a number of telephone exchange offices:

ASST. Stazione Termini. Office in main ticket hall: open 24 hours. Office on lower level: open 8 a.m. to 12 midnight.

*T*he Barcaccia Fountain in Piazza di Spagna is designed in the form of a leaking boat.

ASST. Central Post Office, Piazza San Silvestro: open 8 a.m. to 12 midnight. ASST. Post Office, Viale Mazzini: open Mondays–Fridays 8 a.m. to 9 p.m. Saturdays 8 a.m. to 2 p.m. ASST. Post Office, Via di Porta Angelica: open Mondays–Fridays 8 a.m. to 9 p.m. Saturdays 8 a.m. to 2 p.m. SIP. Corso Vittorio Emanuele: open 8 a.m. to 9.30 p.m. (including Sundays). SIP. Villa Borghese (exit of Spagna Metro station): open Mondays–Saturdays 8.30 a.m. to 8.45 p.m. Fiumicino Airport. ASST: open 24 hours. SIP: 8 a.m. to 8.45 p.m. (including Sundays).

A view from the Pincio of one of Rome's finest squares, the Piazza del Popolo.

Cheap-rate times for international calls. Europe: 10 p.m. to 8 a.m. (all day Sunday). Outside Europe: 11 p.m. to 8 a.m. (all day Sunday). Overseas Operator: 170; International Operator (European and Mediterranean countries): 15; Directory Enquiries (Italy): 12.

Advice to Visitors with Disabilties

Italy unfortunately lags behind many other European countries in the provision of public facilities for people with disabilities. However, there are signs that things are slowly changing. In 1991 wheelchair-accessible symbols appeared for the first time on leaflets issued by the Rome Tourist Board (EPT).

There are lavatories for people with disabilities at both main airports, Stazione Termini, and Piazza San Pietro. St Peter's and the Vatican Museums are wheelchair-accessible but these are still the exceptions rather than the rule. Hotels with facilities for guests with disabilities are listed in the EPT's multi-lingual brochure of hotels, *Alberghi di Roma e Provincia*.

Holidays and Travel Abroad—A Guide for Disabled People is published by RADAR, 25 Mortimer Street, London W1N 8AB (071-637 5400).

Driving in Italy

Drivers in Italy must carry a red warning triangle (which can be hired from ACI frontier offices). The triangle should be placed about 50 m (at least 550 yd) behind the car in the case of a breakdown. A set of spare bulbs is recommended. It is illegal in Italy to carry petrol in cans in a vehicle.

Foreign drivers can buy a concessionary package of Italian petrol coupons (which offer a discount of about 15 per cent on pump prices) and a motorway toll card. The Fuel Card (*Carta Carburante*) that is issued with the package makes you a temporary member of the Italian Automobile Club (ACI) and enables you to call upon its emergency services (incorporating a free breakdown and replacement car benefit). ACI Breakdown Service, Tel. 116. The package may be purchased from Wasteels Travel (121 Wilton Road, London SW1, Tel. 071-834 7066) and from the AA and RAC in the UK and at ACI frontier offices (in foreign currency only). The package is only available if you are driving a foreign-registered car, not if you are hiring a car in Italy itself.

Autostrade

Almost all Italian motorways are toll roads. The charge (payable in Italian lire) varies according to the distance travelled and the horsepower of the vehicle. Toll stations (*pedaggi*) do not accept credit cards. Tickets are issued at entrance control points, often automatically (*Premere qui*: push here; *Prendere biglietto*: take ticket). Keep your ticket and give it up at the exit control point when you leave the motorway. Keep a good supply of change for any automatic tolls you may encounter. A pass called "Viacard" can be used on the majority of Italian motorways and is obtainable from Italian Automobile Association offices, Touring Club offices, and at some large motorway petrol stations and service stations (in denominations of 50,000 and 90,000 lire).

Highway Code

Seatbelts: the wearing of seatbelts has been compulsory in Italy since May 1989 (but the Italians are still finding it hard to adjust to the law, so don't be surprised if you see scores of seatbelt-less drivers).

Drinking and driving: it is illegal to drive if the level of alcohol in the bloodstream is 0.08 per cent or more (another new law with which the Italians are currently coming to terms).

Lights: the use of undipped headlights in towns and cities is prohibited. Dipped headlights are compulsory when passing through tunnels, even if they are well lit.

T he most distinguished profile in Rome: the Dome of St Peter's.

Side mirrors: compulsory on the left-hand of the car.

Speed limits: in built-up areas 50 kph (31 mph); outside built-up areas 90 kph (56 mph). On motorways 110 kph (68 mph) for cars up to 1,099 cc (motor cycles 150–349 cc) and 130 kph (80 mph) for cars over 1,099 cc (motor cycles over 350 cc).

Fines: traffic offences are fined on the spot (the Italian police come down particularly heavily on speeding offences). The police are obliged to hand over a receipt for the amount of the fine paid.

Italian Road Signs

Accendare i fari—Switch on headlights

Banchina non transitabile—Do not drive on the shoulder
Crocevia—Crossroads
Divieto di accesso—No Entry
Divieto di sosta—No Stopping
Entrata—Entrance or turn in
Incrocio—Crossroads
Lavori in corso—Road works ahead
Parcheggio—Parking
Passaggio a livello—Level crossing
Pericolo!—Danger!
Rallentare—Slow down
Senso vietato—One-way street/No entry
Sosta autorizzata—Parking permitted (followed by an indication of times)
Sosta vietata—No Parking
Svolta or *Curva*—Bend
Uscita—Exit or turn out
Vietato ingresso veicoli—No entry for vehicles
Vietato transito autocarri—Closed to heavy vehicles
Zona rimozione—Tow-away zone

Driving in the City

When driving in Rome, be prepared to pull over for official motorcades conveying political bigwigs hither and thither: a dark blue limousine (generally Lancias) flanked by motorcycle police.

At traffic lights expect to encounter foreign immigrants (predominantly North Africans and East Europeans) deftly cleaning windscreens or selling newspapers, cigarette lighters, Kleenex, or flowers in the time it takes the lights to change. You are unlikely to be unduly harassed if you do not display interest in their services.

Never leave anything of value in a parked car: fixed car stereos/radios will vanish in moments (and it's no use hiding a detachable stereo under the driving seat—it's the first place a thief will look). If parking your car overnight try to leave it in a garage or guarded car park, or, at the very least, a well-lit street.

Parking: Romans think nothing of double, even triple, parking but will usually leave their cars unlocked, so they can be moved if you find yourself blocked in.

If you return to find your car missing it may have been towed away by the *Vigili Urbani* (traffic police). Be prepared to encounter red tape and a stiff fine. (Commando dei Vigil Urbani, Via della Conciliazione 4, Tel. 676938.)

Rome's biggest parking space is the underground car park under Villa Borghese (connected with the Piazza di Spagna and the Metro station by a long tunnel).

Fuel: petrol stations with longer than usual opening hours are listed in the newspaper *La Repubblica* on the *"giorno & notte"* page under *Benzina.*

Shopping in Rome

Whether you're interested in hushed and deferential service in exclusive emporia or noisy haggling in a bustling street market, whether it's expensive luxuries you're after or cheap and cheerful bargains: Rome can deliver the goods.

Shopping Districts

The city's most fashionable shopping area is centered on the streets around **Piazza di Spagna**, a district which has acted as a magnet for Rome's visitors since the days of the Grand Tour. Indeed, so popular was the quarter with the English that it was dubbed "the English ghetto" in the 18th century. Today, this grid of streets running between the Spanish Steps and Via del Corso, most of them pedestrianized, is the place to come for Italian high fashion, jewellery, silk and leather.

Via Condotti is the most exclusive of these streets. Here you will find the palatial premises of Bulgari (No 10), Italy's most famous jewellers, while Gucci is at No 8 with its world-renowned range of leather goods and fashion. Across the road is the 18th-century Caffè Greco, haunt of Casanova and Goethe; further down are two fashionable tailors, Battistoni (No 61a) and Cucci (No 67).

Via Borgognona, which runs parallel to Via Condotti, is another elegant

*V*enus in the garden...

high-fashion street with its own share of designer names. Of note is Maud Frizon (No 38), Rome's most celebrated shoe shop, purveyor of expensive, Paris-designed, Italian-made footwear. The neighbouring **Via Frattina** and **Via della Vite** are also good for Italian *alta moda* (high fashion), as are **Via Bocca di Leone** and **Via Mario de Fiori**, which both cross Via Condotti.

Younger fashion can be found along **Via del Corso** in colourful boutiques decorated with wit and panache. American style is a perennial influence in these shops so don't be surprised to see an authentic juke-box or jeep as part of the furnishings.

Via del Babuino, which runs from Piazza di Spagna to Piazza del Popolo, is lined with high-class antique shops and commercial art galleries. Less exclusive antique shops are to be found in **Via dei Coronari** (north of Piazza Navona), a street which once did a thriving trade selling religious objects to the pilgrims on their way to St Peter's. It is the site of an antiques fair each year in May. Picture-framing is the speciality in **Via Margutta**, a traditional artists' street that runs behind Via del Babuino and hosts open-air art exhibitions in the spring and autumn.

Via Nazionale and **Via del Tritone** are streets to try for more affordable fashion, leather goods and shoes, as is the trendy **Via Giubbonari** near Campo dei Fiori. On the other side of the Tiber, **Via Cola di Rienzo** is a good street for quality shopping within walking district of the Vatican.

Specialist Shops

Bises, Via del Gesù 93, has an enormous collection of exquisite silks and fabrics in the splendid setting of a 17th-century palace, the Palazzo Altieri. **Cesari** sells luxurious furnishing fabrics at Via del Babuino 16 and linens at Via Barberini 1. **Bellini**, Piazza di Spagna 77, has expensive, hand-embroidered table linen, sheets and lingerie.

Tupini, Piazza San Lorenzo in Lucina 8, off Via del Corso, is an expensive china shop with beautiful crystal, silverware and hand-painted ceramics. At the other end of the price scale for china and glass is **Stilvetro**, Via Frattina 56. **Myricae**, Via Frattina 36, is a good place to go for regional handicrafts at reasonable prices.

Ai Monasteri, Piazza delle Cinque Lune 76 (off Corso del Rinascimento, near the north-east corner of Piazza Navona) sells the products of Italian monks, including honey, liqueurs, chocolates and olive oil. Try **Amaretto Francescano d'Assisi** or Chartreuse made by the monks of the Carthusian monastery at Farneta near Lucca in Tuscany.

Bookshops

Red Lion Bookshop, Via del Babuino 181, the largest English bookshop in Rome and a few steps from Rome's Anglican church, All Saints.

Economy Book Centre: Via Torino 136 (near the Teatro dell'Opera), for new and second-hand English books.

Anglo-American Bookshop, Via delle Vite 57, a large and eclectic stock of English-language books.

...and in the bathroom. Replica statues in a pair of Roman shops.

Open Door English Bookshop, Via della Lungaretta 25 (in Trastevere).

Rizzoli, Largo Chigi 15 (also entered in Galleria Colonna), the largest book-shop in Italy.

Department Stores

Department stores are something of a rarity in Italy and Rome has nothing remotely approaching a Harrods or a Bloomingdales. Italians prefer to shop at markets and in small specialist shops, of which there are a truly staggering range—indeed, the "nation of shopkeepers" tag would appear to be far truer of the Italians than the English today.

Nevertheless, Rome does have a handful of department stores and they are more likely to stay open all day than the smaller shops (*see* OPENING HOURS).

Coin, Piazzale Appio, near San Giovanni in Laterano (the Metro stop San Giovanni is right outside), Rome's top department store, with good-value clothes, household goods and electrical appliances.

La Rinascente, Coin's main rival, branches at Piazza Colonna (clothes, perfume and accessories) and Piazza Fiume (household goods as well as clothes).

Standa and **Upim** are decidedly downmarket; they sell inexpensive, reasonable-quality clothes and household goods and have branches throughout the city, some of which also sell food.

In Rome you can find shops in the unlikeliest of locations. This one's on the roof of St Peter's.

The most central are Viale Trastevere 60 and Via Cola di Rienzo 173 for Standa, and Via del Tritone 172 and Via Nazionale 211 for Upim.

Arriving daily. Fresh eggs on sale in the food market in Piazza Vittorio Emanuele.

Markets

Piazza Vittorio Emanuele II: mornings Monday–Saturday. Noisy and colourful food market (north side) with all manner of meat, fish, poultry, cheeses, fruit, vegetables and spices. Stalls selling clothes and fabrics on the opposite side. Rome's biggest market.

Porta Portese: Rome's flea market stretches south-west of the Porta Portese, along the Via Portuense towards Stazione Trastevere. Held on Sunday mornings only. New and old clothes, bric-a-brac, small antiques, pets, old cameras, coins and stamps. Get there early if you want to pick up any bargains as this market is extremely popular with Romans. Haggling is half the fun, but be careful of pickpockets.

Via Sannio: Porta San Giovanni in Laterano, mornings Monday–Friday, all day Saturday. Rows and rows of stalls offering all sorts of new and second-hand clothing, including some real bargains.

Via del Lavatore: Lively fruit and vegetable market under the walls of the Palazzo Quirinale.

Piazza Campo dei Fiori: mornings Monday–Saturday. A large, noisy market selling fresh fruit and vegetables, fish and flowers, with colourful stalls nestling beneath the statue of heretical philosopher Giordano Bruno, burned here at the stake in 1600.

Via Trionfale 47/49: (corner of Via Paolo Sarpi). Rome's flower market,

A cornucopia of fruit and veg awaits the Roman diner.

open to the public on Tuesday mornings 10.30 a.m. to 1 p.m.

Via Andrea Doria: (north of the Vatican) mornings Tuesday–Saturday. Large food market.

Largo Fontanella di Borghese: (near Palazzo Borghese) mornings Monday–Saturday. Original and reproduction prints, books and postcards.

Eating in Rome

The glory of Roman cuisine is *la cucina povera*, poor cooking. The city boasts many fine dishes based on such simple ingredients as artichokes, beans, salt cod, tripe, sweetbreads and oxtails. Typical Roman dishes prepared from such fare, and often served in the most exclusive restaurants, include *carciofi alla giudia* (flattened globe artichokes deep fried in oil), *carciofi alla Romana* (artichokes stewed in oil and garlic), *trippa alla Romana* (Roman-style tripe) and *filetti di baccala* (salt cod dipped in batter and fried in oil).

A complete Roman meal begins with *antipasti*, hors d'oeuvre such as salami or *prosciutto crudo* (raw ham).

The next course is *il primo piatto*, and may consist of pasta, rice, *gnocchi* (potato dumplings) or soup. This can often prove the highlight of the meal. Pasta dishes to look out for include *spaghetti alla matriciana* (spaghetti with a sauce made with strips of bacon, chilli pepper and tomatoes, and topped

with grated *pecorino Romano*, a hard and pungent sheep's milk cheese), *spaghetti alla carbonara* (with bacon and eggs), *spaghetti alle vongole* (with clams and tomato sauce) and *penne all' arrabbiata* (pasta quills with a spicy tomato and chilli pepper sauce, "arrabbiata" means "angry"). Another fine *primo piatto* is *stracciatella*, a delicious soup made with eggs, semolina, Parmesan, and broth.

Il secondo is the main meat or fish course and is accompanied by *il contorno*, a vegetable or salad dish, served and eaten on separate plates. Examples of this course include *abbacchio* (roast baby lamb), *involtini ai sugo* (rolled veal cutlets in tomato sauce) and *saltimbocca alla Romana* (rolled slices of veal wrapped around slices of ham and leaves of sage and cooked in white wine), a dish that is said to leap, "*saltare*", into the mouth. A typical accompaniment is *misticanza*, a spring salad of edible weeds, tossed in oil and lemon juice.

The meal concludes with *il dolce* or *la frutta* (sweet or fruit), followed perhaps by coffee and a *digestivo*. Examples include *Grappa*, made from the third or fourth grape pressing, apricot-flavoured *Amaretto* and *Sambuca*, an aniseed-flavoured liqueur drunk with three "flies" (*mosce*), actually coffee beans.

*D*ining all'aperto *in Trastevere.*

Note that meat and fish dishes are sometimes charged *all'etto*, per hundred grammes, which can prove expensive.

Wines

Latium is not one of Italy's best wine-producing regions, certainly not a patch on Tuscany or Piedmont. The Castelli Romani in the Alban hills near Rome produce a number of serviceable white wines, of which Frascati is the most famous. Other white wines include Grottaferrata, Albano and Genzano. Marino and Velletri both produce red wines. The letters DOC (*Denominazione di Origine Controllata*) are not necessarily a great indication of quality. The simple *vino da tavalo* will not necessarily be inferior. Romans often drink their wine diluted with mineral water, either *gassata* (sparkling) or *naturale* (still).

Restaurants

Restaurants in Rome are divided into *ristorante, trattoria* and *osteria*. In theory, these are in descending order of price but a restaurant may call itself a simple *osteria* yet be among the most expensive in the city. At the back of the book is a choice of restaur nts.

Cover Charges and Tipping

A cover charge (*pane e coperto*) and service charge will be included in the bill. Tip the waiter at your discretion (around 10 per cent) but do not tip in family-run establishments.

Restaurants are legally obliged to give you a *ricevuta fiscale*—a bill with the restaurant's tax and IVA (VAT) details. By law, you can be arrested for leaving the restaurant without it. (Remember that in Italy tax evasion is a national pastime.) There are apocryphal stories of restaurants employing someone to accompany departing diners the statutory distance outside the restaurant before retrieving the *ricevuta* so it can then be used again.

Fast Food and Foreign Cuisine

There was an enormous growth of fast-food and ethnic restaurants in Rome during the late 1980s, a gastronomic development which did not please everybody. When Italy's first McDonalds opened in 1986 in Piazza di Spagna there was a storm of protest at this blot on the area and threat to the capital's eating habits. (The restaurant is actually very discreetly situated at the far end of the piazza out of sight of the Spanish Steps, not that all the fast-food joints which followed were quite so tactful.) At the beginning of the decade, non-Italian cuisine in Rome was limited to a few Chinese and Japanese restaurants. Now diners can choose from a veritable United Nations of foreign cuisines, including African, Arab, Korean, Greek, Indian, Lebanese, Mexican, Spanish, French and Austrian.

Bars

During the day Romans tend to use bars as a brief pit-stop. They down a quick coffee and *cornetto* (croissant) and then they are off. They don't stop and linger. Generally, it's only the tourists who are sitting down.

Prices are cheapest if you follow the Romans and drink standing up at the bar. The further you get from the bar, the more the prices increase. They are most expensive if you choose to sit at an outside table. Be prepared, sitting down can triple the cost of your order.

In most busy city-centre bars you will have to pay for your drinks in advance, at the *cassa*, or till, where you will be given a receipt. Repeat your order at the bar and hand over the receipt. It is customary to proffer a small coin as you do so.

There are a bewildering number of ways in which you can order a simple coffee in a Roman bar. The choice is by no means limited to *espresso* or *cappuccino*. Here is a brief guide:

caffè espresso—a small quantity of strong black coffee in a tiny cup

doppio—double quantity

lungo—slightly diluted with hot water

corretto—espresso laced with a shot of spirits

al vetro—in a little glass

macchiato—"stained" with a drop of milk

A bar in Rome isn't just a place for a drink, it's also a stage for the impromptu commedia dell'arte *of everyday Roman life.*

caffè latte—with a lot of milk
latte macchiato—a glass of hot milk
  with coffee added
cappuccino—served with frothed
  milk (this is drunk by Romans for
  breakfast or elevenses and rarely
  at other times of the day; Italians
  look askance at tourists who order
  one after a meal)
cappuccino freddo—iced coffee in a
  glass, a summer speciality.

Refreshing non-alcoholic drinks include a variety of freshly squeezed citrus fruit drinks: *spremuta d'arancia, di limone*, or *di pompelmo* (orange, lemon, and grapefruit). An alternative is a *frullato*, a kind of milkshake made with chopped fresh fruit and milk.

Most bars serve a variety of snacks: *panini* (filled rolls) or *tramezzini* (sandwiches); *tosti* (toasted cheese and ham sandwiches). For English-style toast, ask for *pane tostata* (toasted bread). Some bars have a *tavola calda* serving more substantial quick meals, which can be eaten on the spot or taken away.

The following is a selection of some of Rome's most interesting bars:

Antico Caffè della Pace, Via della Pace. A charming bar with ivy-covered walls not far from Piazza Navona.

Caffè Greco, Via Condotti 86. An historic meeting place for writers and artists for over two centuries, just across the road from Gucci. Founded in 1760 by a Turkish immigrant. Goethe wrote part of his play *Ifigenie auf Tauris* here, Gogol some fragments of *Dead Souls*, while Hans Christian Andersen slept on the first floor (his divan is preserved). Other *habitués* of the café include Casanova, d'Annunzio, de Chirico and Buffalo Bill.

Harry's Bar, Via Vittorio Veneto 150. Those looking for an aftertaste of *la Dolce Vita* should go to this fashionable bar at the top end of Via Veneto. The bar's élite clientele includes a sprinkling of actors and politicians. There is a small and expensive restaurant adjoining the bar.

Sant'Eustachio, Piazza Sant' Eustachio. This famous bar is reputed to have the best coffee in Rome. Your coffee will be already sugared unless you request a *caffè amaro*. Outside the bar is one of Rome's newest fountains, an ancient Roman *vasca* that has recently been rediscovered and restored.

La Tazza d'Oro, Via degli Orfani. A rival to Sant'Eustachio, on the doorstep of the Pantheon. Sit on sacks of

coffee piled against the walls and try one of the bar's specialties, like *granita di caffè con panna* (a scoop of crushed ice flavoured with coffee and mixed with cream).

Babington Tea Rooms, Piazza di Spagna 23. A cool place of repose, next to the bustle of the Spanish Steps, where you can drink Earl Grey or Lapsang Souchong in an atmosphere of sedate Anglo-Saxon gentility. The tea rooms were opened at the end of the 19th century by a Miss Anna Maria Babington.

Ice-cream Parlours

Gelateria della Palma, Via della Maddalena. This popular *gelateria* serves all types of exotic ice cream, including mango and wild strawberry (*fragole dei boschi*). The piano bar is decorated with a quirky *trompe l'oeil* painting depicting illustrious figures from art and history, from the Mona Lisa to Charlie Chaplin, eating ice

*J*ust one cornetto for this customer in Giolitti, Rome's favourite gelateria.

creams at the very marble-topped tables where you sit.

Giolitti, Via Uffici del Vicario 40. Rome's most famous *gelateria* has an equally exotic and mouth-watering range of ice creams. Roman teenagers congregate outside *en masse* on Sunday afternoons.

Entertainment

The constantly fascinating spectacle of Roman life which unfolds before you in the city's streets and piazzas gives new meaning to the term "street theatre". There's nothing Romans, especially young ones, like better to do than to hang about in groups, and their everyday loitering and chatting has a great deal of "performance" about it. The ritual of the *passeggiata*, whereby everyone strolls through the streets before dinner, may not be as noticeable in Rome as in smaller towns and cities, where the streets are packed one minute before eight o'clock and deserted a minute after; in Rome, the presence of thousands of tourists all year round means that the streets are never going to look deserted for long; but the *passeggiata* is still keenly observed by native Romans, particularly along the Corso.

Should you want more structured forms of entertainment then Rome still has much to offer, particularly in summer when *l'estate Romana* fills piazzas and palazzi with music and dance, theatre and film.

Perhaps as a consequence of all that elegant loitering, cutting *una bella figura*, Roman nightlife doesn't really get going until quite late. Nightclubs and discos often don't open until 11 p.m. and even classical music concerts don't start until 9 p.m.

To find out what's going on, consult the supplement *Trovaroma*, published in the Thursday edition of *La Repubblica* newspaper. The monthly *Carnet di Roma* published by EPT in Italian, English, French and German also lists events, as does the fortnightly English-language *Wanted in Rome*, available in Rome's English bookshops.

Cinema

English-language films will be invariably dubbed into Italian—one exception is the tiny Pasquino cinema in Trastevere (Vicolo del Piede 19, Tel. 5803622), which screens American and British films in the original versions and changes its programme every two or three days. Even the graffiti in the lavatories is in English. Occasionally some of the more arty cinemas (*D'Essai*) may show foreign-language films in VO—*"versione originale"* Per formances generally begin around 4/4.30 p.m. with screenings usually on the hour or half hour, every two hours, and a final show at around 10.30 p.m.

Summer Festivals

Estate Romana: cultural festival of music, dance and theatre which runs from June through to September.

Cineporto: summer season of open-air films in the Parco della Farnesina, (entrance in Via Antonio da San Giuliano). Two films every night, starting around 9.30 p.m. with live music in the intervals. Runs from July to September.

Festa dei Noiantri: Trastevere's boisterous ancient festival held in July.

Euritmia: jazz festival with a host of foreign musicians, held at EUR in July.

Opera

Rome's opera season runs from October to June at the Teatro dell' Opera, Piazza Beniamino Gigli (off Via del Viminale), box office Tel. 461755/ 463641. For programme information in English phone 06 67595725; for advanced booking in English phone 06 67595721 (at least ten days before the performance).

In the summer there is a season of open-air operas and ballet in the picturesque and evocative setting of the Baths of Caracalla (July–August). Performances start at 9 p.m. Tickets in advance from the box office of the Teatro dell'Opera or, on the night, from the box office at the Terme di Caracalla.

Classical Music

Romans have a relaxed, decidedly un-stuffy attitude to classical music and this is reflected in some of the venues that are used to stage concerts. Churches, palazzi and the ruins of ancient monuments all become the suggestive backdrops to concerts of classical music. Evening concerts start at 9 p.m. The following is a list of the more conventional venues for classical music.

Accademia di Santa Cecilia, chamber concerts at the Sala dell' Accademia di Santa Cecilia, 18 Via dei Greci (box office Tel. 6541044); orchestral concerts at the Auditorio Pio, Via della Conciliazione 4 (Tel. 6541044). These concerts are very popular and tickets are often hard to obtain.

Auditorium del Foro Italico, Piazza Lauro de Bossis 28 (Tel. 36865625). Venue for well-attended concerts by the RAI Orchestra and Chorus.

Oratorio del Gonfalone, 32 Via del Gonfalone (Tel. 6875952), venue for chamber music.

Auditorio San Leone Magno, 38 Via Bolzano. Venue for afternoon concerts in the Istituzione Universitaria dei Concerti series (Tel. 3610051).

Concerti Alitalia, Teatro Brancaccio, Via Merulana 244 (Tel. 461744).

Teatro Olimpico, 17 Piazza Gentile da Fabriano (Tel. 393304). Venue for concerts by the Accademia Filarmonica Romana and visiting artists.

Il Tempietto organize concerts throughout the year in several venues: Sala dei Concerti di S Maria in Campitelli, 9 Piazza Campitelli; and in summer in the Sala Assunta, Isola Tiberina. Box office Via Urbana 12a (Tel. 4821250).

Istituzione Universitaria dei Concerti, afternoon concerts Auditorium San Leone Magno; evening concerts Aula Magna Universita, la Sapienza, 5 Piazzale A Moro.

Italcable sponsor Sunday morning concerts, Concerti Italcable, Teatro Sistina, Via Sistina 129 (Tel. 4756841). Held at 10.30 a.m.

The Associazione Musicale Romano presents each May an annual festival *Musica a' Palazzo* dedicated to Baroque music at Palazzo della Cancelleria. Tickets available on the night.

Rome Festival, summer season of opera, orchestral and chamber music given by visiting American performers in evocative venues like the courtyard

of Palazzo Baldassini and the court-yard of San Clemente.

Band Music at the Pincio, every Sunday morning from the end of April to mid-July, concerts by military and police bands in the gardens of the Pincio. Information from EPT (Tel.463748).

Music Clubs

Rome has a host of music clubs where you can enjoy everything from salsa to Irish folk duos in intimate surround-ings. Jazz has been popular in Rome for years and there are venues dotted all over the city. Big American stars frequently drop in too. The old work-ing-class districts of Trastevere and Testaccio are good places to explore Rome's music scene.

Alexanderplatz, Via Ostia 9 (Tel. 3729398) Near the Vatican, Jazz, Rhythm'n'Blues.

A *mime artist coaches some volunteers in the square in front of the Pantheon.*

Alpheus, Via del Commercio 36 (Tel. 5783305). Jazz.

Big Mama, Vicolo San Francesco a Ripa 18 (Tel. 582551). Rock venue in Trastevere.

Caffè Latino, Via di Monte Tes-taccio 96 (Tel. 5744020). Jazz club in converted wine cellars beneath Monte Testaccio.

Caruso Caffè Concerto, Via di Monte Testaccio 36 (Tel. 5747720). Another Jazz club in Testaccio.

El Charango, Via di San Onofrio 28 (Tel. 6879908). Salsa, Mexican, Colombian and other Latin grooves.

Folkstudio, Via Frangipane 42 (Tel. 4871036.) Folk music. Host to American, British and Irish singers.

Music Inn, Largo dei Fiorentini 3 (Tel. 6544934). Jazz.

Saint Louis Music City, Via del Cardello 13 (Tel. 4745076). Jazz, fusion, blues.

Yes Brazil, Via San Francesco a Ripa 103 (Tel. 5816267). Venue for Brazilian music in Trastevere.

Discos

Rome's discos change names, decor and musical styles with bewildering regularity. *Trovaroma* provides a weekly guide which will inform you which night spots are currently the in-places.

L'Alibi, Via di Monte Testaccio 44 (Tel. 573448) Gay disco in cellars beneath Monte Testaccio.

Fantasy, Via Alba 42 (Tel. 7016741) Friday and Saturday, Afro-Latin-American disco and live music. Rome's black community comes here.

Gilda, Via Mario de' Fiori 97 (Tel. 6784838) Fashionable disco and restaurant, open late.

Piper '90, Via Tagliamento 9 (Tel. 8414459) Disco, live music and "multivisione video".

Veleno, Via Sardegna 27 (493583) Trendy disco, plus piano bar and restaurant.

Uonna Club, Via Cassia 871 (Tel. 3662837). Disco music and live rock concerts, frequent "theme" evenings.

Nightclubs and Piano Bars

Blue Bar, Via dei Soldati 25 (Tel. 6864221/6864250). Elegant nightclub and piano bar.

Bue Toscano, Via di Tor Margana 3 (Tel. 6798158). Cocktail bar offering late-night, after-theatre meals (closed Saturday and Sunday lunchtimes).

Pubs

Irish pubs are very much in vogue in Rome nowadays. These are currently the in-spots:

Druid's Den, Via di San Martino ai Monti 28. Open 8 p.m. to 12 a.m.

Fiddler's Elbow, Via dell'Olmata 43. Open 5 p.m. to 12 a.m.

Four Green Fields, Via C. Morin 42. Open 8.30 p.m. to 2 a.m.

St Patrick, Via Calabria 30. Open 6 p.m. to 2 a.m. Open all week.

A British pub boasting "typical British food" is **Victoria House**, Via di Gesù e Maria 18. Open 6 p.m. to 1 a.m. Closed Mondays.

Sports and Activities

Bowling

Bowling Brunswick, Lungotevere, Acqua Acetosa (Tel. 3966696); Bowling Roma, Viale Regina Margherita (861184).

Football

Rome has two local teams, Roma and Lazio, both of whom play home games at the Stadio Olimpico, Viale dei Gladiatori.

Golf

Circolo del Golf di Roma, Acqua Santa, Via Appia Nuova (Tel. 783407); Oligiata, Largo dell'Oligiata 15 (Tel. 3789141).

Horse Racing

Flat races and steeplechases at the Ippodromo delle Capanelle, Via Appia Nuova, trotting at the Ippodromo Tor di Valle, Via del Mare.

Swimming

Foro Italico, Lungotevere Maresciallo Cadorna (Tel. 3218591) open-air pool open June–September; indoor pool open November–May; Piscina delle Rose, Viale America, EUR (Tel. 5926717) 50 m (550 yd) open-air pool, open June–September; some hotel pools are open to non-residents including Cavalieri Hilton, Via Cadiolo 101 (Tel. 31512225).

Tennis

Public courts at the Foro Italico, Viale Gladiatori (Tel. 3219021) and at the Tre Fontane Sports Centre, Via delle Tre Fontane (Tel. 5926386).

A motley crew of puppets awaits spectators on top of the Janiculum Hill.

Ideas for Children

Amusement Park

Luna Park, Via delle Tre Fontane, EUR. Large and well-equipped permanent fun fair. The 40 m (44 yd)-high Ferris wheel is a local landmark.

Punch and Judy

Puppet shows on top of the Janiculum Hill and on the Pincio.

Waxworks Museum

Museo delle Cere, 67 Piazza Venezia (Piazza SS Apostoli). Open 9 a.m. to 8 p.m.

Zoo

Giardino Zoologico, Villa Borghese (Tel. 3216564). Open all year round (except 1 May). Summer: 8 a.m. to 6.15 p.m.; Winter 8 a.m. to 5 p.m.

Bitter Sweet: Fellini and *La Dolce Vita*

In the 1950s the international jet-set made Rome's Via Veneto the in-place to be. Along the street and in its chic cafés, aristocrats chased actresses, and play-boys hunted heiresses, while they in turn were pursued by packs of snapping paparazzi. At the end of the decade Italian film director Federico Fellini captured the decadent glamour of the time in the film La Dolce Vita.

Federico Fellini's intention in making La Dolce Vita was, he said, "to take the temperature of an ailing society, a society that has every appearance of running a fever"; a fever his film seemed set on inflaming. On its release in 1960 the Vatican tried to ban it while the Italian Left championed it for laying bare bourgeois decadence; women spat on Fellini at its premiere but Cannes awarded it the Grand Prix. La Dolce Vita was indisputably of the moment. Not only did the film's title, The Sweet Life, pass into common usage but so did the term paparazzo after the name of the pushy, insensitive photographer who accompanies the "hero", gossip columnist Marcello Rubini, in his pursuit of scoops and scandals in Roman high society.

Marcello, played with louche charm by Marcello Mastroianni, was truly the hero of the hour: attractive, unscrupulous and ultimately hollow. Free from ties of church, conscience or women, he lives the sweet life to the full, passing from one beautiful woman to another: from clinging fiancée Yvonne Furneaux to playgirl heiress Anouk Aimée to American starlet Anita Ekberg.

La Dolce Vita caught, and indeed partly created, the mood of the era: the move from post-war austerity to consumer boom, from the end of a rigid, monolithic society whose moral order was imposed from above to one increasingly fragmented into cults and cliques. The film almost seemed to have inauguarated the swinging, permissive sixties but a generation later it's hard to see why everyone got so steamed up. The once shocking orgy scenes now hardly raise an eyebrow while Anita Ekberg's astonishingly pneumatic, cantilevered bust in that famous strapless black dress may represent a miracle of *haute couture* or of structural engineering but is hardly going to cause the moral decline of a nation which has nightly porn-shows on prime-time television.

That the scenes of decadence and debauchery have dated badly seems perversely to work in the film's favour, underscoring the hollowness of the high life, the vapidity of the ceaseless search for new sensation. This mood is reinforced by the film's episodic, plotless nature, at the time seeming almost as daring as Ms Ekberg's cleavage. We follow seven days and seven night's in Marcello's life, passing from a series of parties to their aftermaths, from revelry to hangover, dusk to dawn, effervescence to emptiness: the sweet life always leaves a bitter aftertaste. Years later Ekberg recalled this revealing conversation with Fellini: "I asked to see a script. He said, 'There isn't one. You can write it.' I said, 'I can't even write a letter. I am too lazy.' So he said, 'Never mind, we make it up as we go along.'

Despite this the film is artful rather than anarchic, even if it possesses a symbolic coherence rather than a narrative one, drawing its power from a series of striking and still resonant images: the statue of Christ being flown by helicopter over Rome while the reporters covering the trip snap photographs of girls sunbathing on the rooftops; Anita Ekberg running up the

FEDERICO FELLINI'S
LA DOLCE VITAX THE SWEET LIFE

steps of the dome of St Peter's in a cardinal's soutane or frolicking in the Trevi Fountain; the so-called "miracle" which turns into a media circus.

The savage grotesquerie of Fellini's later films is absent: the beautiful people are beautiful, even if shallow, vain and irredeemably lost. Fellini used real aristocrats in one sequence but the effect was not one of up-market neo-realism, high-society documentary, instead it made the world the film depicts seem more false and brittle, even more of a façade. The names of the actors sound more fantastic, more fictional, than the parts they play: Prince Vadim Wolkonsky, Prince Eugenio Ruspoli di Poggio Suasa, Doris Pignatelli, Princess of Monteroduni.

Fellini's vision of Roman society in *La Dolce Vita* is scathing but never entirely despairing; there is none of the bilious hatred one encounters in his 1986 satire on Italian televison, *Ginger and Fred*. In the end the film's cynicism is tempered. Marcello may be damned but others may still be saved. One strand of the film offers an ambiguous message of hope. Marcello twice encounters a

La Dolce Vita: *the sweet life leaves a bitter aftertaste.*

naive provincial girl from Perugia. On the first occasion he has gone to a seaside restaurant, encouraged by his intellectual friend Steiner to attempt some serious writing. There he meets a young waitress with, he rhapsodizes, a face "like an Umbrian angel". She, seeing his typewriter, declares her ambition to become a typist. Marcello flirts for a while, then leaves, going back to Rome and the high life. At the end of the film his writing ambitions have evaporated completely, he is no longer even a journalist but a publicity agent. After a final party in a seaside villa he and the other guests go down to the beach where a "sea monster" lies stranded on the beach. On the other side of an ever-widening channel the girl from the restaurant appears and shouts enthusiastically to Marcello. She is learning to type. The camera lingers on her beautiful Umbrian-angel face as she yells to Marcello but her voice is drowned by the noise of the waves and the wind.

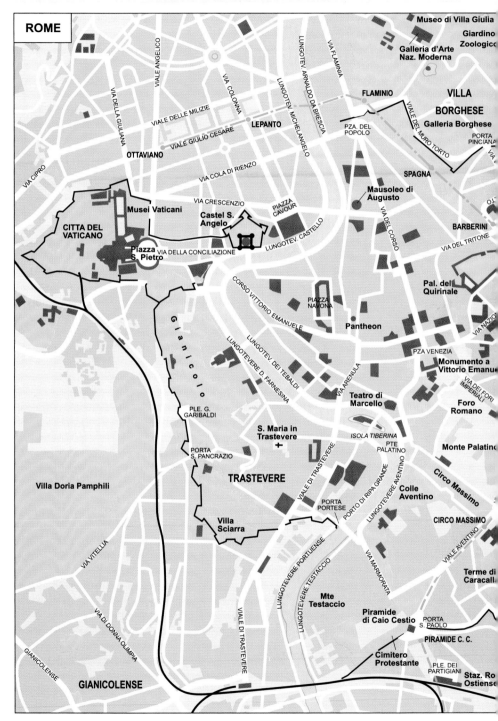

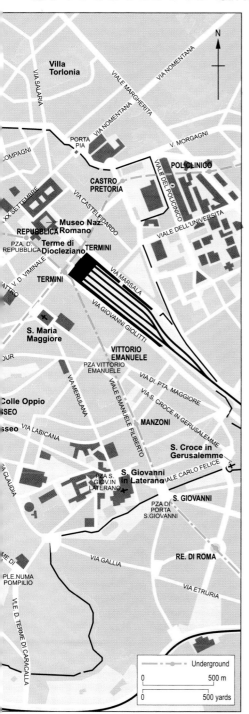

*O*n this and the following four pages are shown maps of Rome to help you find your way around. The map on the left shows most of Rome and the area of most interest to the tourist. The main roads and places of interest are marked. On the following four pages, the north and south of the city are shown in more detail. You should be able to find most of the places referred to in the text on these maps, but anyone wanting to explore Rome in depth should buy one of the many comprehensive maps available locally. For a more detailed map of the ancient heart of Rome, see page 99.

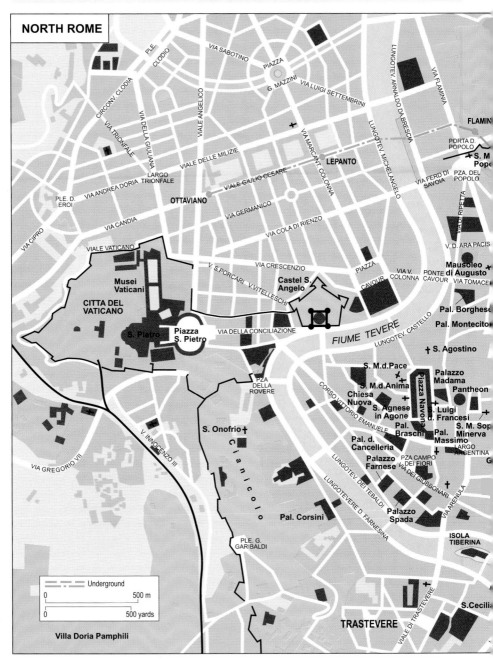

NORTH ROME

PLE. D. CLODIO

VIA SABOTINO

PIAZZA G. MAZZINI

VIA LUIGI SETTEMBRINI

CIRCONV. CLODIA

VIA TRIONFALE

VIA DELLA GIULIANA

VIALE ANGELICO

VIALE DELLE MILIZIE

VIALE GIULIO CESARE

LEPANTO

VIA MARC.ANT. COLONNA

LUNGOTEV. ARNALDO DA BRESCA

LUNGOTEV. MICHELANGELO

VIA FLAMINIA

FLAMIN

PORTA D. POPOLO

S. M Pop

VIA FERD DI SAVOIA

PZA. DEL POPOLO

LARGO TRIONFALE

VIA ANDREA DORIA

PLE. D. EROI

VIA CANDIA

OTTAVIANO

VIA GERMANICO

VIA COLA DI RIENZO

VIA CIPRO

VIALE VATICANO

VIA D. ARA PACIS

V. D. ARA PACIS

Musei Vaticani

CITTA DEL VATICANO

V. S.PORCARI

VIA CRESCENZIO

Castel S. Angelo

V.VITELLESCHI

PIAZZA CAVOUR

VIA V. COLONNA

PONTE CAVOUR

VIA CAVOUR

VIA TOMACE

Mausoleo di Augusto

S. Pietro

Piazza S. Pietro

VIA DELLA CONCILIAZIONE

FIUME TEVERE

LUNGOTEV. CASTELLO

Pal. Borghese

Pal. Montecitor

S. Agostino

PZA DELLA ROVERE

S. M.d.Pace

S. M.d.Anima

Chiesa Nuova

S. Agnese in Agone

Palazzo Madama

Pantheon

Piazza Navona

CORSO VITTORIO EMANUELE

S. Luigi d. Francesi

S. M. Sop

S. Onofrio

Pal. Braschi

Pal. d. Cancelleria

Pal. Massimo

Pal. Minerva

LARGO ARGENTINA

Palazzo Farnese

PZA CAMPO DEI FIORI

VIA DEI GIUBBONARI

G

LUNGOTEV. DEI TEBALDI

LUNGOTEVERE D. FARNESINA

VIA ARENULA

Palazzo Spada

V. INNOCENZO III

Pal. Corsini

C i a n i c o l o

ISOLA TIBERINA

VIA GREGORIO VII

PLE. G. GARIBALDI

S.Cecili

VIALE DI TRASTEVERE

----- Underground

0 _____ 500 m

0 _____ 500 yards

Villa Doria Pamphili

TRASTEVERE

M ain streets and sites of north Rome.

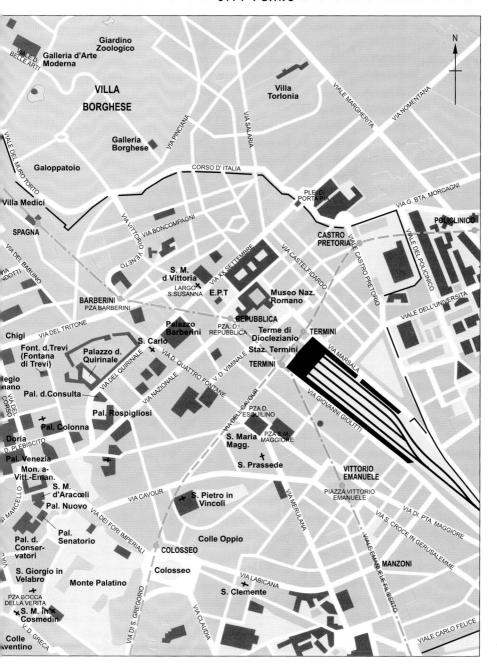

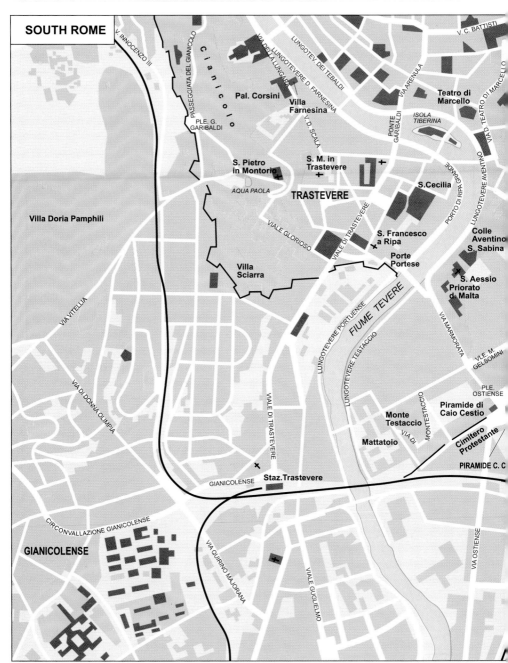

SOUTH ROME

M ain streets and sites
of south Rome.

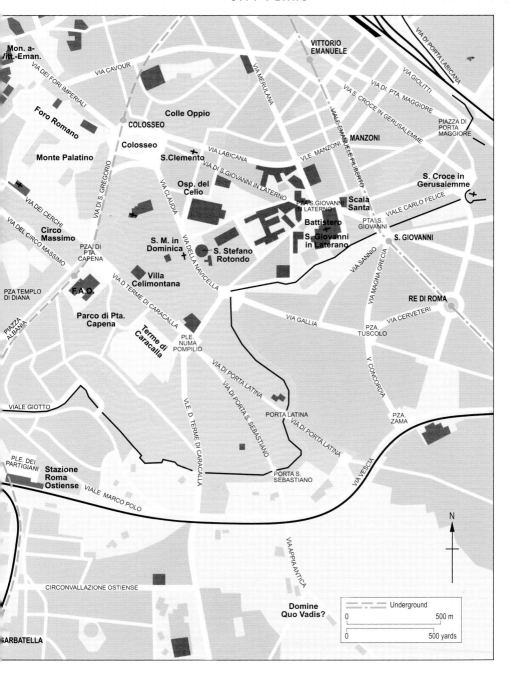

Feast Days and Festivals, Fashion Shows and Fairs

Winter, spring, summer or fall, Romans are never at a loss for an excuse to have a party or put on a show. Visitors are welcome to join in too, whether the celebration is secular or spiritual, mythical or modern. The occasion might be the feast day of a local saint or a grand civic ceremony, a fashion show on the Spanish Steps or open-air opera at the Baths of Caracalla.

January 5—The Christmas Toy Fair in Piazza Navona reaches its climax with a Carnival that goes on into the night.

January 6—Children's Festival of *Befana,* an old woman who brings toys to good children and pieces of coal (in the shape of coal-like sweets) to the naughty. In the towns surrounding Rome, children parade through the streets singing traditional *"Pasquelle".*

Every April the Spanish Steps are ablaze with azaleas; in July they become a catwalk for a night of high fashion: Roma Alta Moda.

January 17—*Festa di San Antonio Abate*: traditional blessing of animals at San Eusebio all'Esquilino, near Piazza Vittorio Emanuele.

January 21—*Festa di Sant'Agnese*: in the saint's church on the Via Nomentana, two lambs are blessed and shorn; the wool is then woven by the Benedictine nuns of Santa Cecilia in Trastevere into the *palliums* worn by the Pope.

January–July—High-fashion shows in major hotels. January: presentation of spring/summer collections

February—*Carnevale*: young children dress up in costume and parade through the centre of Rome; street processions with carnival floats in the Castelli Romani.

February 2—*Festa della Candelora:* traditional procession and blessing of candles, particularly in the Testaccio district.

February 9—Anniversary of the declaration of the Roman Republic of 1849.

March 9—Feast day of Santa Francesca Romana, patron saint of motorists, with a mass blessing of cars, lined up outside the saint's church (more commonly known as Santa Maria Nova) on the Via dei Fiori Imperiali, beside the Colosseum.

March 19—*Festa di San Giuseppe:* celebrations in the Trionfale district (the area directly north of the Vatican), where traditional fritters are cooked and eaten in the open. The festivities centre on the parish church of San Giuseppe.

April—Spring Festival: beautiful display of azaleas on the Spanish Steps.

Holy Week—Palm Sunday: Pope celebrates Mass in Piazza San Pietro.

Maundy Thursday: Pope traditionally attends Mass in San Giovanni in Laterano.

Good Friday: Pope presides over the Stations of the Cross (Via Crucis) to the Colosseum.

Easter Sunday: huge crowds in St Peter's Square to hear the Pope celebrate Mass in St Peter's Square, ending with the blessing "*Urbi et Orbi*", to the City and the World.

Easter Monday—*Pasquetta:* Roman families traditionally go on outings to the country.

April 21—Much pomp and pageantry for the celebration of the Founding of Rome (753 BC) at the Campidoglio.

April 25—Anniversary of the Liberation of Rome (1945). Ceremonies at the Mausoleo delle Fosse Ardeatine, scene of the massacre of 335 Italians by the German occupation.

April 29—Feast of St Catherine of Siena in Santa Maria sopra Minerva, site of the saint's remains.

April–July—Concerts by military bands every Sunday morning, from the last Sunday in April until mid-July, in the garden of the Pincio.

April–May—International Horse Show held at the Piazza di Siena in the Villa Borghese (end of April/beginning of May).

May 1—*Festa del Lavoro:* Labour Day holiday. Traditional to make

52

excursions out of the city—"*for de porta*".

May—Month of the Virgin: hundreds of street shrines to the Virgin are decorated with flowers and illuminated by candles. Pilgrimages to the sanctuary of Divine Love at Castel di Leva (south-east of Rome) and other countryside sanctuaries.

May–July—*Mostre delle Rose*: Rose Show at Via di Valle Murcia on the Aventine. Both an exhibition and an international competition for new varieties of roses.

May—Open-air art fair in Via Margutta.

T he Rose Show on the Aventine may come and go each year but the ruins of the Palatine form a timeless backdrop.

May—International Tennis Championships held at the Foro Italico.

May—Antiques Fair in Via dei Coronari.

May–June—International Trade Fair: Fiera di Roma, Via Cristoforo Colombo.

June–July—*Tevere Expo*: Exhibition of products from the regions of Italy on the banks of the Tiber, between

Ponte Sant'Angelo and Ponte Umberto. Accompanied by dance, theatre, music and sporting events.

June–September—*Estate Romana*: Rome's summer cultural festival of music, dance and theatre in Villa Medici, Accademia di Spagna, Villa Massimo, Palazzo Farnese and Isola Tiberina.

July–September—*Cineporto*: open-air films in the Parco della Farnesina every evening. (*See* FURTHER INFORMATION.)

June 2—*Festa della Repubblica*: military parades in the heart of Rome.

June 24—*Festa di San Giovanni*: festivities in the San Giovanni district, including ancient tradition of eating stewed snails (*lumache in umido*) and suckling-pig.

June 29—*Festa di Santi Pietro e Paolo*: festival of the patron saints of Rome, celebrated by the Pope in St Peter's.

July—*Concerti al Campidoglio*: concerts by the orchestra of the Academy of St Cecilia on the Piazzale del Campidoglio.

July—*Roma Alta Moda*: presentation of autumn/winter collections in the Campo di Moda, Villa Borghese. On the final evening there is a spectacular open-air fashion show on the Spanish Steps, when all the great designers present their evening-wear collections. (Information from Camera Nazionale dell'Alta Moda Tel. 6794390. For invitations contact the Rome fashion houses.)

July—*Festa de Noiantri*: ancient popular festival in the Trastevere district with processions, carnival floats, folk dancing, music, fireworks and open-air dining.

July–August—Season of open-air operas at the Baths of Caracalla.

August 1—*Festa delle Catene*: the holy chains which fettered St Peter are displayed in San Pietro in Vincoli.

August 5—*Festa della Madonna della Neve*: in a ceremony in Santa Maria Maggiore, a shower of white rose petals flutters from the dome of the Borghese Chapel in commemoration of the miraculous summer fall of snow in AD 352 that led to the building of the basilica.

August 15—*Festa dell'Assunta*: notable celebrations of the Assumption in Santa Maria Maggiore and Santa Maria in Trastevere.

Ferragosto: the day when normal life in Rome grinds to a halt and a mass exodus from the city begins.

September—Open-air art fair in Via Margutta.

September 8—Anniversary of the Defence of Rome (1943): the beginning of anti-fascist Resistance commemorated at Porta San Paolo.

October—*Sagra dell'uva*: wine festival in Marino (one of the towns in the Castelli Romani) on the first Sunday in October. The town's fountains flow with wine and there are parades, floats and fireworks.

October 4—*Festa di San Francesco d'Assisi* (patron saint of Italy): celebrations in Santa Maria in Aracoeli and San Giovanni in Laterano.

October–June—Opera season at the Teatro dell'Opera.

October—Antiques Fair in Via dei Coronari.

October—Crafts Fair in Via dell' Orso and adjacent streets.

November 1—*Tutti i Santi*: All Saints' Day.

December 8—Feast of the Immaculate Conception: the statue of the Madonna on the Column of the Immaculate Conception in Piazza dei Spagna is garlanded with flowers.

December—Toy Fair in Piazza Navona (until 6 January).

Christmas—The streets in the city centre, around Piazza di Spagna and Via del Corso, are decked out in Christmas decorations; Christmas cribs are displayed in the churches of Rome, particularly notable are the ones in Santa Maria in Aracoeli, Santa Maria in Via, Santa Alessio and Santa Maria Maggiore.

Christmas Eve—*Vigilia di Natale*: Midnight Mass celebrated by the Pope in St Peter's.

Christmas Eve–Epiphany—Young children recite short poems and speeches before the miracle-working

In the 17th century Via Margutta was home to Dutch and Flemish painters; today it is still an artists' street with galleries and studios and an open-air art fair in May and September.

statue of the Holy Child in Santa Maria d' Aracoeli.

Christmas Day—*Natale*: Christmas Mass celebrated by the Pope in St Peter's at 10 a.m.

New Year's Eve—Traditions for seeing in the New Year include wearing an article of red clothing (particularly red underwear) and throwing old possessions, like furniture or crockery, out of the windows after midnight. A custom more followed in the older districts of Rome, like Trastevere.

Tyrants, Demagogues and Dictators: Rome's Lords of Misrule

Throughout their city's long history Romans have been cursed with more than their fair share of tyrants, demagogues and dictators. Among Rome's many Lords of Misrule, the Emperor Nero, Cola di Rienzo and Benito Mussolini were three of a kind.

The Emperor Nero (AD 37–68)

Cruel, vain and debauched, of the early Roman emperors Nero must surely take the palm for depravity. He did not perhaps sink to the depths of degeneracy plumbed by Tiberius, nor rise to the heights of megalomania reached by Caligula, but as a bad all-rounder Nero was matchless. Yet when he became emperor at the age of 17 in AD 54 Nero gave every sign of proving to be a good ruler. He was both generous and merciful; he abolished oppressive taxes, reprieved condemned criminals and lavished splendid entertainments on the people. He soon showed himself in his true colours though. He put his first wife to death on a false charge of adultery in order to marry his mistress. She too met an early death after Nero kicked her when she was pregnant. Some say he had incestuous relations with his mother, Agrippina (he later had her put to death as well). He debauched virgins of both sexes. One boy, named Sporus, he had castrated before marrying him in a full-blown wedding ceremony, complete with dowry and bridal veil.

Inordinately proud of his abilities as poet, musician and actor, Nero appeared frequently on the public stage. Performances lasted for hours and while the Emperor was singing no one was allowed to leave. Women even gave birth in the theatre, it is said, while some spectators feigned death so that they would be carried out as if for burial.

For all his vanity, Nero cut a pretty unprepossessing figure. Suetonius describes him as "about the average height, his body marked with spots and malodorous, his hair light blond, his features regular rather than attractive, his eyes blue and somewhat weak, his neck over thick, his belly prominent, and his legs very slender. His health was good, for though indulging in every kind of riotous excess, he was ill but three times in all during the 14 years of his reign, and even then not enough to give up wine or any of his usual habits."

Nero was spectacularly extravagant when it came to building palaces. His most luxurious creation, the Domus Aurea, or Golden House, occupied a vast, 80ha (200 acre) park in the centre of Rome and was a magnificent complex of porticoes and pavilions, temples, baths, fountains and gardens. The interior of the palace was decorated with gold, gems and mother-of-pearl. The dining-rooms had fretted ivory ceilings which released showers of flower petals on the guests below, while pipes sprinkled the air with perfumes. The roof of the main dining-room was circular and constantly revolved day and night, 'like the heavens'. In the vestibule stood a 37m (120ft) bronze statue of the Emperor himself.

When the palace was completed Nero exclaimed, "Now at last I can begin to live like a human being!".

To create space for this grandiose palace, Nero is said to have started the great fire which destroyed much of Rome in AD 64. While the city burned he played his lyre and sang songs of the fabled sack of Troy.

Nero, the nonpareil of cruelty and perversion, even by the standards of imperial Rome.

Scapegoats for the fire were found in the members of a strange new sect which was fast gaining adherents in Rome: the Christians. The ancient Roman historian Tacitus described their terrible fate at Nero's hands: "Their deaths were made to afford amusement to the crowd. Some were wrapped in the skins of wild beasts and torn to pieces by dogs; others were fastened on crosses, and when the daylight failed were burned as torches to light up the night."

Eventually even the Romans tired of Nero's excesses. The Emperor met his end in AD 68. Faced with a revolt by the army and deserted by most of his ret-inue, he committed suicide by driving a dagger into his throat with the aid of a servant. Before taking his life, Nero cried out, "What an artist the world is losing in me!".

Cola di Rienzo (1313–54)

The 14th century saw one of the darkest periods in Rome's history. The popes had abandoned the city for Avignon in 1308 and were not to return until 1377. In the absence of the papacy Rome was left in a state of lawless anarchy, dominated by feuding noble families, each with private armies and fortified towers from which to sally

Cola di Rienzo, a medieval demagogue who met a sticky end.

forth to fight pitched battles in the streets. Robbery, rape and murder were rife and corpses were thrown into the Tiber daily.

For one man the contrast between Rome's past glories and present degradation could not have been more painful. He was Cola di Rienzo, the son of an innkeeper and a washerwoman, and a notary by profession. He had read the ancient authors, Livy, Seneca and Cicero, and longed to restore Rome to the greatness these writers had described. He roamed the city, collecting antiquities and deciphering the Latin inscriptions on ancient monuments for the benefit of anyone who would listen. He soon acquired fame for his oratory and in 1343 was sent as an envoy to Clement VI at Avignon to beg him to revisit Rome. The Pope declined but, impressed with Cola's eloquence, he agreed to declare a Holy Year for 1350.

Cola returned to Rome with the title of apostolic notary and began to build a power base in the city. For the forthcoming Jubilee to succeed, Rome had to be made safe for pilgrims. Firm government was needed, but the warring nobles did more to break than uphold the law. In speech after speech Cola railed against the robber barons, promising to cut them down to size when he came to power.

The nobles laughed off the threat posed by this low-born upstart but in May 1347 Cola struck. On Whit Sunday he appeared on the Capitol at the head of a band of well-armed supporters. There he proclaimed himself: "the Tribune of Freedom, Peace and Justice, and the Liberator of the Holy Roman Republic."

Rome's new dictator was at first welcomed by the people, particularly after he had hanged a few noble malefactors. Cola's revolutionary programme of reform proved popular but he was soon brought low by his overweening vanity. With his high-sounding titles went elaborate costumes and ever-more flamboyant behaviour. He declared his ambition to unite all of Italy; Rome would once more be the capital of the world. Cola, the implication went, would of course be the new Emperor. On 1 August he had himself knighted in a magnificent ceremony in San Giovanni in Laterano. On 15 August he was crowned with wreaths made from plants growing on the Arch of Constantine. A few months later Cola's regime had collapsed. Despite victory over the nobles in a battle outside the gate of San Lorenzo on 20 November, Cola realized his power was waning. His craven behaviour on the field of battle had done nothing for his image and for Cola appearance was everything. His grandiose pronouncements on a new Roman empire had meanwhile lost him the favour of the Pope and when a papal bull was issued threatening Cola with excommunication he abdicated on 15 December 1347 and fled the city.

Cola spent part of his exile in the Abruzzi mountains east of Rome; after more wandering he found himself a prisoner of the Pope at Avignon. Then came another change in Cola's fortunes. The Pope died and his successor, Innocent VI, not only freed Cola but sent him back to Rome to restore papal authority there. He arrived in the city on 1 August 1354 and was once again welcomed by the people. But he no longer displayed the charisma which had spellbound everyone seven years earlier. His once handsome figure had run to fat and his rule was even more overbearing and arbitrary. He imposed heavy taxes, arrested citizens on trumped-up charges and then ransomed them back to their families.

On 8 October riots broke out and a mob gathered before Cola's palace on

A typical display of mob oratory by Benito Mussolini.

the Capitol hill, shouting "Death to the tyrant!". Cola appeared on a balcony and attempted to speak to the mob but was shouted down. Stones were thrown and an arrow pierced Cola's hand. When the mob began to set fire to the palace, Cola decided to escape. He took off his armour, cut his beard and blackened his face. Then, dressed in the clothes of a gardener, he sneaked out of the palace and mingled with the mob. Disguising his voice, he even joined in the jeers against the traitor Cola, but someone in the crowd recognized him by the rings he still wore on his fingers. Cola was run through with a sword and hacked to pieces by the mob.

Benito Mussolini (1883–1945)

As modern dictators go, Benito Mussolini was all mouth and trousers: all bombastic rhetoric and flamboyant uniforms. More showman than statesman, his rule was founded on role-playing rather than *realpolitik*.

He was born near Forlì in Romagna on 29 July 1883, the son of a fiercely radical blacksmith who named his son after the Mexican revolutionary Benito Juarez. A truculent bully as a schoolboy, he was expelled from two schools for displaying a tendency to knife his fellow pupils. Such juvenile misdemeanours behind him, in 1901 he became a schoolteacher but fled to Switzerland the following year to avoid conscription. There he dabbled in revolutionary circles, describing himself as "an apostle of violence". He returned to Italy in 1904, took up teaching once again and served in the army after all. He became involved in the socialist party and won renown for his skills as a journalist and orator. By 1912 he had risen through the ranks to become editor of the party newspaper, *Avanti!* When he was expelled from the party in 1914 for his pro-war stance, he started his own paper, *Popolo d'Italia*.

After the war, in which he had served as a corporal in the *bersaglieri*, Benito Mussolini created a new vehicle for his political ideals. This was the Fascist movement, named after the *fasces* or bundle of rods borne by officers of the law in ancient Rome. Mussolini's message was anti-communist, nationalistic and authoritarian. Impressive-sounding if often contradictory, his programme managed to appeal simultaneously to right and left, conservatives and radicals, monarchists and republicans.

In the confused state of post-war Italian politics support for the Fascists grew. In the 1921 elections the party won 35 seats in Parliament and in October 1922 Mussolini's black-shirted followers staged a mass "March on Rome". Mussolini, who arrived by train the next day, was invited by the King to form a government.

Once in power, *Il Duce*, the leader, as he was known, was more concerned with the broad flourishes of propaganda than with the fine detail of actual government. He left a light burning in his office in the Palazzo Venezia to create the illusion of a leader working tirelessly for his people. From the balcony of the palace he mesmerized packed crowds in the piazza below with his fiery speeches.

Despite all the pomp, Mussolini never stood on ceremony. He often went unshaved and unwashed, splashing himself with eau-de-cologne instead of bathing. He wore shoes with elastic bows to save the bother of tying shoelaces. His shoes (and trousers) usually stayed on during the hurried sexual bouts he performed with a string of mistresses on his office floor.

Although the much-trumpeted advances made by his regime (improved communications, land-reclamation schemes, and hydro-electric power stations, and so forth) often had more to do with show than substance, a genuine achievement was the 1929 Lateran Treaty with the Pope which healed the rift between Church and State that had existed since Italy had become one nation in 1870. The pact established the Vatican as an independent sovereign state.

Mussolini's desire for glory abroad (providing the risks were minimal) led Italy to invade Abyssinia in 1935. When the African country (now Ethiopia) was conquered the following year Mussolini announced that Rome had again become the capital of an empire.

In 1936 the ideological empathy of Mussolini and his fellow dictator, Hitler, was cemented by the Berlin-Rome axis and in 1940 Italy entered the Second World War on Germany's side. The war did not go well for Italy. The African Empire was lost and following the Allied landings in Sicily in July 1943 Mussolini was deposed in a bloodless coup. Imprisoned in a mountain fortress in the Abruzzo, he was rescued by the Germans in a daring glider raid and set up as the puppet ruler of the "Republic of Salo" on Lake Garda in north-east Italy. In April 1945, as the end of the war drew near, Mussolini attempted to escape to Switzerland with his mistress, Claretta Petacci, but they were captured by partisans near Lake Como. They were both shot and their bodies ignominiously strung up from the roof of a petrol station in Milan.

THE HISTORY OF ROME

Expansion and Empire, Renaissance and Decadence

Yes. It's official. Rome really was founded on 21 April 753 BC— or thereabouts. Recent archeological discoveries on the Palatine Hill appear to back up the ancient legends. The early settlement was created deliberately, the evidence suggests, on a precise date with sacred significance, rather than coming into being by accidental accretion. With such a confident birth, is it any wonder that Rome should grow up to become the "capital of the world"?

753 BC—Legendary date of the foundation of Rome by the twins Romulus and Remus.

753–509—Era of the Kings: Rome is ruled over by seven legendary kings. Romulus, the first king, is succeeded by Numa Pompilius (716–673) who endows Rome with its religious institutions. There follows the warlike reign of Tullus Hostilius (673–641) and the conquering of the nearby city of Alba

A ristocratic soldier and statesman, Julius Caesar seized control of Rome in 48 BC. He enjoyed four years of power before his assassination on the Ides of March.

Longa. He is succeeded by Ancus Marcius (640–616), a grandson of Numa Pompilius. Lucius Tarquinius Priscus (616–578), Rome's first Etruscan king, initiates a series of public works, including the construction of the Cloaca Maxima, a great sewer to drain the land between the Palatine and Capitoline hills, the origin of the Forum. He also begins the Circus Maximus and the custom of entertaining the Roman people with splendid public games. His reign ends in assassination. Servius Tullius (578–534), a peaceful reign during which the Roman Constitution is reformed and the city's boundaries are extended. Rome now stands on seven hills— Palatine, Aventine, Capitoline, Celian, Quirinal, Viminal and Esquiline—

around which a stone wall is built. Servius is overthrown and killed by Lucius Tarquinius Superbus, Tarquin the Proud (534–510). He continues the public works begun by his father, Lucius Tarquinius Priscus, including the building of the magnificent Temple of Jupiter on the Capitol. But his tyrannical reign provokes increasing resentment and the Tarquins are driven out of Rome in an uprising prompted by the king's nephew Brutus.

510—Rome becomes a republic. The city is ruled by two elected Consuls drawn from the ranks of Rome's aristocratic class, the patricians. In 494 BC Rome's subject class, the plebeians, revolt against the severity of patrician rule and withdraw to the Aventine Hill threatening to establish a separate community. In the ensuing accord between patricians and plebeians, Rome's constitution is revised and two Tribunes are elected as representatives of the people.

5th C BC—Rome is engaged in struggles with its neighbours, the Etruscans, Volscians and Latins, and gradually extends its dominion over the peoples of central Italy.

390—Italy is invaded by Gaulish tribes from beyond the Alps and Rome is sacked and almost totally destroyed. But the city recovers. Rome's walls are rebuilt and strengthened and its legions mount successful campaigns against its rivals in central Italy, including the Samnites and Latins.

3rd C BC—Rome extends its dominion over the Italian peninsula, subjugating the Greek cities of the south of Italy (Magna Græcia). In 275 BC the Romans defeat Pyrrhus, king of Epirus.

312—Appius Claudius begins to build the great military road known as the Appian Way and also constructs Rome's first aqueduct, the Acqua Appia.

264–241—The First Punic War. Rome goes to war with Carthage, the north African city state and naval power which controls the western Mediterranean. A treaty ends the war in 241 BC and wins the Romans control over most of Sicily.

218–201—The Second Punic War. A second war with Carthage breaks out in 218 BC. The brilliant young Carthaginian general Hannibal marches over the Alps with his troops and elephants and inflicts a series of severe defeats on the Roman legions. The Roman general Publius Cornelius Scipio turns the tide in Rome's favour with victories in Spain and Africa, defeating Hannibal decisively at Zama in 202 BC.

149–146—The Third Punic War. Carthaginian power is conclusively destroyed and Carthage itself razed to the ground.

2nd C BC—Rome continues to increase its foreign dominions. Southern Greece becomes a province of Rome after the capture of Corinth in 146 BC. Rome in turn comes increasingly under the influence of Greek art, architecture, religion and philsophy.

88—Civil war breaks out in Rome. The low-born soldier and consul Marius and the patrician Sulla contest for power.

82—Sulla wins control of Rome and has himself appointed dictator. He abdicates in 79 BC.

73–71—The Thracian gladiator Spartacus leads a violent insurrection of gladiators and slaves. He wins a

The Capitoline Venus, a Roman copy of a Greek original.

number of victories over the Roman legions but is finally defeated in Apulia by the Roman general Marcus Licinius Crassus. Another section of Spartacus's army is vanquished by Cnaeus Pompeius (Pompey the Great) who thereby shares credit for the extirpation of the revolt. Crassus and Pompey are elected Consuls in 70 BC.

58–50—The ambitious aristocratic general Julius Caesar pursues successful campaigns in Gaul and Britain.

49—Julius Caesar crosses the Rubicon, the stream which divides Cisalpine Gaul from Italy, and marches on Rome. Pompey is defeated at the Battle of Pharsalus in 48 BC and Caesar becomes effective sole ruler of Rome.

44—Julius Caesar is assassinated in the Senate on the Ides or 15 March (in a conspiracy led by M. Junius Brutus and C. Cassius Longinus). Brutus and Cassius are defeated at the Battle of Philippi in 42 BC and Rome is ruled by the triumvirate of Mark Antony, Marcus Aemilius Lepidus and Caesar's adopted son, Octavian.

40—Soon afterwards, the Roman Empire is split between a western part ruled by Octavian and an eastern one governed by Antony, who becomes increasingly infatuated with the Egyptian queen Cleopatra (formerly the lover of Caesar). War between the two sides inevitably breaks out and in 31 BC Antony and Cleopatra are defeated at the naval battle of Actium. Octavian is undisputed master of the Roman world.

27 BC—Octavian is proclaimed emperor and later adopts the title Augustus, meaning "the sacred" or "the venerable". His long reign (until AD 14) sees Rome enjoy peace and prosperity. He begins an ambitious building programme which, he boasts, transforms Rome from a city of brick into one of marble. The Augustan Age also witnesses the flourishing of writers like Virgil, Horace, Livy and Ovid.

AD 14–68—The Giulio-Claudian dynasty: Augustus is succeeded by the debauched Tiberius, the insane Caligula, the crippled Claudius and the megalomaniac and cruel Nero. During his reign, Christians are made scapegoats for the terrible fire of AD 64 which destroys much of Rome. Among the victims are Saints Peter and Paul.

69–79—Rome's fortunes revive during the reign of the Emperor Vespasian. He restores many of the city's important buildings and constructs new ones, including the Colosseum, which is inaugurated during the reign of Vespasian's successor, his son Titus.

79–96—The brief reign of Titus (died AD 81) is followed by the longer rule of his brother Domitian. The magnificent Arch of Titus is erected at the end of the Forum in AD 81 to commemorate the victories of Vespasian and Titus over the Jews in AD 70.

96–180—Following the assassination of Domitian and the brief reign of Nerva, Rome is ruled by a series of wise and able emperors, who each choose an adoptive heir as his successor. Edward Gibbon called this "the period in the history of the world during which the condition of the human race was most happy and prosperous." Under the Antonines, as the emperors are collectively known, "the vast extent of the Roman Empire was governed by absolute power under the guidance of virtue and wisdom."

98–117—The reign of the Emperor Trajan sees an extension of the Empire abroad and an impressive programme of public works at home. Trajan builds a new Forum, the grand Basilica Ulpia, extensive markets and a monumental column. Rome's population reaches one million.

117–38—The rule of the brilliant Emperor Hadrian, builder (and quite possibly also architect) of the Pantheon, the vast Temple of Venus and Rome, and a giant Mausoleum (which survives today as the Castel Sant' Angelo). The Empire flourishes in peace and prosperity.

138–80—Rome's prosperity continues during the reign of Hadrian's adoptive heir Antoninus Pius and that of his successor Marcus Aurelius. This Stoic philosopher and soldier (whose magnificent bronze equestrian statue can be seen on the Capitol) is the last of the adoptive emperors.

180–284—A time of unrest at home and abroad. Barbarian tribes threaten the outreaches of the Empire and in Rome rulers follow one another in rapid and bloodthirsty succession.

284–305—The Emperor Diocletian initiates a series of reforms which help to restore Rome's fortunes. In 286 he divides the Empire into Western and Eastern parts and shares rule with co-emperor Maximian. Between 298 and 306 the Baths of Diocletian, the largest in Rome, are built. Diocletian vigorously persecutes the followers of the cult of Christianity which is growing rapidly in Rome and the Empire.

306–37—Reign of Constantine the Great, the first Christian emperor. Christianity is legalized in 313. Rome's first great churches are built, modelled on the city's secular basilicas. In AD 330 Constantine transfers the seat of imperial government to Byzantium on the Bosphorus Strait. He names his new capital Constantinople.

337–476—Christianity completes its triumph over paganism while the Empire goes into irreversible decline. Rome is threatened by barbarian tribes from the north. In 410 a Visigoth army under Alaric occupies and sacks Rome, the first time the city has been captured by a foreign force in 800 years. In 452 the forces of Attila the Hun turn back before reaching Rome but in 455 the city is sacked by the

Constantine made Christianity the state religion and transferred the seat of empire to Byzantium.

Vandals. In 476 the German warrior Odoacer deposes the boy emperor Romulus Augustulus and makes himself ruler of the Italian peninsula. The Western Empire is at an end.

6th C—Odoacer is succeeded as King of Italy by the Ostrogoth Theodoric. The Byzantine emperor Justinian I sends troops to invade Italy in an attempt to drive out the Ostrogoths and regain control of Rome. The Ostrogoths are finally defeated in 552 but in 568 another Germanic tribe, the Lombards, invades Italy from the north. Rome suffers from famine, flood and plague, its buildings crumble and its population shrinks.

590–604—Papacy of Pope Gregory the Great. Missionaries are despatched abroad to convert pagan tribes, including the Angles in England. The Pope becomes the undisputed religious leader of western Europe. The Lombards overrun Northern and Central Italy but are bought off from attacking Rome.

753—The Lombards lay siege to Rome, Pope Stephen III appeals for help to Pepin the Short, who has recently deposed the last Merovingian king of the Franks. The Lombards are defeated and forced to restore to Rome large tracts of central Italy. The temporal power of the papacy increases.

800—Pepin's son Charlemagne is crowned Holy Roman Emperor in St Peter's by Pope Leo III.

9th C—The Carolingian Empire declines. In 846 Saracen pirates sail up the Tiber and sack the basilicas of St Peter's and St Paul without the Walls. In response Pope Leo IV builds a defensive wall around the Basilica of St

Peter's and its surroundings. Powerful families vie for control of the papacy.

10th C—Control of Rome and the papacy is contested between powerful Roman families and the German emperor. In 962 King Otto I is crowned Holy Roman Emperor by John XII. Two years later Otto deposes the Pope and replaces him with his own nominee. The Romans rise up in revolt against the Emperor but the rebellion is put down. There are further insurrections in the coming years. The Crescenzi family rise to prominence in the city and challenge the power of successive emperors.

11th C—Struggles between popes and anti-popes continue. In 1045 there are simultaneously three rival popes in Rome. The German Emperor, Henry III, dismisses all three claimants and puts a fourth candidate on the papal throne. In 1073 Gregory VII is elected Pope and strives to reform and strengthen the Church. He excommunicates the Emperor, Henry IV, who is forced to beg humbly for forgiveness. Clad only in a thin penitential shirt, he is kept waiting for three cold January days outside the fortress of Canossa in which the Pope is residing. Eventually he is granted absolution but the rapprochement is short-lived. Excommunicated a second time, Henry VI lays siege to Rome. The city is divided between support for the Emperor and for the Pope, who holds fast in the fortress of Castel Sant'Angelo. In 1084 the Norman leader Robert Guiscard advances on the city and frees the Pope. But his troops rampage through the city, laying whole districts to waste.

12th C—An uneasy compromise between emperors and papacy is reached in the Concordat of Worms in 1122. In 1143 the Roman people rise up in revolt against the Pope and nobles and establish a republic. Inspired by the radical monk Arnold da Brescia, they declare the temporal power of the Pope to be at an end and sack the palaces and forts of the cardinals, bishops and nobles. In 1154 Nicholas Breakspeare is elected to the papacy as Adrian IV, the only Englishman to become pope. He demands that the heretical Arnold be expelled from Rome. The Romans refuse and the Pope finds himself a virtual prisoner in the Vatican. He retaliates with an interdict, effectively excommunicating the city. The people give in. Adrian also subdues, for a while, the Emperor Frederic Barbarossa. In 1188 Pope Clement III recognizes the city as a commune while the Republic concedes the temporal power of the Pope. Under Innocent III (1197–1216) the temporal and spiritual power of the papacy reaches its greatest extent.

13th C—In 1252 the Bolognese aristocrat Brancaleone degli Andalo is appointed Senator of Rome and rules the city successfully for three years, subduing the power of papacy and nobles. After Brancaleone's period of office, Rome once more relapses into civil war and anarchy.

1300—Pope Boniface VIII proclaims 1300 the first Holy Year. Pilgrims flock to Rome and the Church's coffers fill.

1308—The French Pope Clement V moves the papacy to Avignon, where it will remain for 68 years, the so-called Babylonian Captivity.

1347—Demagogic leader Cola di Rienzo proclaims himself Tribune of

The Coronation of the Virgin in Santa Maria Maggiore, the finest medieval mosaic in Rome.

the Roman People, promising to restore Rome to its ancient glory. He champions the cause of the people and subdues the nobility but he is undone by an insatiable vanity. Cola's power wanes and he abdicates before the end of the year and secretly flees the city.

1350—Pilgrims descend on Rome in hundreds of thousands for the second Holy Year.

1354—Cola di Rienzo is recalled to Rome but his second period as Tribune is an abject failure. After less than three months he is murdered by a mob on the Capitol.

1377—The papacy returns to Rome under Pope Gregory XI. He dies a

year later and for 40 years the Church is rent by the Great Schism, as once more rival candidates lay claim to the papacy.

1417—Martin V becomes Pope and begins a period of renewal for the city. He restores the ruined basilicas and reconstructs the aqueducts, including the Acqua Vergine, built by Marcus Agrippa in 19 BC.

1447–55—The papacy of the learned and generous Nicholas V marks the start of the Renaissance in Rome. The squalid and decrepit medieval city is slowly transformed. Many churches are restored and work begins on a new basilica to replace the old ruined St Peter's. Money for these ambitious projects comes from the tens of thousands of pilgrims who flock to Rome for the Holy Year of 1450.

1471–84—The Ligurian Francesco della Rovere is elected Pope and takes the name Sixtus IV. His papacy is

The Baptism of Christ by Perugino and Pinturicchio in the Sistine Chapel.

marked by shameless nepotism and worthy public works. He promotes nephews, rebuilds churches, improves roads and constructs the Ponte Sisto over the Tiber. But his chief work is the Sistine Chapel in the Vatican, which he has decorated by the leading artists of the day, including Botticelli, Ghirlandaio, Pinturicchio, Signorelli and Perugino.

1492–1503—The Spaniard Rodrigo Borgia bribes his way into the papal chair as Pope Alexander VI. He is the first Pope to publicly acknowledge his illegitimate children, including his beloved daughter Lucrezia. He makes Cesare, the favourite of his sons, first an archbishop then a cardinal. Father and son gain notoreity for supposedly poisoning cardinals at will and seizing their property. In 1494 King Charles VIII of France lays claim to the Kingdom of Naples and leads his army into Italy. The French troops occupy Rome while the Pope shelters in Castel Sant' Angelo.

1503–13—Giuliano della Rovere becomes Pope Julius II. Work advances in earnest on the rebuilding of St Peter's under the direction of Bramante. Raphael is brought to Rome to paint a series of rooms in the Vatican (the Raphael Stanze) and Michelangelo is commissioned to paint the Sistine Chapel ceiling.

1513–21—Giovanni de'Medici is elected Pope and takes the name Leo X. A great patron of the arts, like his predecessor, he makes Rome the social, artistic and intellectual capital of Europe. To raise funds for his grandiose projects, he sells indulgences on a massive scale: one of the abuses which helps pave the way for the Reformation.

1527—The Sack of Rome. The city is occupied and pillaged by the Lutheran troops of the German Emperor Charles V. When the imperial troops finally leave nine months later, the papacy has been brought low and the glories of the Renaissance almost totally eclipsed.

1534–49—The papacy of Paul III. In 1535 Michelangelo begins to paint the *Last Judgement* in the Sistine Chapel. Eleven years later, the 72-year-old Michelangelo is commissioned to direct the continuing rebuilding of St Peter's. The Counter-Reformation gets under way. Ignatius Loyola founds the Society of Jesus in Rome in 1540. The Jesuits, "a cohort combined for combat against spiritual foes", are recognized by the Pope and spearhead the moral regeneration of the Church. The Jesuits heavily influence the findings of the Council of Trent, convened by the Pope in 1545. In 1542 the Inquisition is restored in Rome. Heretics are publicly burned in the Campo dei Fiori. Under Paul IV, in 1557, a list of condemned writings is drawn up, the Index of Prohibited Books. It is made a penal offence to possess any forbidden book.

1568–75—The first church of the Baroque, the Gesù, is built in Rome. It has an enormous influence on subsequent architecture all over Europe.

1585–90—Sixtus V reorganizes the papal finances and embarks on a radical programme of Baroque town planning in Rome, entirely transforming the appearance of the city. He builds new aqueducts and fountains, widens and reroutes streets, constructs new bridges over the Tiber, and has obelisks set up as focal points for the new network of roads. He also has scores of medieval and classical buildings pulled down—much to the horror of many Romans.

1594—Death of Pierluigi Palestrina, the father of polyphonic music and the greatest of Italian Renaissance composers.

1600—The heretical philosopher, astronomer and mathematician, Giordano Bruno, is burned at the stake in the Campo dei Fiori. In 1633 Galileo is brought to trial in Rome and forced to denounce the Copernican system. Though made to recant the subversive notion that the earth moves around the sun, he is legendarily supposed to utter under his breath, *"Eppur se muove"*. Yet it moves.

1623–44—The papacy of the Barberini pope, Urban VIII, sees the flourishing of Baroque architecture, dominated by the genius of Bernini. In 1626 the Pope consecrates the new St Peter's.

1656–67—Bernini builds St Peter's Square.

18th C—Rome's political importance declines but foreign visitors continue to pour into the city, particularly notable are English gentlemen on the Grand Tour. Among the visitors is Edward Gibbon, who conceives the idea for *The Decline and Fall of the Roman Empire* while sitting on the Capitol in 1764. There is a new interest in the remains of ancient Rome, typified by the enthusaistic work of the Prussian archaelogist Johann Winckelmann, Europe's leading expert on classical art, who in 1763 is appointed

Chief Superintendent of antiquities in the city.

1797—After a series of victories in Italy, Napoleon Bonaparte imposes the Treaty of Tolentino on the Pope. Rome is stripped by the French of countless antique sculptures, Renaissance paintings and other works of art.

1798—French troops, under General Berthier, occupy Rome and proclaim a republic. The 80-year-old Pope Pius VI is expelled from the city. His successor, Pius VII, comes to terms with Napoleon by the Concordat of 1801 and three years later crowns Napoleon Emperor in Paris.

1809—Napoleon annexes the Papal States to the French Empire and exiles the Pope. In 1811 he proclaims his new-born son King of Rome.

1814—Following the defeat of Napoleon, the Papal States are restored and Pius VII returns to Rome.

1848—Revolutions break out all over Europe. The Risorgimento gains momentum—the dream of throwing off foreign domination and creating a united Italy, with Rome as its capital. Pius IX is driven out of Rome and a republic established. As a French army advances on Rome to restore the Pope, Mazzini becomes the political leader of the Roman Republic. Its defence is

The Victor Emmanuel monument was built as a proud symbol of Italian unity, but for the Romans it is a huge monstrosity.

entrusted to Garibaldi, a veteran of revolutions in South America. But despite valiant efforts the Republic falls to the French in July 1849. The following year Pius IX returns to Rome and papal rule is re-established.

1861—Victor Emmanuel II, King of Sardinia and Savoy, is proclaimed King of Italy. Rome is declared the capital of the new kingdom but remains in the control of the Pope.

1869—The dogma of papal infallibility is defined at the First Vatican Council.

1870—French troops are withdrawn from Rome during the Franco-Prussian War, to be replaced on 20 September (XX Settembre) by the forces of King Victor Emmanuel II. The Pope retires into the Vatican and Rome becomes the capital of a united Italy. In the coming years, palaces and convents are converted into government ministries and an army of civil servants descends on the city. New buildings are erected all over Rome, altering forever the appearance of the city. Attracted by the building boom, large numbers of peasants flood into the capital. Between 1870 and the end of the century, Rome's population more than doubles, from around 200,000 to over 460,000.

1922—Mussolini's Fascists stage the March on Rome and Mussolini is invited by King Victor Emmanuel III to form a government.

1929—The Lateran Pact is signed, formalizing relations between the Vatican and the Italian State. The Vatican City becomes an independent sovereign state.

1943—Mussolini is deposed. Italy surrenders to the Allies but Rome is occupied by the Germans. Over 2,000 Jews are arrested and deported to Germany. In reprisal for the killing of 32 Germans by the Italian Resistance, 335 people are shot in caves along the Fosse Ardeatine on 24 March 1944.

1944—Rome is liberated by the Allies.

1946—Victor Emmanuel III abdicates. The Italian people vote by referendum to establish a republic.

1957—The Treaty of Rome establishes the European Economic Community.

1960—Rome hosts the Olympic Games. Federico Fellini's film *La dolce vita* paints a portrait of a glamorous and decadent Rome enjoying the "sweet life" to the full. The Vatican attempts to have the film banned. The Via Veneto becomes the in-place for international café society.

1962—Pope John XXIII calls the Second Vatican Council, which introduces many reforms to the Church.

1976—Rome elects a Communist mayor for the first time in its history.

1978—The Christian Democrat leader Aldo Moro is kidnapped and assassinated by the Red Brigades. Karol Wojtyla becomes Pope John Paul II.

1981—A Turk attempts to assassinate John Paul II in St Peter's Square.

1986—*Il Sorpasso*. The 1980s are a period of economic boom for Italy. In 1986 Italy claims to have overtaken Britain and become the fifth world economic power.

1990—Italy hosts the World Cup and the final is staged in Rome. In the years leading up to the championships, billions of lire are spent on refurbishing the capital.

Just the Essentials

First-time visitors to Rome may be overwhelmed by the sheer wealth of the city's cultural heritage. For those whose time is limited here's a list of places one simply shouldn't miss.

Capitoline Hill
Capitoline Museums: oldest (public) selection of classical sculpture worldwide.
Capitoline Wolf: Etruscan, bronze.
Belvedere di Monte Tarpeo: excellent views from garden.

The Roman Forum
Forum: ancient centre of public life.

The Palatine
Hill over Forum; she-wolf's cave.

Colosseum
Colosseum: most famous monument; cruel beauty.
Trajan's Column: with reliefs of victorious soldiers.

Piazza Venezia to Campo dei Fiori and the Ghetto
Gesù: flamboyantly designed Jesuit Church.
Campo dei Fiori: site of public executions 17th century; now a busy food market.
Fontana delle Tartarughe: delightful fountain.

Around Piazza Navona
Piazza Navona: ancient stadium; vibrant activity, a haunt for all types of people.
Contarelli Chapel: paintings of life of St Matthew, Caravaggio's first Rome Commission.

The Pantheon
The Pantheon: awesome architecture/memorial temple built by Agrippa/Hadrian.

Around the Spanish Steps and the Corso
Piazza di Spagna and Spanish Steps: Keats-Shelley Memorial Museum; district popular with English aristocrats.
Villa Borghese Park: splendid views from the terrace of the Pincio.
Saint' Ignazio church: *trompe l'oeil* ceiling.
Fontana di Trevi: an unforgettable sites in Rome.

Villa Borghese

Galleria Borghese: summer house containing early sculptures of Bernini.

Museo Nazionale di Villa Guilia: Etruscan art, summer villa built for Julius III.

From the Quirinal to the Baths of Diocletian

Galleria Nazionale d'Arte Antica: work from Lippi, Raphael, Titian, Caravaggio and Holbein.

Santa Maria della Vittoria church: Ecstasy of St Theresa by Bernini—massive sculpture.

Santa Maria Maggiore to the Baths of Caracalla

Santa Maria Maggiore: graceful patriarchal basilica.

Santa Prassede church: striking Byzantine mosaics.

Saint Peter in Chains church: church built on top of another— archaeological interest.

San Giovanni in Laterano

San Giovanni in Laterano: Rome's official cathedral.

San Giovanni in Forte: Baptistery of cathedral; most ancient part.

Trastevere

Janiculum Hill: vantage point for viewing Rome.

Piazza Bocca della Verita. The Aventine and Testaccio

Santa Maria in Cormedia: 12th-century elegant church.

Aventine Hill: peaceful site considered the Ancients "Sacred Mount".

San Paolo Fuori le Mura

San Paolo Fuori le Mura church: cloisters; renowned as the most beautiful in Rome.

Castel Sant'Angelo

Castel Sant'Angelo: tomb and fortress; wide and varied history.

St Peters

St Peters: church

Piazza San Pietro: oval piazza with obelisk.

Pietá: sculpture of Madonna, by Michelangelo in St Peter's.

The Vatican

Laocoön: celebrated sculpture in Pio-Clementine Museum.

Raphael Stanze: rooms decorated by Raphael.

Sistine Chapel: containing Michelangelo's astounding frescoes.

Vatican Picture Gallery: collection from 11th–19th centuries.

Environs

Appian Way: Roman road to Capna.

Ostia Antica: ruins of Rome's ancient Port.

Tivoli: Hadrian's Villa, most notable; Villa d'Este, in forum.

Colli Albani: south-east of Rome; volcanic hills.

Going Places with Something Special in Mind

Rome has so many sights and sites to choose from that it's difficult to know where to begin. One way to plan your visit is to organize your sightseeing around particular themes, whether the works of a great artist or the best shopping districts. Here are a few suggestions to help you on your way.

Panoramic Rome

Given that Rome was built on seven hills it's no surprise that the city should boast a number of vantage points offering splendid panoramic views.

1 BELVEDERE DI MONTE TARPEO
Views of the Forum, Palatine, Colosseum, Aventine and, in the distance, the Baths of Caracalla from the promontory on the Capitoline Hill

*P*iazza del Campidoglio, Michelangelo's beautiful Renaissance square on the Capitoline Hill.

where ancient Rome's enemies were thrown to their deaths.

2 PINCIO
The dome of St Peter's dominates the Rome skyline seen from the terrace at the south-west corner of the Villa Borghese.

3 GIANICOLO
Superb views of St Peter's (to the north) and the city (to the east) beside the equestrian statue of Garibaldi on top of the Janiculum Hill.

4 CASTEL SANT'ANGELO
Spectacular view of the city from the terrace of this papal castle; Puccini's heroine Tosca leaped from the battlements to her death.

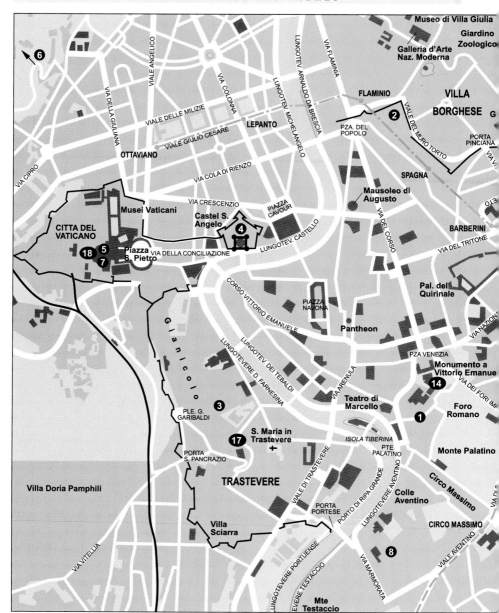

5 ST PETER'S

The Dome of St Peter's affords an unbeatable view of the city and its surroundings; closer at hand are the Vatican city and the Pope's back garden.

6 MONTE MARIO

Hill to the north of the Vatican; the site of Raphael's Villa Madama, popular with painters in the 17th and 18th centuries and still pleasant today.

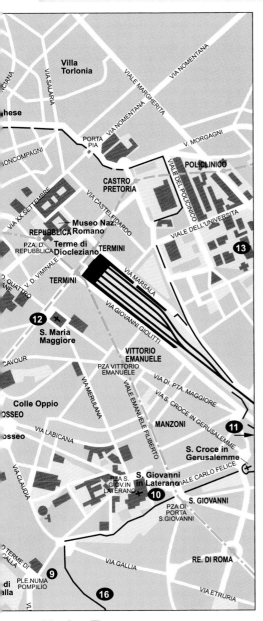

*P*ositions of the sites described in Panoramic Rome, Holy Rome *and* In the Steps of St Peter.

martyred saints. Only the Pope may celebrate mass at the high altar of the four patriarchal basilicas: St Peter's, San Paolo fuori le Mura, San Giovanni in Laterano and Santa Maria Maggiore.

7 ST PETER'S
Most famous church in Christendom, built over the tomb of St Peter; Michelangelo's dome is the most celebrated outline on the Rome skyline.

8 SAN PAOLO FUORI LE MURA
The great basilica founded over the tomb of St Paul in the 4th century was destroyed by fire in 1823; the rebuilt church preserves the ancient cloisters, the most beautiful in Rome.

9 SAN SEBASTIANO
Named after the Roman soldier martyred for his Christian faith in 288 AD; the nearby 'catacombs' gave their name to all Rome's underground cemeteries.

10 SAN GIOVANNI IN LATERANO
The Pope's official seat as Bishop of Rome and thus the city's cathedral; founded by Constantine, the first Christian Emperor.

Holy Rome

The seven pilgrimmage churches of Rome have been sites of special reverence for Christians for centuries. Most were built over the tombs of

11 SANTA CROCE IN GERUSALEMME
Named after a relic of the True Cross brought to Rome by St Helena, the mother of Constantine.

12 SANTA MARIA MAGGIORE
Founded on the site of a miraculous midsummer fall of snow and dedicated to the Mother of Christ.

13 SAN LORENZO FUORI LE MURA
Built over the legendary tomb of St Lawrence; the basilica consists of two early-Christian churches joined together in the 13th century by the demolition of their apses.

In the Steps of St Peter

St Peter, the fisherman from the shores of Lake Galilee; the 'rock' upon whom Christ said he would build the Church; bearer of the keys of heaven and first pope. He met martyrdom in the persecutions of Christians ordered by Nero after the great fire of AD 64. He asked to be crucified head downwards as he was not worthy to suffer the same death as Christ.

14 SAN PIETRO IN CARCERE
The Mamertine Prison, where St Peter was imprisoned by Nero; later consecrated as a chapel.

15 SAN PIETRO IN VINCOLI
Contains the chains said to have bound St Peter during his imprisonment in Jerusalem (and, some say, the chains of his confinement in Rome).

16 DOMINE QUO VADIS
Fleeing Rome to escape Nero's persecutions, St Peter encountered a vision of Christ at this spot; he thereupon returned to the city to face martyrdom.

St Peter Enthroned: *bronze statue by Arnolfo da Cambio in St Peter's.*

17 SAN PIETRO IN MONTORIO

Built on the supposed site of St Peter's crucifixion (authorities now say the apostle was martyred in the Circus of Nero, just to the south of the site of the basilica of St Peter's).

18 ST PETER'S

The greatest church in Christendom stands over the site of the apostle's tomb.

Parks and Gardens

Rome's green spaces were once the preserve of popes and princes, now many of the city's aristocratic parks are open to all.

1 VILLA BORGHESE

Rome's finest public park, created for Cardinal Scipione Borghese in the 17th century and presented to the city by King Umberto I in 1902. The park in-

Piazza di Siena in the Villa Borghese.

cludes the gardens of the Pincio and the city's zoo.

2 VILLA ADA

Vast public park in the grounds of the former residence of Italy's last king, Victor Emmanuel III.

3 VILLA TORLONIA

The villa was once Mussolini's private residence; the gardens are now a public park.

4 PARCO COLLE OPPIO

Park on the summit of the Oppian

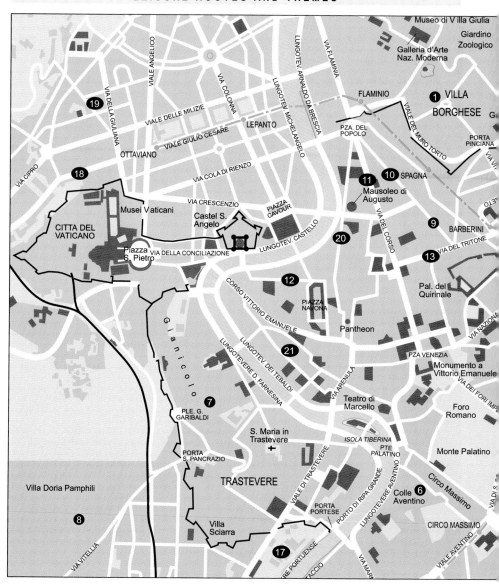

Hill, contains the remains of Nero's Golden House and the Baths of Titus and Trajan.

5 VILLA CELIMONTANA
Picturesque gardens on the Celian Hill, the grounds of a patrician villa built in 1582.

6 ROSETO DI VALLE MURCIA
Rose garden on the Aventine Hill.

7 PASSEGGIATA DEL GIANCIOLO
Winding promenade through a park laid out in the late-19th century on the Janiculum Hill.

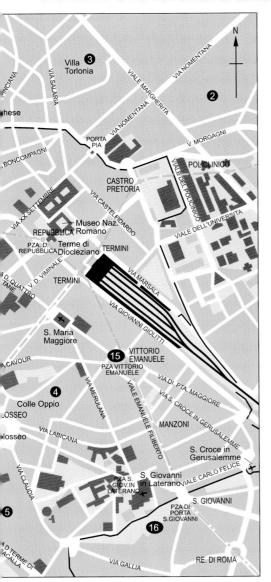

Positions of the sites described in Parks and Gardens *and* Shopping.

*V*alentino in Via Bocca di Leone.

Shopping

From up-market and exclusive shops to street markets, Rome offers the complete shopping experience.

Shops

9 VIA CONDOTTI
Rome's most fashionable shopping street, home to Bulgari and Gucci and other high-class shops. The neighbouring streets also boast elegant and exclusive emporia.

10 VIA DEL BABUINO AND VIA MARGUTTA
High-class antiques shops and galleries; Via Margutta specializes in picture-framing.

11 VIA DEL CORSO
Lively high-street fashion rather than *alta moda*.

12 VIA DEI CORONARI
Site of a celebrated antiques fair in May.

8 VILLA DORIA PAMPHILI
Rome's largest park, created for Prince Camillo Pamphili in the 17th century.

83

*C*ampo dei Fiori.

13 VIA DEL TRITONE AND VIA NAZIONALE
Affordable fashion, leather, and shoes.

14 VIA COLA DA RIENZO
Classy shopping street near the Vatican.

Markets

15 PIAZZA VITTORIO EMANUELE
Noisy and colourful market selling everything from food to fabrics.

16 VIA SANNIO
Huge market for clothes near the basilica of San Giovanni in Laterano.

17 PORTA PORTESE
Rome's famous Sunday-morning flea market.

18 VIA ANDREA DORIA
Food market north of the Vatican.

19 VIA TRIONFALE
Flower market open to the public on Tuesday mornings.

20 LARGO FONTANELLA DI BORGHESE
Weekday morning market specializing in old prints and books.

21 CAMPO DEI FIORI
Lively fruit and vegetable market in an historic square.

Wine Tour

Among the Alban Hills south-east of Rome are the Castelli Romani, a series of towns famous for their wines.

1 GROTTAFERRATA
Noted for its castle-like abbey and splendid white wine.

2 MARINO
Scene of a bacchanalian wine festival in October when the town's fountains flow with wine.

3 CASTEL GANDOLFO
Site of the ancient Latin city of Alba Longa; today the town is the summer residence of the Pope.

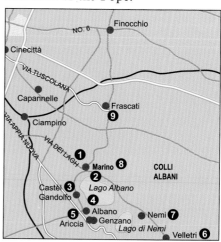

4 ALBANO

Founded as a legionary camp in the 2nd century AD by the Emperor Septimius Severus.

5 ARICCIA

Ancient town pleasantly sited on wooded slopes; famous for its *porchetta*, sucking-pig.

6 VELLETRI

Historic wine-making town esteemed for its dry red wine and 13th-century cathedral.

7 NEMI

Nearby Lake Nemi was in ancient times the site of the Grove of Diana; today the area is renowned for its *fragole di bosco*, wild strawberries.

8 ROCCA DI PAPA

The highest of the Castelli Romani, named after a 12th-century papal castle.

9 FRASCATI

Hill town famous for its soft and golden white wine and historic villas.

The Seven Hills of Rome

The seven hills of ancient Rome may not be as prominent today as they once were but they remain at the heart of the city.

1 PALATINE

Where Romulus founded his new city and the emperors built their palaces.

2 CAPITOLINE

The smallest of the seven hills but the symbolic head of Rome.

3 AVENTINE

In ancient times the "Sacred Mount"; today a tranquil oasis in the heart of the city.

4 CELIAN

Crowned by the church of Santa Maria in Domnica and the gardens of the Villa Celimontana.

5 ESQUILINE

Most expansive of the ancient hills.

6 VIMINAL

Today the ancient Viminal Hill is almost indistinguishable from the neighbouring Quirinal.

7 QUIRINAL

The highest of the seven hills; on the summit stands the palace of Italy's president.

Fountains

Thanks to the engineering skills of the ancient Romans (who built the city's aqueducts) and the patronage of the Renaissance popes (who restored them), Rome is simply awash with water. No other city can boast so many fountains. Here is a half-dozen of the very best.

8 FOUNTAIN OF THE TORTOISES

Four dolphins, four boys and some tortoises in Piazza Mattei.

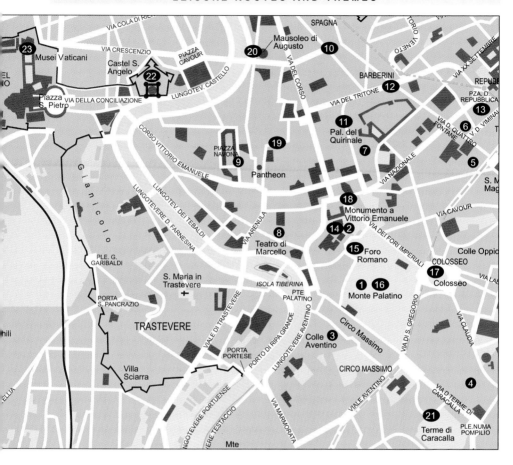

9 FOUNTAIN OF THE FOUR RIVERS

Bernini's brilliant Baroque centrepiece to Piazza Navona.

10 BARCACCIA FOUNTAIN

A fountain in the shape of a leaking boat at the foot of the Spanish Steps.

11 TREVI FOUNTAIN

A visit to Rome would be incomplete without tossing a coin into the city's most famous fountain: Nicola Salvi's Rococo extravaganza.

*P*ositions *of the sites* described *in* The Seven Hills of Rome, Fountains *and* Ancient Rome.

12 TRITON FOUNTAIN

Bernini's triton blows water from a conch in Piazza Barberini (his charming Bee Fountain is nearby too).

13 FOUNTAIN OF THE NAIADS

Voluptuous bronze nymphs splashing about in the Piazza della Repubblica.

Ancient Rome

You can hardly move in Rome without stubbing your toe on some ancient remains, but you simply must look up and take note of these famous monuments, archaelogical sites and works of art.

14 CAPITOLINE
The equestrian statue of Marcus Aurelius; the Capitoline Wolf; the Esquiline Venus; the colossal statue of Constantine.

15 ROMAN FORUM
The centre of ancient Rome's political, religious and business life.

16 PALATINE
The overgrown remains of imperial palaces on the hill of Rome's legendary birthplace.

17 COLOSSEUM
The imposing remains of the gladiator's bloody circus.

18 TRAJAN'S COLUMN
Decorated with spiralling reliefs illustrating Trajan's military campaigns.

19 PANTHEON
A pagan temple to all the gods; an unparalleled feat of architecture and engineering.

20 ARA PACIS AUGUSTAE
The Altar of Augustan Peace.

21 BATHS OF CARACALLA
The most luxurious baths of ancient Rome.

22 CASTEL SANT'ANGELO
Built by Hadrian as an imperial mausoleum; later used as a papal fortress.

23 VATICAN MUSEUMS
The Laocoön group, found in 1506 and a great influence on Renaissance artists; the Belvedere Torso, a 1st-century BC statue much admired by Michelangelo.

Medieval Rome

Medieval Rome has tended to be overshadowed by earlier and later periods, but in its art and architecture there is much to admire, from Byzantine-influenced mosaics to a rare Gothic church.

1 SANTA MARIA SOPRA MINERVA
Behind a plain Renaissance façade lies the only truly Gothic church in Rome (late-13th C).

2 SANTA MARIA MAGGIORE
Important medieval mosaics decorating nave and triumphal arch (5th C); apse mosaic by Jacopo Torriti (late-13th C).

3 SANTA PRASSEDE
Chapel of St Zeno, decorated with splendid Byzantine mosaics and known in the Middle Ages as the "Garden of Paradise" (9th C).

4 SAN CLEMENTE
Well-preserved medieval basilica (early-12th C) built above early-Christian church (late-4th C).

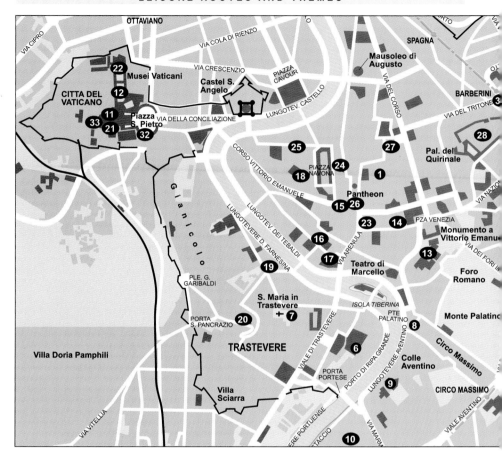

5 SAN GIOVANNI IN LATERANO
Baptistery, founded by Constantine (c. 315–24) and rebuilt by Sixtus III (432–40); cloisters by Jacopo and Pietro Vasselletto (c. 1230).

6 SANTA CECILIA IN TRASTEVERE
Fresco of the Last Judgement by Pietro Cavallini (c. 1295).

7 SANTA MARIA IN TRASTEVERE
One of the oldest churches in Rome and the first to be dedicated to the Virgin (4th C).

8 SANTA MARIA IN COSMEDIN
Beautiful medieval church (8th C) with elegant Romanesque bell tower and fine Cosmatesque mosaic work (12th C).

9 SANTA SABINA
Fine example of an early-Christian basilica; ancient door made of cypress wood (5th C).

10 SAN PAOLO FUORI LE MURA
The most beautiful cloisters in Rome, the work of the school of Cosmatesque mosaic workers (13th C).

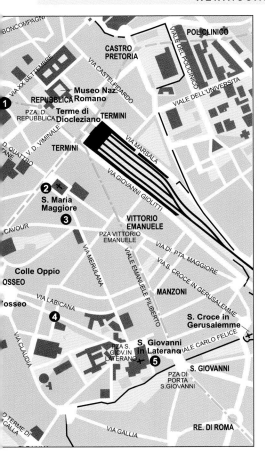

*P*ositions of sites described in Medieval Rome, Renaissance Rome *and* Baroque Rome.

Renaissance Rome

The Renaissance was inspired by the rediscovery in the 15th century of the art of ancient Greece and Rome. It began in Florence and came late to Rome, but from around 1500 to 1527, under the leadership of Bramante, Michelangelo and Raphael, the city was the undisputed capital of the High Renaissance.

13 PIAZZA DEL CAMPIDOGLIO
Michelangelo's glorious Renaissance square (1546).

14 PALAZZO VENEZIA
The first major Renaissance palace in Rome (begun 1455).

15 PALAZZO DELLA CANCELLERIA
Splendid Renaissance palace, the architect is unknown but Bramante is reputed to have worked on the beautiful courtyard (1485–1513).

16 PALAZZO FARNESE
One of the masterpieces of High Renaissance architecture, created by Antonio da Sangallo, Michelangelo and Giacomo della Porta (1514–89).

17 PALAZZO SPADA
Huge Renaissance palace with impressive stucco decorations on the façade (1549–59).

18 SANTA MARIA DELLA PACE
Bramante's beautiful and harmonious cloisters (1504).

19 VILLA FARNESINA
Raphael's Galatea fresco (1514).

11 ST PETER'S
St Peter Enthroned, bronze statue by Arnolfo da Cambio (c. 1296).

12 VATICAN MUSEUMS
Stefaneschi Altarpiece, triptych by Giotto which prefigures the Renaissance (c. 1330).

Cloisters in San Paolo fuori le Mura.

(1508–12); Raphael Stanze (1508-34); Vatican Picture Gallery: Raphael's Transfiguration (1519–20).

20 SAN PIETRO IN MONTORIO
Bramante's Tempietto, a beautifully proportioned circular temple (1502).

21 ST PETER'S
The Dome, designed by Michelangelo and completed by Giacomo della Porta (1546–90); Michelangelo's Pietà (1499).

22 VATICAN MUSEUMS
Chapel of Nicholas V: frescoes by Fra Angelico (1447–51); Sistine Chapel: frescoes by Pinturicchio, Botticelli, Perugino and Luca Signorelli (1481–83), and Michelangelo's sublime ceiling

Baroque Rome

The spiritual confidence of the Counter Reformation found expression in the theatricality and dynamism of the Baroque. In Rome, the Baroque era was dominated by artists such as Bernini but contemporaries like Carlo Maderno, Borromini and Pietro da Cortona also bestowed their share of masterpieces on the city.

23 GESU
Jesuit church prefiguring the Baroque (1568–75) with Giovanni Battista Gaulli's illusionistic ceiling fresco, the

Triumph of the Name of Jesus, and Andrea Pozzo's tomb of St Ignatius of Loyola (1695–1700).

*B*ernini's Piazza San Pietro, "the meeting place of all mankind".

24 PIAZZA NAVONA
Bernini's *Fountain of the Four Rivers* (1648–51); Borromini's dramatic façade to Sant'Agnese in Agone (1653–57).

25 SANTA MARIA DELLA PACE
Pietro da Cortona's elegant facade and semicircular portico (1656–57).

26 SANT'IVO
Baroque masterpeice by Borromini, crowned by remarkable spiralling campanile (1642–60).

27 SANT'IGNAZIO
Andrea Pozzo's spectacular *trompe l'oeil* ceiling fresco, the Apotheosis of St Ignatius (1691–95).

28 SANT'ANDREA AL QUIRINALE
Compact Baroque masterpiece by Bernini (1658–71).

29 SAN CARLO ALLE QUATTRO FONTANE
Ingenious use of cramped site on Via del Quirinale by Borromini (1638–68).

30 PALAZZO BARBERINI
Grand Baroque palace begun by Carlo Maderno in 1624; Pietro da Cortona's illusionistic ceiling fresco, *The Triumph of Divine Providence* (1633–39).

31 SANTA MARIA DELLA VITTORIA
Cornaro Chapel, Bernini's *Ecstasy of St Theresa* (1645–52).

32 PIAZZA SAN PIETRO

Bernini's majestic oval piazza symbolizes the embrace of the Church (1656–67).

33 ST PETER'S

Bernini's *baldacchino*, a dazzling fusion of sculpture and architecture (1624–33), and his magnificent Chair of St Peter (1665).

The Genius of Michelangelo

The idea of the artist as genius can be said to have originated with Michelangelo Buonarroti (1475–1564). His apparently superhuman talents as painter, sculptor and architect astonished his contemporaries and he was the first artist to be made the subject of a biography during his own lifetime.

Piazza del Campidoglio: overall design for square and the three palaces which bound it.

Palazzo Farnese: cornice and central loggia of façade.

Santa Maria sopra Minerva: statue of *Christ the Redeemer*.

Porta Pia: city gate, one of the artist's last works.

Santa Maria degli Angeli: converted from the central hall of the Baths of Diocletian.

San Pietro in Vincoli: Tomb of Julius II, including statue of Moses.

St Peter's: Dome; Pietà sculpture.

Vatican: Sistine Chapel ceiling frescoes and fresco of the *Last Judgement* on altar wall; Michelangelo is also said to have designed the uniforms of the Swiss Guards.

The Prodigious Talent of Raphael

Born 31 years after Leonardo da Vinci and eight years after Michelangelo, Raphael (1483–1520) was the youngest of the three great creators of the High Renaissance, but while still in his 20s he was acknowledged as their peer. Dead at 37, he left a legacy of inestimable value to Western art.

Santa Maria della Pace: frescoes of the Sibyls.

Sant'Agostino: fresco of the Prophet Isaiah.

Sta Maria del Popolo: Chigi Chapel.

Accademia di San Luca: *St Luke Painting the Virgin*.

Galleria Borghese: *Lady with a Unicorn*; *Portrait of a Man*; *Deposition*.

Galleria Nazionale d'Arte Antica at Palazzo Barberini: *La Fornarina*.

Villa Farnesina: Galatea Loggia.

Vatican: Raphael Stanze; Loggia; Vatican Picture Gallery: *Coronation of the Virgin*; *Madonna of Foligno*; *The Transfiguration*, Raphael's last work.

Caravaggio's Shocking Art

Michelangelo Merisi da Caravaggio (1571–1610) scandalized his contemporaries as much by his art as by his dissolute and violent lifestyle. He revolutionized religious painting by his deployment of realistic characters and settings and by his use of dramatic lighting and startling forshortening.

Capitoline Picture Gallery: *St John the Baptist*.

Sant'Agostino: *La Madonna dei Pellegrini*.

*R*aphael's Leo I repulsing Attila.

The Baroque Brilliance of Bernini

San Luigi dei Francesi: *The Calling of St Matthew*; *St Matthew and the Angel*; *The Martyrdom of St Matthew*. Santa Maria del Popolo: *The Crucifixion of St Peter*; *The Conversion of St Paul*.
Galleria Doria Pamphili: *St John the Baptist*; *Mary Magdalene*; *Rest on the Flight into Egypt*.
Galleria Nazionale d'Arte Antica at Palazzo Barberini: *Narcissus*; *Judith with the Head of Holofernes*.
Galleria Borghese: *Boy with a Basket of Fruit*; *The Sick Bacchus*; *David with the Head of Goliath* (the head is believed to be a self-portrait).
Galleria Nazionale d'Arte Antica at Palazzo Corsini: *St John the Baptist*. Vatican Picture Gallery: *Descent from the Cross*.

On no other city has one artist stamped his mark so emphatically as Gian Lorenzo Bernini (1598–1680) did on Rome. The supreme master of Baroque art (in some eyes, its virtual inventor), Bernini changed the look of the city forever with his boldly theatrical designs for fountains and squares, churches and chapels.
Piazza Navona: *Fountain of the Four Rivers*; *Moor Fountain*.
Piazza Minerva: Elephant supporting Egyptian Obelisk.
Santa Maria del Popolo: Cappella Chigi, statues of *Habakkuk* and *Daniel and the Lion*.
Galleria Doria Pamphili: bust of *Innocent X*.
Villa Borghese: sculptures—*Aeneas and Anchises*, *Rape of Proserpine*, *David*, *Apollo and Daphne*; two portrait busts

of *Cardinal Scipione Borghese*; paintings—two self-portraits.
Santa Andrea al Quirinale: Bernini's finest church.
Piazza Barberini: *Triton Fountain*; *Bee Fountain*.
Santa Maria della Vittoria: Cornaro Chapel, *Ecstasy of St Theresa*.
San Francesco a Ripa: Altieri Chapel, statue of *Beata Ludovica Albertoni*.
St Peter's: Piazza San Pietro; Basilica: Baldacchino; Chair of St Peter; statue of *St Longinus*; Tombs of Urban VIII and Alexander VII; equestrian statue of *Constantine*.

Gastronomy

The Caesars may have feasted on larks' tongues in aspic but today real Roman gastronomy is based on the simple food of the poor; nevertheless, fine dishes based on plain ingredients can be found in the very best restaurants.

IL BAFFETTO
Via del Governo Vecchio 114 (Tel. 6561617); lively pizzeria near Piazza Navona.

L'EAU VIVE
Via Monterone 85 (Tel. 6541095); restaurant run by French nuns.

LA ROSETTA
Via della Rosetta 9 (Tel. 6861002); expensive fish restaurant.

EL TOULA
Via della Lupa 29b (Tel. 6873498); reckoned by many the best restaurant in Rome.

PIPERNO
Monte dei Cenci 9 (Tel. 6542772); Roman-Jewish cuisine.

VECCHIA ROMA
Piazza Campitelli 18 (Tel. 6864604); historic restaurant in medieval square.

DA MARIO
Via delle Vite 55 (Tel. 6783818); Tuscan food.

ROMOLO
Via Porta Settimiana 8 (Tel. 5818284); historic restaurant in Trastevere.

APULEIUS SUL COLLE AVENTINO
Via Tempio di Diana 15 (Tel. 5742160); fish restaurant on the Aventine.

CHECCHINO
Via Monte Testaccio 30 (Tel. 5746318); 100-year-old restuarant in Testaccio, the best in town for offal.

*B*ernini's statue of the prophet Habakkuk in the Chigi Chapel of Santa Maria del Popolo.

Scenes of Triumph and Disaster on Rome's Capitol Hill

The smallest of the Seven Hills of Ancient Rome, the Capitoline makes up for what it lacks in size in historical importance. Rome's legendary founder, Romulus, made the hill a refuge for fugitive slaves as a way of boosting the population of his new city. When Rome had grown in size and power, her generals came in triumph to the temple of Jupiter; on another part of the hill, the city's traitors were thrown from a cliff to their deaths. The Capitoline has always been the symbolic head of Rome, but in the greatest days of the Empire it was more, it was the "head of the world".

From **Piazza d'Aracoeli** a gentle flight of steps leads to the Capitol. This is **La Cordonata**, designed by Michelangelo but not completed until after his death. The steeper flight of steps on the left, which lead to the church of Santa Maria in Aracoeli, were built as a thanksgiving for the end of the plague in 1348. In the garden between the two staircases is a small bronze statue of that medieval demagogue Cola di Rienzo, erected in 1887. It was on the

*T*hese giant marble fragments were once part of a colossal statue of Constantine, the first Christian emperor.

Capitol in 1347 that Cola proclaimed himself Tribune of the Roman People, promising to restore Rome to its ancient glory. But his grandiose dreams ended in disaster. Just a few years later, in 1354, Cola met his end, stabbed to death by his disgruntled subjects. The statue marks the spot where he was killed.

At the top of the **cordonata** are colossal statues of the **Dioscuri**, the name given to the demigods Castor and Pollux, the twin sons of Jupiter and Leda. The statues were found in the Ghetto and brought here in 1585.

Pause here to reflect that climbing the Capitoline has not always been so easy. In 390 BC Rome was threatened by tribes of Gauls from beyond the Alps. The Roman armies had been

Double Helping

When Leda was ravished by that wily old bird Jupiter in the guise of a swan, she gave birth to two eggs. From one of the eggs sprang Castor and Clytemnestra (wife-to-be of the Greek leader Agammenon), from the other came Pollux and Helen (femme fatale of the Trojan War). Castor and Pollux were stars in their own right (indeed, they finally made it up there among the constellations). Known together as the *Dioscuri* (from the Greek *Dios Kouros*, sons of Zeus), they had adventures aplenty, including the time they came to the aid of the Romans at the Battle of Lake Regillus in 496 BC. The battle, which saw off the tyrannical Tarquin dynasty once and for all, was only won when the twins joined the fray on their horses Cyllaros and Harpagus. The twins then rode to Rome with tidings of the victory, stopping to water their horses at the Fountain of Juturna in the Forum.

defeated in the field and the Gauls had almost totally overrun the city, but the Capitol held out. One starlit night, relates Livy, the Gauls launched a surprise attack and had almost succeeded in scaling the hill, unperceived by its defenders. But, in the nick of time, the honking of the sacred geese of Juno, which had not been killed despite the shortage of food, alerted an officer named Manlius. He swiftly raised the alarm and rushed to the crest of the hill, hurling from the precipice the leading Gaul. The attacker fell, dragging down others in his wake. Manlius's comrades then joined him in raining down javelins and stones on

*T*he Cordonata: Michelangelo's graceful approach to the Campidoglio.

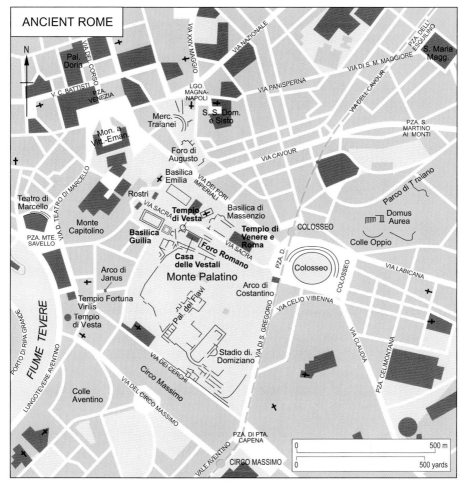

The main sites of ancient Rome.

the invaders and presently the whole company of Gauls lost their footing and were flung down headlong to destruction.

The Capitoline is actually twin peaks, the **Capitolium** to the south and the **Arx** to the north, with a hollow called the **Asylum** between them. When Romulus had founded his new city on the nearby Palatine Hill (traditionally in 753 BC), he set apart the Asylum as a haven for fugitive slaves. A canny strategem to increase the population of Rome.

The Asylum is now a glorious Renaissance square, the **Piazza del Campidoglio**, designed by Michelangelo for Pope Paul III as a splendid setting for the reception of the Holy Roman Emperor Charles V on his visit to Rome in 1536. The square was conceived as a fitting setting for a modern triumphal procession rivalling those of the ancient world. Michelangelo also planned the building, or re-building, of the three palaces that bound the square: the **Palazzo Senatorio** in front, the **Palazzo dei Conservatori** on the right and the **Palazzo Nuovo** on the left.

In fact, Michelangelo's conception was not to be fully realized until the middle of the next century. It was completed with contributions from various other architects, including Giacomo della Porta and Girolamo Rainaldi.

The centrepiece of Michelangelo's design for the square was the antique equestrian **statue of Marcus Aurelius**, which had been standing outside the Lateran palace since about the 12th century. This magnificent pagan monument, the oldest bronze equestrian statue in existence, had only survived down the centuries by virtue of its mistaken identification with the first Christian emperor, Constantine. (It was not recognized as a representation of Marcus Aurelius until the papacy of Sixtus IV in the 15th century.)

The statue, in gilded bronze, shows the Emperor in civilian dress, and was erected in commemoration of his military victories over the Germans (AD 173–180). It is said that Michelangelo found the statue so lifelike that he stood before the horse and commanded it to walk, "Cammina !"

Only traces of the ancient gilding remain on the bronze but, according to legend, when the end of the world is nigh, the statue will be miraculously covered again with gold. The statue, much damaged by pollution, spent most of the 1980s undergoing extensive restoration and is now on display, behind glass, in the Palazzo Nuovo.

The **Palazzo Senatorio** is in origin a medieval castle, itself built on the remains of the *Tabularium*, the ancient Roman State Record Office, erected in 78 BC. In the mid-12th century, Rome's medieval Senate was established in the fortress. Today, the building, redesigned by Michelangelo in the 16th century, is the official seat of the Commune of Rome.

The **Palazzo dei Conservatori**, designed by Michelangelo but completed by Giacomo della Porta, occupies the site of the ancient *Temple of Jupiter Optimus Maximus Capitolinus*. The most venerated temple in ancient Rome, it was founded by the Etruscan king Tarquinius Priscus, completed by his son Tarquinius Superbus and consecrated in 509 BC. According to legend, when the foundations for the temple were being dug a human head was unearthed, still bloody. This was taken to be a sign that Rome would become the head (*caput*) of Italy. Hence the name of the hill and the origin of the word "capital".

The **Palazzo Nuovo**, or the Palazzo del Museo Capitolino as it is sometimes known, was designed by Michelangelo. With its twin palace opposite, the Palazzo Nuovo houses the **Capitoline Museums**, the oldest public collection of classical sculpture in the world. (The first exhibits were made over to the people of Rome by Sixtus IV in 1471.)

The Capitoline Museums

In the courtyard of the Palazzo Nuovo is a fountain by Giacomo della Porta,

which incorporates a 1st-century BC statue of a river god. Known as **Marforio**, this is one of Rome's famous "talking statues", statues to which placards containing satirical comments on the events of the day were attached during the Renaissance. Marforio was popularly supposed to keep up a dialogue with his fellow *statua parlante,* Pasquino, a mutilated torso which stands near Piazza Navona.

The Palazzo Nuovo contains a number of very fine ancient statues. The most notable are to be found on the first floor. They include the **Capitoline Venus**, a Roman copy of a Greek original, the *Dying Gaul*, originally thought to be a statue of a gladiator ("Butchered to make a Roman holiday", in Byron's words), and a **Satyr Resting**, a copy of an original by

M arforio, one of the "talking statues" which gave the Romans a chance to laugh at their rulers.

Praxiteles. This is the statue which inspired Nathaniel Hawthorne's novel *The Marble Faun*. "It is impossible to gaze long at this stone image," wrote Hawthorne in the novel, "without conceiving a kindly sentiment towards it, as if its substance were warm to the touch, and imbued with actual life."

The **Hall of the Emperors** contains portrait busts of Roman emperors and their families, while the **Hall of the Philosophers** includes busts of Socrates, Sophocles, Demosthenes, Euripedes and Homer.

*T*his terrace on the Capitoline Hill offers a tremendous vantage point from which to view the ruins of the Roman Forum.

In the courtyard of the Palazzo dei Conservatori are the surreal fragments of a colossal **statue of Constantine**, which once stood in his Basilica in the Forum. The gigantic marble head is 2 m (6 ft) high and weighs 9 tons.

On the way up the stairs of the museum there are **reliefs** from the

triumphal arch of Marcus Aurelius. The reliefs depict scenes from the emperor's triumph, including one showing him making a sacrifice before the Temple of Jupiter Capitolinus. (Victorious Roman generals ended their triumphal processions through the city by making a sacrifice in the temple of Jupiter, their faces painted red in semblance of the god himself.)

The rooms of the museum are crammed with classical statuary. In the *Sala dei Trionfi di Mario* (the third room) is the celebrated **Spinario**, a delightful 1st-century BC statue of a boy plucking a thorn from his foot. The *Sala della Lupa* houses the **Capitoline Wolf**, a bronze statue of Etruscan origin dating from the 6th or 5th century BC. The figures of Romulus and Remus were added by Antonio Pollaiuolo in the early 15th century. The *Sala degli Orti Lamiani* displays statues found in the Lamiani Gardens on the Esquiline Hill, including the beautiful **Esquiline Venus**, dating from the 1st century BC.

The *Braccio Nuovo*, or New Wing, contains remains from the foundations of the Temple of Jupiter Capitolinus and recently discovered sculptures. The **Capitoline Picture Gallery (***Pinacoteca***)** includes works by Titian, Veronese, Velazquez, Rubens and Caravaggio.

Towards the Forum

Descend the Via del Campidoglio (to the left of the Palazzo Senatorio) to the terrace below, which affords a splendid view across the Forum. Immediately below the terrace is the Arch of Septimius Severus, in the distance looms the imposing hulk of the Colosseum; between these two monuments lie the ruins of the basilicas and temples of the Forum (*see* THE ROMAN FORUM).

Take the Via di Monte Tarpeo on the right for the Belvedere di Monte Tarpeo, or the Via San Pietro in Carcere for the nearby Mamertine Prison.

The **Mamertine Prison**, or *Tullianum*, is said to contain the dungeon in which St Peter was imprisoned by Nero. It was consecrated in the 16th century as the chapel of *San Pietro in Carcere*. In origin a water cistern, it was used as a prison by the ancient Romans. Prisoners were thrown into a dismal cell beneath the prison, called the *Tullianum*, there to die of strangulation or starvation. Among those who met their ends here were Vercingetorix, Julius Caesar's valiant Gaulish adversary, the African king Jugurtha, and the Emperor Tiberius's treacherous deputy Sejanus.

The **Belvedere di Monte Tarpeo** is a small garden which offers more fine views. The cliff below is thought to be the Tarpeian Rock, from which traitors to Rome were hurled to their deaths. The origin of the cliff's name goes back to Rome's earliest days.

When Romulus opened the Asylum to fugitives he succeeded in increasing Rome's population, but the settlement still lacked women. So Romulus invited neighbouring tribes to a festival in honour of the god Consus. When the celebrations were at their height, the Roman men swooped down and carried off the women of the Sabine tribe—the legendary Rape of the Sabine Women.

The Sabines plotted revenge and set seige to the Capitoline. Romulus had entrusted defence of the citadel to a commander named Spurius Tarpeius and it was thanks to the treachery of his daughter, Tarpeia, that the fortress fell to the Sabines. Dazzled by the golden bracelets of the Sabines, Tarpeia agreed to open the gate to the enemy if they gave her "what they wore on their left arms". When Tarpeia let in the Sabines, her reward was to be crushed to death by the Sabines' shields, which they also wore on their left arms.

The next day, a long and furious battle took place, with advantage going first one way, then the other. But just as the Romans seemed to have their opponents at their mercy, the Sabine women rushed into the midst of the combatants to entreat peace between their new husbands on the one side and their fathers and brothers on the other. The two tribes henceforth lived united as one nation: the Romans on the Palatine and the Sabines on the Capitoline. The valley between the two hills, where Romans and Sabines met, developed into the Forum.

Santa Maria in Aracoeli

The church stands on the site of the ancient Temple of Juno Moneta. (The Roman mint was attached to the temple, the origin of the word "money".) According to a medieval legend, it was here that the Tiburtine Sibyl prophesied the birth of Christ to the emperor Augustus. The Emperor thereupon saw a vision of the Virgin Mary, which prompted him to erect an altar on the spot. This was the *Ara Coeli*, or Altar of Heaven.

In existence from at least the 6th century, **Santa Maria in Aracoeli** for some time belonged to the Benedictines but in the 13th century it was transferred to the Franciscans who rebuilt it in the Romanesque style. In the Middle Ages the church was the meeting place of the Roman Parliament and it was here on Whit Sunday in 1347 that Cola di Rienzo set forth his revolutionary programme for the transformation of Rome. Cola is supposed to have been the first to ascend the flight of steps leading to the church from the Piazza d'Aracoeli but he had in fact fled the city before they were built in 1348. It was here, on the 15 October 1764, as he sat musing on the Capitol, listening to the chants of the barefoot friars in Santa Maria, that Edward Gibbon conceived the idea for his monumental *History of the Decline and Fall of the Roman Empire*.

Inside the church the nave is lined with 22 columns taken from ancient temples and palaces. Above your head is a richly gilded ceiling, created in 1575 to commemorate the Christian naval victory over the Turks at the Battle of Lepanto four years earlier. Below your feet is a 13th-century Cosmatesque pavement, a fine example of the art of the school of mosaic workers which flourished in Rome from the 12th to 14th centuries. Indeed, the church is rich in religious works of art and magnificent funerary monuments. Look out for the 15th-century fresco cycle depicting the **Life of St Bernard of Siena** by Pinturicchio in the Buffalini Chapel (the first chapel in the right aisle) and the beautiful early-14th-century tomb of Cardinal Matteo di Acquasparta (mentioned by Dante in "Paradiso"). The tomb is by Giovanni Cosma and contains a fresco by Pietro Cavallini.

The church's most venerated relic is the **Santo Bambino**, a statue of the Holy Child which was reputedly carved by a 14th-century Franciscan monk out of the wood of an olive tree from the garden of Gethsemene. This sacred image, embellished with precious jewels, is held in particularly deep affection by the Roman people and is taken to visit the sick in the hospitals of Rome. In former years the Santo Bambino travelled in his own carriage; today, more prosaically, he gets about by taxi. From Christmas Eve to Epiphany (6 January) the statue is displayed in the *Cappella del Presepio* (in the left aisle). Here young children recite *sermoni*, short poems and speeches, before his crib. For the rest of the year the statue is kept in the *Cappella del Santissima* (off the transept).

Romantic Ruins at the Heart of Ancient Rome

Visitors come to the Forum to contemplate ancient Rome's navel. This was the city's hub, around it revolved Rome's political, religious and business life. The city's main street was here, the Via Sacra or Sacred Way, so were its most important temples and public buildings. Here, symbolically, was the very centre of the city: the Umbilicus Urbis.

Originally a marshy valley between the Capitoline and Palatine hills, the area occupied by the **Forum** was drained by the Cloaca Maxima, the great sewer traditionally begun by the legendary Etruscan king Tarquinius Priscus in the 6th century BC. The site became a market place and thence developed into the centre of the city's public life in all its aspects—business transactions, political meetings, religious ceremonies, important funerals, public

Of all the women in Imperial Rome, the vestal virgins were second only to the empress in social rank and political importance.

executions and the early gladiatorial games all took place here.

Earthquakes, pillage and centuries of use as a stone quarry reduced the Forum to rubble. When the early archaeologists arrived on the scene towards the end of the 18th century (the first people to take a scientific rather than a romantic interest in the ruins), the Forum was in use as a cattle field, the *Campo Vaccino*, its original level hidden by some 15 m (50 ft) of earth and debris. Since then painstaking excavations have uncovered the traces of around 1,000 years of Roman history.

It takes a considerable effort of the imagination to rebuild in the mind's eye the grandeur that was ancient Rome from these shattered remains, but walking about the Forum today

*T*he ruins of the Forum, the hub of ancient Rome.

one can suddenly come across a detail which brings the past vividly to life again—like the copper coins fused into a pavement by the heat of the flames when Rome was sacked and razed by the invading Goths in AD 410.

The entrance to the Roman Forum (so called to distinguish it from the later imperial fora) is around half-way down the Via dei Fori Imperiali, opposite Via Cavour. (Before attempting to pick your way through the remains it is worth while to get an overview of the site from the vantage point of the terrace behind the Capitol.) Having entered the Forum, the visitor should proceed in a general anticlockwise direction to take in the major remains.

On the right is the **Basilica Aemilia**, a great hall used as a place of business, originally built by the censors M. Aemilius Lepidus and M. Fulvius Nobilitor in 179 BC. Restored several times in the next century, it was rebuilt by Augustus after a fire. Augustus's building was itself largely destroyed by fire during the conquest of Rome in AD 410 by Alaric's army of Goths. Look out for the green stains left by coins fused into the stone by the heat of the flames.

In front of the basilica is the site of the original Forum. Through it runs the oldest and most important street in ancient Rome—the **Via Sacra**, the Sacred Way, along which passed the triumphal processions of victorious Roman generals on their way to offer sacrifice in the Temple of Jupiter on the Capitol. In a triumph (the highest honour the State could bestow) the general rode in a chariot drawn by four horses, his prisoners and the spoils of war before him, his soldiers following on behind. He wore a purple toga embroidered with gold and carried a branch of laurel (in his right hand) and an ivory sceptre surmounted by an eagle (in his left hand). Beside him rode a slave, holding a gold wreath above the general's head and whispering, as a warning against overweening pride, *"Respice post te. Hominem te memento"* ("Look behind. Remember that you are but a man").

Beyond the Basilica Aemilia is the **Curia**, the ancient Senate House of Rome, traditionally founded by Tullius Hostilius, the third king of Rome. The building we see today dates to the time of Diocletian, who rebuilt the Curia after a fire in AD 283. In 638 the Curia was converted into a church (to which it owes its survival) but it was restored to its imperial form earlier this century. The doors are copies of the original bronze doors which were filched by Pope Alexander VII for the basilica of San Giovanni in Laterano.

In front of the Curia is the **Comitium**, the precinct where the popular assembly met and the centre of political life in republican Rome. This was the original site of the *rostra*, the platform from which speakers addressed the assembled citizens. Of even earlier origin is the **Lapis Niger**, a pavement of black marble built over an ancient holy place. Discovered in 1899, the monument below the pavement bears the oldest-known Latin inscription. Tradition holds this to be the site of the tomb of Romulus, legendary founder of Rome.

The Arch of Septimius Severus was erected by the Senate in AD 203 in honour of the Emperor and his sons Caracalla and Geta (Geta's name was effaced after his murder by Caracalla in 211 but traces of the original inscription can still be made out). This imposing triple arch is 21 m (69–70 ft) high and 23 m (76 ft) wide and decorated with reliefs representing the Emperor's victorious campaigns in the East over the Parthians, Arabs and Assyrians.

To the left of the arch are the remains of the **Imperial Rostra**, the raised speaker's platform moved here from the Comitium by Julius Caesar. It was originally decorated with the prows or beaks (*rostra*) of ships captured at the Battle of Antium in 338 BC.

Behind the rostra is a curved platform, at the northern end of which is the *Umbilicus Urbis*, the navel of the city. Opposite is the site of the *Milliarium Aureum*, the golden milestone, a column of gilded bronze set up by Augustus on which were marked the distances from Rome of the chief towns of the Empire.

Eight Ionic columns are all that remains of one of the most ancient and venerated temples of Republican Rome, the **Temple of Saturn**. Consecrated in 498 BC, the temple housed the Roman state treasury and was the focus for the festival of Saturnalia, held each year on 17 December —the pagan precursor of Christmas.

Beyond the Temple of Saturn are the remains of two other temples. On the right is the **Temple of Concord**, a reconstruction by Tiberius in AD 10 of the sanctuary erected in 367 BC to mark the peace between the patricians and the plebians. To the left are three Corinthian columns from the **Temple of Vespasian**, erected in memory of the

---

A Brave Sacrifice

In 362 BC Rome was hit by a succession of disasters: a pestilence raged, the Tiber burst its banks and earthquakes shook the city. But the worst portent was still to come—a yawning chasm opened up in the middle of the Forum.

After all attempts to close it had failed, the Romans turned in desperation to their divine oracles. The soothsayers delivered the answer: the gulf could only be filled by throwing into it that which Rome most prized. Only then would the city be preserved. While the people debated what the gods could mean, a young soldier named Marcus Curtius came forward. Fully armed, he mounted his horse and, declaring that Rome possessed nothing so valuable as a brave citizen, rode into the abyss. The earth closed over him and the city was saved.

The spot where this heroic sacrifice took place is known as the Lacus Curtius, or Curtian Lake. The site (just to the east of the Column of Phocas) is marked by a copy of a 1st-century-BC relief depicting the legend.

Emperor after his death in AD 79 by his sons Titus and Domitian, both of whom later became emperors. Vespasian was one of the better rulers of imperial Rome, bringing peace and prosperity to the city after the excesses of Nero and his three short-lived successors. He financed some of his munificent public works with a tax on the urine that was collected by Roman fullers from the city's public urinals. When one of Vespasian's sons turned up his nose at this way of raising revenue, the Emperor replied, "*Pecunia non olet.*" ("Money doesn't smell".)

Turning now towards the Colosseum, the remains on the right are the foundations of the **Basilica Giulia**, a vast hall (begun by Julius Caesar and completed by Augustus) that held four law courts. To the left is the **Column of Phocas**, the last monument to be erected in the Forum, a 13½ m (44 ft) high Corinthian column taken from some more ancient temple or basilica and set up here in AD 608 in honour of Phocas, the sanguinary Emperor of the East who presented the Pantheon to the Church.

Beyond the Basilica Giulia are three surviving columns from the **Temple of Castor and Pollux**, built in 484 BC after the Battle of Lake Regillus, at which the miraculous appearance by the heavenly twins won the day for the Romans. This famous victory foiled the last attempt to restore the Tarquins to the throne of Rome and so secured the Republic. A block of marble from the temple was used by Michelangelo as the base for the equestrian statue of Marcus Aurelias in the Piazza del Campidoglio.

Behind the temple is the **Fountain of Juturna** (*Lacus Juturnae*), the well at which Castor and Pollux (known together as the *Dioscuri*) watered their horses after bringing the tidings of victory at Lake Regillus to the city.

On the other side of the temple are the remains of the oldest Christian church in the Forum, **Santa Maria Antigua**, which contains much-damaged 7th–8th-century wall paintings.

The **Temple of Vesta**, the virgin goddess of the hearth, was the most holy place in the Forum. Here was kept the sacred fire brought by Aeneas from Troy, watched over by six vestal virgins. These priestesses, guardians of the symbolical city hearth, were a priviliged and venerated body. Vestals,

who had to be of noble birth and free of any physical defect, were chosen by the *Pontifex Maximus* (High Priest) between the ages of six and ten. Those selected swore an oath of chastity for 30 years, after which they were free to enter ordinary society and even marry. If a vestal lost her virginity she was buried alive and her lover strangled. The immured vestal would be given a burning lamp, a loaf of bread, and a

The mutilated statue of a vestal virgin in the courtyard of the House of the Vestals.

little milk and water, so as to prolong the agonies of pain and remorse. The **House of the Vestals**, the once luxurious and richly ornamented building where the vestal virgins lived, lies beyond the temple.

The **Temple of Julius Caesar** was erected by his adopted son, the Emperor Augustus, on the spot where his body was cremated following his assassination on the Ides of March in 44 BC. The funeral pyre was kept alight for days as the grieving Romans threw their own personal possessions on to the flames.

The Fall of a Sorcerer

During the reign of Nero, the sorcerer Simon Magus challenged Saints Peter and Paul to a levitation contest in the Forum. The sorcerer (who makes a brief appearance in the Acts of the Apostles) succeeded in flying up into the air but the prayers of the apostles brought him to earth with a bump. Simon Magus was killed outright (his name lives on in the sin of simony). The apostles had prayed so hard that the imprint of their knees was left in the paving stones. The marks they made can still be seen, say Romans, in the church of Santa Francesca Romana.

The **Regia**, to the left, was the official seat of the Pontifex Maximus. It was traditionally regarded as the house of Numa Pompilius, the legendary second king of Rome, formulator of the state's religious practices. Solemn rites were carried out here by priests and vestals.

The **Temple of Antoninus and Faustina** was built by Antoninus Pius in AD 141 in memory of his wife. On the Emperor's death in 161 it was also dedicated to him. In the 11th century

the temple was converted into the church of **San Lorenzo in Miranda**. The Baroque façade dates from 1602. Beyond the temple is the **Archaic Necropolis**, the site of a prehistoric cemetery of the area's early Iron Age inhabitants, pre-dating the foundation of Rome.

The **Temple of Romulus** next door has nothing to do with Rome's legendary founder. This small octagonal temple is thought to have been built by the Emperor Maxentius in memory of his son Romulus who died in AD 309 at the age of four. The ancient bronze doors, an important influence on the design of cathedral doors in the Middle Ages, have survived. The temple acts as a vestibule to the church of **Santi Cosma e Damiano**, which was converted in the 6th century from a hall in the Forum of Vespasian.

The ruins of the **Basilica of Constantine** are the largest remains in the Forum. The basilica was begun by the Emperor Maxentius in AD 306 (it is sometimes referred to as the Basilica of Maxentius) and was completed in 330 by his successor. (Constantine, the first Christian emperor, wrested control of the Empire from Maxentius at the Battle of Milvian Bridge in 312.) The basilica was looted for building materials in the Middle Ages; the tiles of gilded bronze which covered the roof were taken by Pope Honorius I for use on the old basilica of St Peter's.

Founded on the site of a pagan temple, **Santa Maria Nova** (also known as Santa Francesca Romana) is a 10th-century church with a 12th-century bell tower and a 17th-century Palladian façade. Its convent houses the **Antiquarium Forense**, a museum containing

T he Arch of Titus was known in medieval times as the "Arch of the Seven Lamps" from the relief depicting the seven-branched Jewish candlestick.

objects discovered in excavations of the Forum (admission included in entrance to the Roman Forum).

Beyond Santa Maria Nova are the remains of the **Temple of Venus and Rome**, the largest temple of ancient Rome, built by the Emperor Hadrian and consecrated in AD 136. It remained in use into the Christian era and was not closed until 391. As with the Basilica of Constantine, Honorious stole the bronze tiles from the temple's roof for the old St Peter's.

The **Arch of Titus** was built to commemorate the capture of Jerusalem in AD 70. Reliefs inside the arch show Titus in his imperial quadriga (chariot) crowned by Victory, the chariot's horses led by the goddess Roma. The spoils of the Temple of Jerusalem, including the golden seven-branched candlestick, are shown being carried in triumphal procession.

Acanthus and Oleander among the Ruins of Ancient Palaces

Rome's imperial rulers lived in pomp and luxury on the Palatine Hill. Here successive emperors strove to outdo one another by building larger and ever more ostentatious palaces. Little remains of this splendour today, only ruins overgrown with wild flowers and shrubs. "Behold the Imperial Mount!" wrote Byron. " 'Tis thus the mighty falls."

The drama of Rome's mythic origins was enacted on the **Palatine**, the hill that rises above the Forum. Here stood the cave in which the she-wolf suckled the twins Romulus and Remus; here Romulus stationed himself to watch for a sign from the gods to determine where to build a settlement; and it was around the hill that he ploughed a furrow to mark the limits of his new city, the four-walled *Roma Quadrata.*

With the fall of the Republic the centre of political power in Rome slipped from the Forum to the Palatine.

When the story of Rome moves out of the mists of legend into the clearer light of history, the Palatine continues to figure prominently. During the Republic the Palatine was an exclusive residential district, the home of Rome's wealthiest and most prominent citizens. Augustus, Rome's first imperial ruler, was born on the Palatine and continued to live there on becoming emperor. Augustus lived in a comparatively simple fashion. His sucessor, Tiberius, wasn't nearly so modest, and built for himself the magnificent *Domus Tiberiana*, the first in a series of increasingly ostentatious imperial palaces that were to cover the hill. Not for nothing did the Palatine bequeath us the word "palace".

The palaces may have crumbled but the Palatine remains a beautiful and evocative spot. It's best to soak up the atmosphere rather than pore studiously over every detail. Indeed, after exploring the ruins of the Forum in the open, it comes as a relief to wander along the shaded walks of the Palatine, amidst the umbrella pines and cypresses, oleander and acanthus. Here is how Byron found the place, as described in *Childe Harold*:

Cypress and ivy, weed and wallflower grown
Matted and mass'd together, hillocks heap'd
On what were chambers, arch crush'd, columns strown
In fragments, choked-up vaults, and frescoes steep'd
In subterranean damps, where the owls peep'd,
Deeming it midnight:—Temples, baths, or halls?
Pronounce who can; for all that Learning reap'd
From her research has been, that these are walls.—
Behold the Imperial Mount! 'Tis thus the mighty falls.

The Palatine is approached from the Forum by the *Clivus Palatinus*, which begins near the Arch of Titus (alternatively, it may be entered through a gateway in Via di San Gregorio). To the right of the path are the **Farnese Gardens** (*Orti Farnesiani*). These are beautiful pleasure gardens laid out in the 16th century by Giacomo da Vignola, for Cardinal Alessandro Farnese, over the ruins of the Palace of Tiberius (*Domus Tiberiana*).

A She-Wolf of a Different Sort
Everyone knows the story of Romulus and Remus and the She-Wolf: how the twins, sons of a vestal virgin raped by the god Mars, were abandoned to die in a basket on the River Tiber; how the basket came to rest on the root of a wild fig tree at the foot of the Palatine Hill; how a she-wolf, coming to drink, found the twins and took them to her den, where she suckled them until they were discovered by the shepherd Faustulus, who gave them to his wife to rear.

This is the familiar legend recounted by Livy, the chronicler of Rome's early history. Less well known is the theory Livy gives to account for the legend's origin. He suggests that Faustulus's wife, Larentia, may have been given the nickname "she-wolf" (which in Latin sometimes bore the connotation of strumpet), for having been too free with her favours with the other local shepherds.

Beyond the gardens are the remains of the **Temple of the Magna Mater** (Great Mother), sometimes called the Temple of Cybele (mother of the gods), dating from 191 BC. The southwest corner of the hill is the oldest part of the Palatine and excavations earlier this century have revealed traces of early Iron-Age settlements (9th century BC). A genuine Iron-Age hut is traditionally regarded as the **Hut of Romulus**, the dwelling of the shepherd who raised Romulus and Remus. Nearby is the legendary site of the **Lupercal**, the cave sanctuary dedicated to the she-wolf that suckled the twins.

The **House of Livia** (widow of Augustus) lies to the east of the Temple of Cybele and contains beautiful wall paintings. Further east is the **Palace of Domitian**, in effect two palaces: the **Domus Flavia**, the Emperor's official

116

*T*he she-wolf, emblem of Rome.

palace, and the **Domus Augustana**, his private residence. Designed for Domitian by the architect Caius Rabirus between AD 81 and 96, this vast palace extended over much of the Palatine, a luxurious complex of porticoes and colonnades, fountains and gardens, private temples and sumptuous apartments. Domitian had an obsessive and superstitious fear of assassination (not unwarranted given his favourite method of raising money—accusing senators of treachery and promptly confiscating their property) and the walls of his palace were lined with polished marble to reveal the approach of any potential assailant. To no avail, no sooner was his magnificent residence completed than he was stabbed to death in a palace conspiracy.

Adjoining the Domus Augustana is the **Palatine Stadium** or Hippodrome, usually considered to have been built by Domitian for horse races but thought by some to have been a sunken garden. Beyond the Stadium is the **Domus Severiana**, built by Septimius Severus (AD 193–211). The palace contains a specially built terrace, known as the "Imperial Box", from which the Emperor and his entourage could watch the games and races in the Circus Maximus below.

Circus Maximus

Set in the valley between the Palatine and Aventine hills, the Circus Maximus (*Circo Massimo*) was the oldest and largest circus in Rome. Tarquinius Priscus, the first Etruscan king of Rome, is traditionally regarded as its founder (around 600 BC), but the earliest mention of the circus is in 329 BC. Rebuilt and enlarged many times over the centuries, at its peak the circus could hold some 380,000 spectators. The last games were held by the Ostrogoth king Totila in AD 549.

Though the circus also hosted athletic contests, wild-beast fights and mock naval battles (after flooding the arena), it was primarily designed for chariot and other horse races. The length of a race was seven circuits of the *spina*, the low platform which ran down the centre of the circus. At either end of the *spina* was a conical pillar known as a *meta*, the site of frequent accidents as the charioteers strove to turn sharply and gain on their opponents. The charioteers were divided into four factions, red, white, blue and green, and the rivalry between the teams provoked intense emotions and frenzied betting among the spectators. One can descend to the arena's grassy remains by means of steps leading down from Via del Circo Massimo and, guided by images from *Ben Hur*, try to conjure up the noise and excitement of the circus in its heyday.

117

"The Gladiator's Bloody Circus Stands, A Noble Wreck in Ruinous Perfection"

The Colosseum's monumental grandeur and bloody past have impressed and appalled visitors for almost 2,000 years. Christians may not actually have been fed to the lions here—whatever popular myth might tell you—but the stadium certainly did see acts of cruelty no less horrifying. While crowds bayed for blood, gladiators fought to the death, their lives hanging on an emperor's whim. Wild beasts suffered too; 5,000 animals were slaughtered on the stadium's opening day alone.

The visitor to the **Colosseum** cannot help but have mixed feelings at the sight of the most famous monument of ancient Rome: full of admiration for the engineering and architectural skill that went into its construction, yet full of horror at the barbarous acts of cruelty that were committed within.

Charles Dickens was profoundly affected by the Colosseum's "awful beauty", vividly imagining "thousands

*O*ver *the centuries, this enduring symbol of ancient Rome has been battered by the elements and by man—damaged by earthquakes, plundered for its valuable travertine stone and corroded by modern pollution.*

of eager faces staring down into the arena, and such a whirl of strife, and blood, and dust going on there, as no language can describe. It is the most impressive, the most stately, the most solemn, grand, majestic, mournful sight conceivable."

The Colosseum's name in antiquity was the Flavian Amphitheatre, after the family of the three emperors involved in its construction. It was begun around AD 72 by the Emperor Vespasian on the site of a great lake in the grounds of Nero's grandiose palace, the *Domus Aurea* (the Golden House). The building was thus a reparation to the Roman people for Nero's original confiscation of the land. It also demonstrates the skill in drainage of the Roman engineers. Vespasian's son,

Titus, opened the great stadium in AD 80, but it was left to his brother, Domitian, to complete the project.

The name by which the building is known today actually dates from the Middle Ages. It is first found, around AD 700, in the writings of the Venerable Bede, who related this prophecy, brought back from Rome by Anglo-Saxon pilgrims:

While stands the Colosseum, Rome shall stand;
When falls the Colosseum, Rome shall fall;
And when Rome falls – the world.

It was not the building's great size which gave it the name "Colosseum" but the giant 40-m (120-ft) high bronze statue of Nero that used to stand before it.

*W*ill Rome's love-affair with the car prove curtains for the Colosseum?

The elliptical building is composed of four storeys: the first three are all of arches, respectively Doric, Ionic and Corinthian; the top storey (dating from the 3rd-century restoration by Alexander Severus) is made up of Corinthian pilasters. The many holes in the Colosseum's surface, which give it a pockmarked appearance, were made in the Middle Ages by the extraction of the iron clamps that were used to hold together the large blocks of travertine that make up the body of the building.

The amphitheatre is 188 m (617 ft) long, 156 m (513 ft) wide, has a circumference of 527 m (1,730 ft) and is 57 m (187 ft) high.

In its heyday the Colosseum could contain over 50,000 spectators. Seating was arranged in the different tiers according to social class: the higher up the building the lower the status of the spectator.

Of the Colosseum's 80 entrances, two were reserved for the emperor and his entourage, while two were for the gladiators: the *Porta Saniviviaria* for the living, the *Porta Libitina* for the corpses. The remaining 76 entrances were all numbered, the numbers corresponding to the spectators' tickets.

Having entered, the spectators would find their way along corridors and staircases to their seats in one of the three tiers in the *Cavae*. The first stage was for knights and tribunes, the second was for the middle classes and the third for the populace. Women sat apart from the men in a colonnade above the highest tier. Higher still was the *velarium*, a giant awning, handled by sailors, which was drawn over the arena to shelter the spectators from the sun or rain.

Nearest the arena was the podium, a marble platform with places of honour for the Vestals, senators and other high-ranking officials. The emperor's throne was under a canopy above the podium.

The *Arena* was originally a wooden floor, covered with sand to give the fighters a firm footing and to soak up the blood spilled in combat. Beneath this floor were underground passages (now exposed) containing the dens of wild animals and the machinery which raised and lowered scenery into the arena. On occasions, the arena was even flooded for the staging of mock naval battles.

The gladiators were originally slaves, prisoners of war and condemned criminals, but, later on in the history of the games, some free men entered the "profession" voluntarily, willing to risk death for the high pay and prospect of fame. (They were very much the popular idols of their day.) The gladiators marched into the amphitheatre in procession and paraded around the arena. When they were opposite the imperial tribune, they saluted the emperor with the words, "Hail Caesar! Those about to die salute thee!"

Trained in schools called *Ludi*, gladiators specialized in different forms of combat. The *Retiari* entangled their adversaries in nets thrown with the left hand, while defending themselves with tridents in the right; the *Laqueatores* threw slings against their adversaries; the *Dimachae* were armed with a short sword in each hand; the *Bestiari* only fought against animals.

Wild beasts were brought to Rome to be used in the games from all parts of the Empire, a traffic which led to the extermination of the elephant and lion from North Africa. When Titus opened the stadium in AD 80, the games lasted 100 days and on the first day alone, according to Suetonius, 5,000 animals were slaughtered.

Women sometimes fought in the arena and there were mock battles between Amazons and pygmies. The megalomaniac and cruel Emperor Commodus (AD 180–182), took part in almost 1,000 gladiatorial combats, dressed in a lion's skin and calling himself Hercules.

The popular image of the Colosseum is of Christians being fed to the lions. There is actually little historical evidence to support this supposition, but the practice undoubtedly did take place in Rome and could have occurred here. There is in any case a long tradition of the Colosseum as a site of Christian martyrdom.

Gladiatorial combats came to an end in 404, after a Christian monk, Telemachus, was stoned to death by the spectators at a show. He had rushed into the arena in an attempt to separate the combatants. Wild beast shows continued in the Colosseum, however, until 523.

The history of the Colosseum in the Middle Ages alternates between neglect and abuse. It was damaged by earthquakes in 1231 and 1349, and was even used as a fortress, first by the powerful Frangipani family, then by the Annibaldi. But its main function in the Middle Ages was as a stone quarry. Its valuable travertine was used

T he finest reliefs on the Arch of Constantine were pinched from the monuments of earlier emperors.

in the building of the Palazzo di Venezia, the Palazzo Barberini, St Peter's and the Cancelleria. Sixtus V planned to turn the Colosseum into a wool factory, while Clement XI thought of turning it into a manufactory of saltpetre. Both schemes fortunately came to nothing.

Pope Benedict XIV stopped the use of the building as a quarry in 1749 and dedicated it to the Passion of Jesus, pronouncing it sanctified by the blood of the Christian martyrs who were reckoned to have died here.

The ruin was much admired by visitors in the Romantic era, including Byron, who described it in his poem *Manfred*: "The gladiator's bloody circus stands, a noble wreck in ruinous perfection."

The Arch of Constantine

Before the Colosseum stands the Arch of Constantine, erected in AD 315 by the Senate and people of Rome in honour of the Emperor's victory over Maxentius at the Mulvian Bridge. The triumphal arch was largely decorated with sculptures and reliefs taken from other monuments. The crudeness of the few original reliefs is taken to be a sign of the decline of artistic skill in the late Empire.

The Imperial Fora

As Rome grew in power and its population increased, the original Forum became too small to serve the city's needs and new fora were built by a succession of rulers: Caesar, Augustus, Vespasian, Nerva and Trajan. Their remains lie on either side of the Via dei Fori Imperiali, the grandiose boulevard built by Mussolini between the Victor Emmanuel Monument and the Colosseum and opened in 1933. **Trajan's Forum**, the last to be built, was the most impressive in size and splendour, with temples, libraries and a vast basilica, surrounded by marble colonnades.

Trajan built the forum, designed by the great architect from Damascus, Apollodorus, between AD 107 and 113 on the proceeds of two successful campaigns in the Kingdom of Dacia (modern-day Romania). **Trajan's Column**, erected in 113 to commemorate the Emperor's Dacian victories, was also designed by Apollodorus. The column is 38 m (125 ft) high, the height representing the size of the hill that was levelled to make way for Trajan's Forum. It is decorated with beautiful reliefs which spiral up around the column and contains some 2,500 figures, illustrating Trajan's Dacian campaigns in great detail. The column was topped with a statue of the Emperor himself (replaced in 1588 with a statue of St Peter). The reliefs, much damaged by car fumes over the last half-century, have recently emerged from a mammoth restoration.

Trajan also built extensive markets, the remains of which can still be visited (entrance in Via Quattro Novembre). Indeed, parts of Trajan's multi-storey shopping complex, built in three tiers in a large semicircle, are remarkably well preserved and give a good idea of the sophisticated commercial life of ancient Rome.

Putting On A Show— Public Spectacle in Rome

Free food and lavish entertainments— "bread and circuses" in Juvenal's famous phrase—was how the Roman emperors kept their subjects contented.

His belly full, the Roman plebeian could feast his eyes on thrilling spectacles: gladiatorial combats and wild beast shows, chariot races, boxing matches, athletic contests, even full-pitched naval battles in a flooded amphitheatre. Denied a part in the affairs of state, the people still had a voice in the public arena of the games.

It was the Etruscans who originally introduced the tradition of splendid public games to Rome. The Circus Maximus, venue for chariot and other horse races, was begun by Tarquinius Priscus, the first of three Etruscan kings who ruled Rome in the 7th and 6th centuries BC. The Etruscans also introduced the gladiatorial games to Rome, a development of the human sacrifices which accompanied the funeral of an Etruscan dignitary.

Under the Republic, wealthy and politically ambitious men put on games as a way of currying favour with the people. In imperial Rome this was still a means of gaining political and social advancement, but by then the games had come to embody the social bond between an emperor and his subjects.

The games lasted from sunrise to sunset and sometimes went on for weeks on end. No expense was spared in putting on a grand spectacle, though sometimes the entertainment did not go exactly to plan.

Before draining Lake Fucinus, a lake to the east of Rome, the Emperor Claudius staged a sham sea-fight on the water. Prior to the battle the combatants lined up and gave the traditional salute to the Emperor, "Hail, Caesar, those about to die salute thee", to which Claudius jokingly replied, "Or not".

The combatants took this to mean they need not risk their lives in battle and refused to fight. Somewhat taken aback by this unexpected bolshiness, the Emperor jumped up from his throne and, lame though he was, tottered along the side of the lake entreating the men to fight. At length, induced partly by threats and partly by promises, the men agreed and the battle, between two fleets of twelve triremes, was launched. Some emperors took their involvement in the games even further. Nero took part in chariot races (and was awarded first prize even when he crashed and failed to complete the course); Commodus, the brutal son of Marcus Aurelius, fought almost a thousand combats as a gladiator, dressed in a lion skin and calling himself Hercules.

Not every Roman was quite so bloodthirsty when it came to the games. "Magnificent are these shows, nobody denies it," agreed Cicero in the 1st century BC, "but what delight can it be for a refined mind to see a feeble man torn by a beautiful beast, or a noble animal pierced with a javelin?"

Not that refined minds were any better off in the Roman theatre, where the spectacle was every bit as gory as that found in the arena. Mythological subjects allowed the presentation of almost unlimited sex and violence: Leda ravished by the swan, Ixion bound on a wheel of fire. At a play's climax, condemned criminals were sometimes substituted for actors and executed publicly on the stage.

Back in the arena, those gladiators who managed to live and fight another day became popular idols. And not only

Blood-thirsty Romans took a savage thrill in gladiatorial combat.

with the masses. Juvenal writes of the senator's wife who created a scandal by eloping with a battle-scarred gladiator.

The gladiatorial combats were killed off by Christianity, but, after the Caesars, it was the popes who were to prove the next great patrons of public spectacle in Rome. Indeed, the Roman Carnival, with all its pagan and profane elements, was largely shaped by a Renaissance pope, Paul II.

The carnival, eight days of revelry and riot before the penitential fasting of Lent, had hitherto taken place on the Capitol or on Monte Testaccio, but in 1466, two years after his election, Paul II decreed it should take place in and around the Via Lata, one of the busiest and most important streets in the city. From his newly built palace, the Palazzo Venezia, the Pope could now enjoy the spectacle of the races, or *corse*, along the Via Lata. A special feature of the carnival, they were to give the street its new name—the Corso.

There were races for humans and animals; for old and young, Christians and Jews, horses, donkeys and buffaloes.

The most eagerly awaited event of all was the race of the Barberi, riderless Arab horses wearing saddles studded with nails to make them run faster. Cruelty to animals had not ended with the ancient Romans.

In the 20th century Mussolini, ever anxious to emulate imperial Rome, planned a giant sports complex in the north of the city, a "Forum of Mussolini" which would dwarf the Colosseum. Neither Il Duce nor Fascism survived long enough to see this dream completed, but today a huge marble monolith, inscribed "Mussolini Dux", still rises at the entrance of the complex.

The centrepiece of the Foro Italico (as Mussolini's projected Forum is now known) is the Stadio Olimpico. Completed for the 1960 Olympic Games and lavishly renovated for the 1990 World Cup, it is home to the city's two football teams, Roma and Lazio.

Football, introduced to the industrial cities of northern Italy by English factory owners at the turn of the century, now inspires passionate support all over the country. Indeed, Italians describe their football league as "*il campionato più bello nel mondo*"—the greatest championship in the world.

Just as the Colossuem has proved the template for all modern sports stadia, so has the adulation won by the gladiators foreshadowed the hero-worship of modern footballers. And the fans—*i tifosi*? They too share certain similarities with their ancient counterparts. They don't shout *Jugula*, or "kill him", any more, but the din they do make—drums, fireworks, the tribal chant of *alé-oo-oo, alé-oo-oo*—must surely rival that created in the heyday of the Colosseum. Add to this the name of the street the fans walk to reach the stadium and the comparison is complete—it is none other than the Viale dei Gladiatori—the avenue of the gladiators.

The Wedding Cake and the Field of Flowers

Nicknamed the "wedding cake" in the Second World War, the Victor Emmanuel Monument is shamelessly conspicuous. Use it as a landmark for city-wide orientation but don't neglect the area close at hand. It's full of splendid palaces and significant churches. Every stone has a history to tell. Mussolini harangued the crowds from the balcony of the Palazzo Venezia. Nearby is the Gesù, mother church of the Jesuits, shock troops of the Counter Reformation. Heretics were burned in the Campo dei Fiori, not far from the Ghetto, where Rome's Jews were confined by a Renaissance pope.

Piazza Venezia is dominated by the colossal **Victor Emmanuel II Monument**, or Altar of the Nation, erected in 1911 as a symbol of Italian unification. Made of gleaming white *botticino* marble from Brescia, the monument was dubbed the "wedding cake" by British soldiers during the Second World War. Among the other derisive appellations it has attracted are "Mussolini's typewriter" and "a mountain of sugar". The monument contains the

A thirst-quenching fountain near the Victor Emmanuel monument. The pine cone is the emblem of the surrounding district, the Rione della Pigna.

tomb of Italy's Unknown Soldier from World War I.

On the west side of the piazza is the **Palazzo Venezia**, the first great Renaissance palace in Rome. It was begun in 1455 for the Venetian Cardinal Pietro Barbo, later to become Pope Paul II. Mussolini used the palace as his official headquarters after 1929 and made many of his most rabble-rousing speeches from the balcony overlooking Piazza Venezia. The dictator's office was the huge Sala del Mappamondo, empty save for a large desk placed 60 ft from the door. If the Duce wished to put the wind up visitors he would take no notice of them as they crossed this vast, intimidating space, their footsteps echoing coldly on the marble floor. Mussolini was full of such poses.

He would leave a light burning in the Sala at night to show that the great man was working tirelessly for the Italian people.

The palace houses the **Museo del Palazzo Venezia** (entrance in Via del Plebiscito). The museum contains a permanent collection of ceramics, jewellery, German, Flemish and Italian tapestries, wood sculptures and bronzes. The museum also bears the famous Odescalchi collection of arms and armour and many fine paintings.

Adjoining the palace is the ancient church of **San Marco**, founded in 336 by Pope St Mark. It was rebuilt by Gregory IV in the 9th century and further restorations followed in the 15th, 17th and 18th centuries, leaving the church with a Romanesque bell tower, a Renaissance façade and a Baroque interior. The beautiful mosaic of the apse dates from the 9th century and

> *This busty bust was nicknamed Madama Lucrezia in the 16th century.*

Anni di Piombo

The 1970s were Italy's "years of lead", the so-called *anni di piombo*, which saw political terrorism of the left and right cast a shadow over the country. The darkest hour came in 1978 when the Christian Democrat leader Aldo Moro was kidnapped and murdered by the Red Brigade in Rome. In a cruelly symbolic gesture, the terrorists dumped the politician's lifeless body in a car parked in Via Caetani, halfway between the headquarters of Italy's two leading political parties, the Christian Democrats in Piazza del Gesù and the Communists in Via delle Botteghe Oscure.

---

shows Gregory IV offering a model of the church to Christ.

Near the church is the curious statue known as **Madama Lucrezia**, one of Rome's celebrated talking statues: monuments to which scurrilous satires were attached by the populace during the Renaissance. This battered female figure is thought to represent a bust of Isis.

The area to the west of Piazza Venezia, bordering Corso Vittorio Emanuele, is rich in splendid Renaissance palaces and important churches, not to mention several fine museums and galleries.

From the north-west corner of the piazza, Via del Plebiscito leads to the **Gesù**, the main Jesuit church in Rome. Built between 1568 and 1575 with funds provided by the rich and powerful Cardinal Alessandro Farnese, the church was an important landmark in the development of the architecture of the Counter-Reformation. The flamboyance of its design and decoration look forward to the Baroque churches of the next century. The façade is by

The remains of four republican temples in the Area Sacra di Largo Argentina.

Giacomo della Porta and the interior by Vignola, while the vault of the nave is decorated with an elaborate *trompe l'oeil* **fresco** by Giovanni Battista Gaulli representing the Triumph of the Name of Jesus. Equally opulent is the **tomb of St Ignatius of Loyola**, founder of the Jesuits. The monument includes a huge globe made from the largest block of lapis lazuli in existence.

The busy Corso Vittorio Emanuele leads to the Largo Argentina, a congested square built around the **Area Sacra di Largo Argentina**, the remains of four republican temples, the earliest of which dates back to the end of the 4th century BC. The temples were uncovered during excavations in 1926.

On the western side of the square is the 18th-century **Teatro Argentina**, the venue for the first performance of Rossini's Barber of Seville in 1816. The opera was roundly booed at its premiere, as the singer performing the role of the heroine Rosina herself described. "We arrived at the finale, a classical

composition which would do honour to the first musicians in the world. Laughter, howls, and piercing whistles, and, whenever silence intervened, it was the signal for even noisier ones to begin."

In the nearby Via del Sudario the Casa del Burcardo houses the **Burcardo Theatrical Collection** (*Raccolta Teatrale del Burcardo*), a theatrical museum and library.

Back on the Corso Vittorio Emanuele, the magnificent baroque church of **Sant'Andrea della Valle** has the second largest dome in Rome, after St Peter's, of course. It was begun in 1591 and Giacomo della Porta, Francesco Grimaldi and Carlo Maderno all had a hand in the design. The church is the setting for the first act of Puccini's much-loved opera *Tosca*.

Diagonally opposite the church is the **Palazzo Massimo alle Colonne**, built by Baldassare Peruzzi (1532–36) for the ancient Massimo family on the site of an earlier palace, which had been burned down during the sack of Rome in 1527. Each year on 16 March the Massimo family throw open their doors to visitors in memory of the miraculous revival from the dead of young Paolo Massimo by St Philip Neri on that day in 1583. The family chapel where this miracle took place is on the second floor of the palace.

A short way further along the Corso Vittorio Emanuele the late-18th-century **Palazzo Braschi** stands in the tiny Piazza San Pantaleo. The palace houses two museums: the **Galleria Communale d'Arte Moderna,** Rome's Municipal Gallery of Modern Art, containing 20th-century works by Italian and foreign artists; and the **Museo di Roma**, which documents the history of Rome from the Middle Ages to the present day.

Opposite the Palazzo Braschi is the Renaissance **Palazzo Piccola Farnesina**. This delightful palace was built in 1523 by Anthony da Sangallo the Younger for the French prelate Thomas le Roy. Le Roy's role in negotiating the concordat of 1516 between Pope Leo X and the French king, Francis I, had won him the right to incorporate the fleur-de-lis into his coat of arms. The palace's unusual name is the result of a confusion of the French fleur-de-lis with the Farnese lilies. The palace houses the **Museo Barracco**, a museum based on the personal collection of ancient sculpture gathered by Barone Giovanni Barracco and presented to the city in 1902.

Nearby is yet another splendid Renaissance palace, the **Palazzo della Cancelleria**, built between 1486 and 1513 by Cardinal Raffaele Riario with the proceeds of a fortune won in a single night's gambling. The palace's architect is unknown but the courtyard has been attributed to Bramante.

Corso Vittorio Emanuele continues towards the Tiber and *en route* passes the **Chiesa Nuova**. This church, also known as Santa Maria in Vallicella, was built for St Philip Neri, founder of the Oratorians, or Filippini, one of the great spiritual orders of the Counter-Reformation. St Philip Neri set great store by the spiritual benefits of singing and in 1574 introduced the concept of the "Oratorio", sacred dramas set to music. His New Church was begun in 1575 and consecrated in 1599, seven years after the saint's death. The façade, however, was not completed until 1606.

St Philip Neri had wished the church's interior to be simple, with plain whitewashed walls, but in the century after his death the principles of the Oratorians changed and Pietro da Cortona was commissioned to paint the magnificent series of frescoes which decorate the vault, apse and dome of the church. Also among the church's treasures are three altarpieces by Rubens. Adjoining the church is the **Oratorio dei Filippini**, designed by Borromini (1637–62).

Campo dei Fiori

Retracing one's steps along the Corso Vittorio Emanuele, the celebrated **Campo dei Fiori** can be reached by the Piazza della Cancelleria. Once a meadow (the name translates as "field of flowers"), Campo dei Fiori was the site of public executions during the 17th century. One of the first victims was the philosopher Giordano Bruno, who fell foul of the Inquisition because of his professed belief in the Copernican system. The Church could not countenance the revolutionary idea that the earth moves around the sun and condemned Bruno for heresy. He was burned at the stake here in 1600. The piazza is now a busy food market, in the centre of which is a bronze statue to Bruno, erected in 1889, much to the displeasure of the Vatican, which still considered that he was a heretic.

From Campo dei Fiori, the Vicolo del Gallo leads to the **Palazzo Farnese**, one of the masterpieces of High Renaissance architecture. It was built for the Cardinal Alessandro Farnese, who used his position as Treasurer of the Church to amass an enormous fortune. The palace cost so much that for a while even the Farnese finances were strained. A temporary embarrassment which the Cardinal, who became Pope Paul III in 1534, soon rectified with the sale of indulgences. The palace was begun in 1514 by Antonio da Sangallo the Younger, continued by Michelangelo after 1546 and finished by Giacomo della Porta in 1589. It is now the French Embassy, rented from the Italian Government for the sum of one lira every 99 years. (In return, Italy has the use of the Hotel Galiffet in Paris.) Inside, the **Galleria** contains superb frescoes of mythological scenes by Annibale Carracci. These works rank among Rome's greatest treasures; you need written permission to see them.

The Vicolo di Venti leads to another huge Renaissance palace, the **Palazzo Spada**, built for Cardinal Girolamo Capodiferro between 1549 and 1559. The building's façade is notable for its handsome stucco decoration of garlands, medallions and cartouches. In the 17th century the palace was restored by Borromini, who added the ingenious *trompe l'oeil* Perspective Gallery (though some now say this was the work of the Augustinian priest Giovanni Maria da Bitonto). The palace is now the seat of Italy's Consiglio di Stato (Council of State). It also houses the **Galleria Spada**, a

It's easy to overlook the Chiesetta di Santa Barbara dei Librari.

One of Rome's best-loved fountains, the Fontana delle Tartarughe.

makers, who worked in this area. On the other side of the busy Via Arenula, Via dei Falegnami ("street of the joiners") leads to one of Rome's most delightful fountains. The **Fontana delle Tartarughe**, the fountain of the tortoises, stands in Piazza Mattei. It was created in 1585 by Taddeo Landini from a design by Giacomo della Porta and depicts four slender youths supporting four dolphins, from whose mouths water flows into marble shells. The tiny bronze tortoises, also supported by the boys, were added in a restoration of 1658.

The Ghetto

The district to the south and east of the fountain is occupied by the old **Ghetto**. During the Middle Ages Rome's Jews generally enjoyed religious tolerance and personal freedoms. But in 1555 they were confined to the Ghetto by order of Pope Paul IV.

Jews were often forced to attend services for their conversion in the church of **Sant'Angelo in Pescheria**. This church had been built on the ruins of the **Porticus of Ottavia**, a rectangular portico enclosing temples to Jupiter and Juno, dating back to 149 BC. Rome's fish market was set up in the portico in the 12th century (hence the name of the church) and remained here until the last century.

South of Sant'Angelo in Pescheria stands the **Theatre of Marcellus**. This ancient theatre was begun by Julius Caesar and finished in AD 13 by Augustus, who dedicated it to his late nephew. The theatre held around 15,000 spectators. The spectacles here

distinguished patrician collection begun by Cardinal Bernardino Spada (1594–1661), containing many fine 17th- and 18th-century paintings including works by Titian and Rubens.

The Vicolo Grotte leads back to Campo dei Fiori and to Via de' Giubbonari, a lively shopping street with a number of trendy shops. Halfway down the street, note the tiny **Chiesetta di Santa Barbara dei Librari**, which is squeezed into a small piazza.

Via de' Giubbonari ends at Piazza Cairoli, where stands the Baroque church of **San Carlo ai Catinari**, named after the *catinari*, or bowl

offered violence and sensationalism to rival the gladiatorial games in the Colosseum. In the Middle Ages the building was converted into a fortress by the powerful Fabi family. It was then turned into a palace in the 16th century by Baldassare Peruzzi for the aristocratic Savelli.

The walls of the Ghetto were destroyed in the revolutionary year of 1848 during the short-lived Roman Republic. When Rome fell to King Victor Emmanuel's troops in 1870, ending papal dominion over the city, the Jews were finally given the same rights as other Italian citizens. Today the area retains its Jewish heritage. It boasts a number of fine restaurants, including Piperno in Monte dei Cenci and Giggetto in Via del Portico d'Ottavia, which serve such Roman-Jewish specialties as *carciofi alla giudia* (deep fried artichokes).

The large **Synagogue** on Lungotevere Cenci, nearby beside the Tiber, contains a museum illustrating the history of Rome's Jewish community through the ages.

The **Isola Tiberina**, an island in the middle of the Tiber, is reached by the Ponte Fabricio, erected in 62 BC and the oldest surviving bridge in the city. In ancient times the island was sacred to Aesculapius, the god of healing. A temple to the god was dedicated here in 291 BC. The island's association with healing continues today. It is the site of the **Ospedale Fatebenefratelli,** a hospital founded in 1548. On the other side of the island, the Ponte Cestio leads into the heart of Trastevere, the traditional working-class district.

Downstream of Tiber Island is Rome's **Ponte Rotto**, the broken bridge, a single surviving arch of the ancient **Pons Aemilius**, the first stone bridge over the Tiber. Beyond the Ponte Rotto lies the late-19th-century Ponte Palatino. From the parapet of this bridge, the mouth of the famous **Cloaca Maxima** is visible at low tide. The largest of Rome's sewers, the Cloaca Maxima was begun by the legendary Etruscan king Tarquin to drain the swampy area that was to become the Forum. Completed in 33 BC, it is still in use today.

*T*he Isola Tiberina, Rome's river island.

Bedazzled by the Baroque Genius of Bernini in Rome's Liveliest Square

If Piazza Navona is Rome's liveliest square then it surely takes its spirit from the flamboyance and dynamism of Bernini's *Fountain of the Four Rivers*. But Bernini isn't the piazza's only genius loci: his great rival Borromini achieved here, in the dramatic façade of Sant'Agnese in Agone, the quintessence of Baroque architecture.

 Piazza Navona derives both its name and its shape from the Circus Agonalis, the Emperor Domitian's athletics stadium, which opened here in AD 86. The name may have been corrupted (through "in agone" to "n'Agona" to "Navona") but the site remained a sporting arena well into the Middle Ages, when it was used for jousts and other games. In the 17th century the piazza was flooded every August to provide a site for aquatic pageants for the entertainment of the people. This practice continued well into the 19th century, when it was observed by the Victorian writer Augustus Hare:

"In the hot months, the singular custom prevails of occasionally stopping the escape of water from the fountains, and so turning the square into a lake, through which the rich splash about in carriages, and eat ices and drink coffee in the water, while the poor look on from raised galleries."

The Piazza Navona has been one of Rome's great public spaces from the time of the Emperor Domitian.

Today the piazza not only retains the outline of the ancient stadium, it also preserves much of the colour and gaiety it must have had in the past. It is the haunt of native Romans and foreign visitors, of artists and buskers,

A close-up view of Bernini's Fountain of the Four Rivers.

cartoonists and palm-readers. Every Christmas it stages a celebrated toy fair, which climaxes on the night before Epiphany with a vibrant carnival.

The piazza owes its predominantly Baroque appearance to the Pamphili pope, Innocent X (1644–55), who sought here to outdo what his predecessor Urban VIII had achieved in the neighbourhood of the Palazzo Barberini on the Quirinal. In Piazza Navona, Innocent enlarged his family's palace, rebuilt the church of Sant' Agnese in Agone and commissioned the square's brilliant centrepiece, Bernini's **Fountain of the Four Rivers.**

Bernini won the commission, much to the annoyance of his great rival Borromini, despite being out of favour with the new pope. Indeed, at first, Bernini was not asked to submit a design for the project. But, so the story goes, his friend, Prince Niccolo Ludovisi, left Bernini's model for the fountain in a room where it was certain to be seen by the Pope. The Pope was duly impressed and enagaged Bernini to execute the work. "We must indeed employ Bernini," he said. "The only way to resist executing his works is not to see them."

The four rivers of the fountain, symbolized by colossal allegorical figures, are the Danube, Ganges, Nile and Plate, representing the continents of Europe, Asia, Africa and America. The River Plate is identified by a pile of coins and an armadillo, the Nile by a lion and the Danube by a horse (the Ganges, however, lacks an accompanying emblem). That the power of the papacy extends over these lands is shown by the prominent position in the design given to the papal keys and tiara, and the arms of the Pope. Rising above the statues is an ancient obelisk, taken from the Circus of Maxentius. The obelisk is topped by the figure of a dove with an olive branch (from the Pope's family coat of arms) to show that this once pagan monument has been converted into a Christian one.

Romans like to say that the statue of the River Nile has his head veiled to avoid seeing Borromini's façade of the church of Sant'Agnese. A further sign of Bernini's disdain for his rival's architectural abilities is supposedly indicated by the posture of the River Plate, raising his arm as if to shield himself from a building that will come crashing down at any moment. Actually, the fountain was finished in 1651, before work on the church began, and the Nile is veiled as an allusion to its unknown source.

Bernini also had a hand in the fountain at the southern end of the piazza, designing the central figure of the Moor. The fountain at the northern end of the piazza shows Neptune and Nereids; the figures were completed in 1878.

The tales associated with Bernini's fountain mentioned above may be apocryphal but the genuine history of the building of the church of **Sant' Agnese in Agone** is no less illustrative of the fierce rivalries and political infighting that went on between the architects of the Baroque era.

Girolamo Rainaldi began work on the church in 1652, assisted by his son, Carlo. But when Girolamo's design came in for a critical drubbing he resigned in a huff. His son was soon outmanoeuvred and replaced by that temperamental genius Borromini, whose

Profiting by the Pope

When Cardinal Giambattista Pamphili was elevated to the throne of St Peter's as Innocent X in 1644, his money-grubbing sister-in-law, Olimpia Maidalchini, knew she had hit the jackpot. The 72-year-old pope was totally in her thrall and she meant to profit by her influence.

With the pope in her pocket, Donna Olimpia had but one aim: to convert the patronage of the papacy into hard cash. Every papal appointment meant a kickback and Donna Olimpia was as ruthless as any mafioso when it came to extorting money. Bishoprics and benefices went to the highest bidder; cardinals' hats were sold as fast as they became vacant. During the ten years of Innocent's reign, Donna Olimpia's rapacity knew no bounds.

As the money poured into the family coffers, Olimpia rigorously shielded the pope from anyone who might threaten her hold over him. Throughout the last year of Innocent's life, the only times she left the pope's side were to make her weekly trips from the Vatican to her own palace in Piazza Navona with the proceeds of the week's hard graft. She made the trips in secret at the dead of night, accompanied by several porters carrying away the loot in sacks. The pope, meanwhile, was safely locked in his chamber. Innocent might bear the keys of St Peter but Donna Olimpia held the keys to the door.

altered in the course of all this to-ing and fro-ing. Nevertheless, his masterly concave façade and soaring dome contribute enormously to the heightened Baroque ambience of Piazza Navona and were a great influence upon his fellow architects.

After the size and grandeur of the façade the interior of Sant'Agnese is surprisingly small and compact. It is arranged on a Greek-cross plan and is extravagantly decorated in the Baroque style.

The church occupies the site of the martyrdom of St Agnes, who was executed during the persecutions of Diocletian in AD 304. Before her death, the 14-year-old martyr was publicly exposed in a brothel but her hair grew miraculously to hide her nakedness. A marble relief by Alessandro Algardi depicting this miracle is contained in the ancient Oratory of St Agnes which lies beneath the church.

Palazzo Pamphili, to the right of the church, was designed for the Pamphili family by Girolamo Rainaldi and built between 1644 and 1650. Borromini had a hand in the work's completion, designing much of the sumptuous interior. His long gallery is decorated with a magnificent ceiling fresco by Pietro da Cortona depicting the story of Aeneas (from whom the Pamphilis claimed descent). Innocent X gave the palace to his notoriously grasping sister-in-law Olimpia Maidalchini. It is now the Brazilian Embassy.

Piazza Pasquino, immediately to the south-west of Piazza Navona, contains one of Rome's celebrated "talking statues", the mouthpieces of popular discontent in the city during the Renaissance. This mutilated marble torso,

overall plan is largely responsible for the look of the church today. Borromini, however, was himself forced to resign in 1657 and Carlo Rainaldi was recalled to the project. The church was finally completed by a variety of other hands, including, needless to say, Bernini.

Borromini's daringly original designs for the church were considerably

thought to represent Menelaus supporting the dying Patroclus and to date from the 3rd century BC, was placed here by Cardinal Carafa in 1501. The custom arose of attaching to the statue barbed comments on the events of the day and the doings of the authorities. Pasquino, as the statue was dubbed after a sharp-tongued local tailor, conducted satirical dialogues with his fellow talking statue, Marforio, who lies on the Capitol.

The nearby **Palazzo Braschi** houses the Museum of Rome, which was established to document the changes in the city's appearance and customs from the Middle Ages to the present day. The museum has been closed in recent years.

Via Santa Maria dell'Anima leads to the church of the same name, one of a number of interesting churches in the vicinity of Piazza Navona. A Renaissance church dating from the early 16th century, **Santa Maria dell'Anima** is the German national church in Rome. Its unusual name (St Mary of the Soul) comes from the statue found over the central door which shows the Madonna between two souls in purgatory. The figures are attributed to the Florentine sculptor Andrea Sansovino, who came to Rome in 1505.

The nearby church of **Santa Maria della Pace** is reached by the narrow Vicolo della Pace. The church was built around 1480 by Sixtus IV as a thanksgiving for the end of the war with Florence that had resulted from the papal-inspired Pazzi conspiracy against the Medicis. The Baroque façade and the beautiful semicircular portico date from Pietro da Cortona's

17th-century restoration. Inside the church are Raphael's celebrated **frescoes** of the Sibyls of Cuma, Persia, Phrygia and Tibur, painted in 1514. The harmonious **cloisters** attached to the church are by Bramante (1500–04), one of his first works on coming to Rome.

The church of **Sant'Agostino,** off Piazza delle Cinque Lune, at the northeast corner of Piazza Navona, is notable for a sublime painting by Caravaggio. **La Madonna dei Pellegrini** (found in the first chapel on the left) is one of Caravaggio's most profoundly moving and fascinating works. It shows two pilgrims, an old man and a woman, both carrying staves, kneeling before the Madonna, who stands in a typical Roman doorway holding a rather mature Child. The inspiration for the painting is the statue of the Virgin and Child at the pilgrimage shrine of Loreto, which Caravaggio probably saw on the trip to the Marches region he made shortly before executing the painting in around 1605.

Caravaggio's startlingly realistic portrayal of the dusty pilgrims apparently caused a great deal of controversy at the time. According to an early biographer of the painter, the public made a great deal of fuss (*"estremo schiamazzo"*, an extreme racket) about the supposed lack of respect and propriety shown by the man's muddy feet and the woman's torn and dirty cap. What is more likely to strike the contemporary viewer of the painting is the remarkable depiction of the Virgin. She is dark-haired for a start, has bare shoulders and feet, and full, sensual features.

The model for the Madonna is rumoured to have been the painter's mistress, a prostitute called Lena who plied her trade in the Piazza Navona. Lena was evidently the cause of a violent dispute between Caravaggio and a notary named Pasquelone, which took place in the summer of 1605. The quarrel climaxed with Caravaggio wounding the notary on the side of the head with a blow from his sword. A criminal complaint was brought against Caravaggio in which Lena is described as the "donna di Michelangelo" (the painter's first name). This was just one of Caravaggio's many brushes with the law. The following year he killed a man in a quarrel and was forced to flee Rome. He died of a fever in Port'Ercole four years later, just as efforts were being made in Rome to obtain him a pardon.

A short distance away in Via della Scrofa, a veritable treasure trove of paintings by Caravaggio can be found in San Luigi dei Francesi, the French national church in Rome. The Contarelli Chapel (the last one on the left) contains three paintings illustrating the life of St Matthew, Caravaggio's first public commissions in Rome.

The **Calling of St Matthew** (on the left) shows the saint, in contemporary Roman dress, sitting at a table

---

Benvenuto Cellini

Bevenuto Cellini was a true Renaissance man, someone who "lived the whole life of his age, who felt its thirst for glory, who shared its adoration of the beautiful, who blent its Paganism and its superstitions, who represented its two main aspects of exquisite sensibility to form and almost brutal ruffianism", at least, that was the verdict of the 19th-century British art historian John Addington Symonds.

Born in Florence in 1500, Cellini won renown throughout Europe as a sculptor and goldsmith. But thanks to his candidly scandalous autobiography his fame now rests largely on his prowess as amorist and assassin, braggart and brawler. Swaggering, quarrelsome and vain, yet he idolized his fellow Florentine Michelangelo. In 1519 he refused an invitation to go to England with the sculptor Pietro Torrigiano because Torrigiano was the man who, in his youth, had broken the nose of the "divine Michelangelo".

Instead, Cellini came to Rome and, in 1527, played a dashing role in the Siege of Rome. He boasted of having saved the Castel'Sant Angelo almost single-handed by his own "unimaginable energy and zeal". It was his shot, he declared, that killed the Constable of Bourbon, commander of the invading imperial forces. When, some years later, Cellini was imprisoned in the castle for murdering a rival goldsmith, he kept up his reputation for derring-do by managing to escape.

Cellini took considerable pride in his accomplishments as an assassin. His first admitted murder was committed, not far from the Piazza Navona, in revenge for the killing of his brother, Cecchino. The deed done but with four soldiers in hot pursuit, Cellini took refuge in the Palazzo Madama, residence of Duke Alessandro de' Medici. When the soldiers arrived they found themselves apologizing to Cellini for having interrupting him at his task.

Taken to account for his murders by the sculptor Bandinelli, Cellini replied, "At any rate, the men I have killed do not shame me so much as your bad statues shame you; for the earth covers my victims, whereas yours are exposed to the view of the world."

collecting taxes and surrounded by rakish hangers-on. There are coins on the table; Matthew even has one stuck in the brim of his hat. Christ, partly obscured by St Peter, stretches out his hand in beckoning, prompting Matthew to point to himself in surprise as if to say, "Do you mean me?" The languid pose of Christ's outstretched arm is a direct visual quotation of the figure of Adam on the Sistine Chapel ceiling: a symbolic reference to the belief that Christ was the new Adam who would redeem original sin. "For as in Adam all die, even so in Christ shall all be made alive," reads the passage in Corinthians Caravaggio undoubtedly had in mind.

St Matthew and the Angel (over the altar) accords with traditional representations of the evangelist but Caravaggio still manages to imbue it with a striking originality. The painting shows the now aged Matthew bending awkwardly over a table, pen in hand, an open book before him, while looking over his left shoulder at the angel, hovering overhead dictating the gospel to him. Caravaggio's depiction of the saint, wrinkled and barefoot, caused much controversy at the time. This is, however, a toned-down version of his original conception: the rude realism of his first version of the painting was rejected by the Church on grounds of indecorum.

The Martyrdom of St Matthew (on the right) is violent and dramatic. A muscular and near-naked executioner stands over the prone saint while bystanders recoil or flee in horror. The painting's brutal power is such that viewers cannot help but feel as though they are participating in the drama.

Interestingly, Caravaggio includes a self-portrait in the painting. He is the dark, bearded, villainous-looking man who can be seen immediately above the executioner's sword arm. Unlike the other spectators, he appears to be reacting with indifference to the horrifying scene.

Beyond the church, the 16th-century **Palazzo Madama** (main entrance in Corso del Rinascimento) is now the seat of the Italian Senate, the upper house of the country's parliament. Nearby, the courtyard of the Palazzo della Sapienza (formerly the seat of the University of Rome, now the State Archive) leads to Borromini's church of **Sant'Ivo** (1642–66). The church's curious spiral bell tower is seen to best advantage from the Piazza Sant' Eustachio just around the corner. The eponymous bar here is reputed to serve the best coffee in Rome.

*M*ounted police in the *Piazza Navona.*

The Timeless Grace of a Pagan Temple

Built as a temple to all the gods, the Pantheon has survived as a monument to the vaunting self-confidence of the ancient Romans. A staggering feat of engineering, it remained unparalleled for centuries, the largest cast concrete construction in existence until this century. Severe and majestic, it has astonished and inspired visitors to Rome for almost 2,000 years.

The **Pantheon** impresses from first sight, whether glimpsed in part as you approach through the warren of surrounding streets, or taken in slowly from the Piazza della Rotonda in front. The building's portico is stately and imposing, 16 massive Corinthian columns: 8 across at the front, the others staggered in 4 rows behind. All but 3 of the columns (the ones on the extreme left) are original. That the portico was used as a poultry market

*A*round the corner from the Pantheon, Santa Maria sopra Minerva is Rome's only Gothic church. This chubby cherub is among the decorative additions of a later age.

during the Middle Ages has done nothing to diminish its dignity.

But, as impressive as the building's exterior undoubtedly is, nothing can quite prepare the visitor for the experience of stepping inside. Once you have passed through the mighty bronze doors (restored in the 16th century), the sense of awe and wonder that floods over you is almost overwhelming. The sheer size of the building has much to do with it. But there is grace and harmony as well as grandeur. As art historians and architects have never tired of repeating, the height of the dome is the same as its diameter: 43.3 m (142 ft).

Who was responsible for this immortal symmetry? The inscription you will have noticed outside on the frieze

An Egyptian obelisk rises from Giacomo della Porta's Baroque fountain in Piazza della Rotonda.

over the portico is misleading. It reads M. AGRIPPA L.F. COS TERTIUM FECIT—Marcus Agrippa, son of Lucius, consul for the third time built this. Agrippa, statesman and general, son-in-law of the Emperor Augustus, did indeed build the original temple—in 27 BC, in honour of the victory he had won over Antony and Cleopatra at Actium.

Agrippa's building, however, was severely damaged by fire in AD 80. It was rebuilt around AD 125 by the Emperor Hadrian, who, modest to a fault, did not put his own name on the temple. A complex and brilliant man, Hadrian has been credited by posterity as the building's architect, not just

its patron. His genius also went into the creation of the Temple of Venus and Rome (the largest temple in the city) and his celebrated Villa at Tivoli.

The most striking aspect of Hadrian's building is, of course, the giant concave dome. A metre wider than that of St Peter's, it had a profound impact on the architects of the Renaissance, influencing Brunelleschi's cathedral in Florence and Michelangelo's design for the dome of St Peter's itself.

The dome was originally covered with bronze, the walls coated with marble and stucco: it is now green lead and the walls bare brick. But though it has been plundered over the centuries, by emperors and popes, as well as by pillaging Goths, the Pantheon has come down to us remarkably intact: the best-preserved monument of ancient Rome. That the edifice has survived at all is due to its conversion from pagan temple to Christian church. It was consecrated in 609 as *Santa Maria ad Martyres* (St Mary of the Martyrs) by Pope Boniface IV, who thereupon transported 28 cartloads of martyrs' bones from the catacombs to be re-interred in the church.

The Pantheon's new status as a church didn't prevent it from further despoilation. In 663 the Byzantine emperor Constans II stripped the dome of its gilded bronze, which he then carted off to his capital, Constantinople; almost 1,000 years later, in 1632, the Barberini pope, Urban VIII, removed 200 tons of bronze from the roof of the portico to make Bernini's *baldacchino* (canopy) in St Peter's and 80 cannons for the Castel Sant'Angelo. This act of papal vandalism gave rise to the celebrated pasquinade *"Quod non fecerunt barberi, fecerunt Barberini"*—"what the barbarians didn't do, the Barberini did".

Urban VIII did leave the bronze rim around the central opening of the dome. This is the **oculus**, the great all-seeing eye of heaven. Eight-and-a-half metres wide (28 ft) and open to the elements, it is the building's only source of light. On fine days a beam of sunlight moves around the interior of the building like a slow searchlight, illuminating the frescoes and tombs inside.

The Pantheon contains the tombs of painters and kings. Raphael (d. 1520) and Annibale Carracci (d. 1609) are buried here, as are the first two kings of the united Italy, Vittorio Emanuele II (d. 1878) and Umberto I (d. 1900).

In the nearby **Piazza Minerva** stands a most unusual monument, a marble elephant, supporting on its back a 6th-century BC Egyptian obelisk. The obelisk was found in a nearby garden in 1665 and erected here shortly after. The delightful elephant which bears this great burden is by Bernini.

Santa Maria sopra Minerva is the only truly Gothic church on Rome. It was built in the 8th century on the site of a temple of Minerva, hence the church's unusual name, Saint Mary above Minerva. Its present form dates from around 1280 when it was rebuilt by the Dominicans on the lines of their church of Santa Maria Novella in Florence.

The church contains the tombs of several popes and cardinals, and a number of prominent members of Rome's leading families (from whose ranks the popes and cardinals were very often drawn). In the left aisle (between the third and fourth chapels) is found the **Tomb of Giovanni Vigevano** (d. 1630), which contains a striking bust by Bernini.

The **Carafa Chapel**, in the right transept, contains a series of beautiful **frescoes** by Filippino Lippi depicting the *Annunciation*, the *Assumption* and scenes from the life of St Thomas, painted between 1488 and 1492. Michelangelo's statue of **Christ the Redeemer** is found at the foot of the choir, on the left of the high altar. Michelangelo's Christ was carved as a nude figure in Florence and then sent to Rome, where it was ineptly finished by pupils. The gilded drapery was added later, as were the sandals, which were attached to the statue to preserve Christ's foot from being worn away by the kisses of the faithful.

Beneath the high altar are preserved the relics of St Catherine of Siena, the patron saint of Italy. St Catherine died in a nearby house in 1380.

Classy Shopping and Classical Monuments around the English Ghetto

Those Grand Tourists of the 18th century, the English aristocracy, stayed in the area around the Spanish Steps on their visits to Rome, giving it the nickname the "English ghetto". (The Romans did tend to dub all rich foreigners "*Inglesi*".) Keats, Balzac, Wagner and Liszt, and other great 19th-century artists, followed in their footsteps. Today the district is the haunt of big-league shoppers, conspicuously consuming in the elegant and expensive shops of Via Condotti and its neighbouring streets.

For centuries the area around the **Piazza di Spagna** and the famous **Spanish Steps** has been the haunt of foreigners. The piazza and steps take their name from the Spanish Embassy to the Vatican, which was established here in the 17th century. In the 18th century the surrounding district was popular with English aristocrats on the Grand Tour. The area's hotels and *pensioni* continued to attract foreigners throughout the 19th century, including

*T*he Piazza di Spagna *is truly international. The French church of the Trinita dei Monti looms over the Spanish Steps, while McDonalds imparts an American flavour to the area.*

an impressive roster of writers and artists. Tennyson, Stendhal, Balzac, Liszt and Wagner all stayed in the vicinity.

The English poet Keats lived the last months of his life at No 26 Piazza di Spagna. Keats and his friend, the painter Joseph Severn, had meals sent up to their lodgings from a trattoria across the piazza in Via Condotti, now Rome's most fashionable and exclusive shopping street. The site of this humble trattoria is now occupied by the opulent premises of the jewellers Bulgari.

Keats died of consumption in a small room overlooking the Spanish Steps on 23 February 1821. The house is now a Keats–Shelley memorial and museum, and contains relics of Keats and Shelley, and their contemporaries Byron and Leigh Hunt. Among the exhibits are two contrasting masks: the death mask of Keats and the wax carnival mask that Byron wore at the Carnival of Ravenna in February 1820.

In the centre of Piazza di Spagna is a charming fountain which takes the form of a leaking boat. The **Barcaccia Fountain** was once thought to be the work of Pietro Bernini but is now attributed to his more famous son, Gian Lorenzo Bernini.

The Spanish Steps, or **Scalinata della Trinità dei Monti** as they are more properly called, were built in the early 18th century. Today, they are a popular gathering place for young Italians and foreigners. In spring the steps are decorated with a display of azaleas.

To the left of the Spanish Steps is **Babington's Tea Rooms**, opened in 1896; to the right of the steps, is the first McDonalds in Italy, which dates from 1986.

At the top of the Spanish Steps is the church of the **Trinità dei Monti,** its striking Baroque façade one of the city's most distinctive landmarks. The church was founded by Charles VIII, King of France, for the Order of Minims created by San Francesco di Paola. Work began on the church and adjoining convent in 1502 but was not completed until 1587. The ancient **obelisk** in front of the church was erected here by Pius VI in 1788.

Viale della Trinita dei Monti leads to the 16th-century **Villa Medici**, home to the French Academy since 1803 and the venue for important art exhibitions. The centrepiece of the charming fountain in front is a cannonball said to have hit the wall of the villa when Queen Christina of Sweden fired a cannon from Castel Sant'Angelo. Beyond the villa, Viale della Trinita dei Monti continues into Viale d'Annunzio, which leads to the Pincio.

Standing at the south-west corner of the Villa Borghese park, the **Pincio** contains formal gardens laid out in the early 19th century. The tradition of gardens here goes back to classical times when it was known as the *Collis Hortulorum*, the Hill of Gardens. The **terrace** of the Pincio, overlooking Piazza del Popolo, affords splendid views of the city, particularly at sunset. On Sunday mornings in summer military bands perform at the nearby bandstand.

From the Pincio, a winding path leads down to **Piazza del Popolo,** one of Rome's most splendid piazzas. It was created by Paul III in 1538 but given its present appearance in the early 19th century by Giuseppe Valadier. The 12th–13th-century BC **obelisk** in the centre of the piazza, the second oldest in the city, was brought here from the Circus Maximus in 1589.

The magnificent **Porta del Popolo**, which stands on the site of the ancient Porta Flaminia, was built in 1561 for Pius IV. The inner façade of the gate was created by Bernini to mark the arrival in the city of the celebrated Roman Catholic convert, Queen Christina of Sweden, in 1655.

Santa Maria del Popolo, which gives its name to the piazza, was built as a chapel by Paschal II in 1099 on what was believed to be the site of Nero's tomb. Enlarged in the 13th century, it was rebuilt by Sixtus IV in 1474. The church contains many fine works of

A friendly lion licks Daniel's leg in Santa Maria del Popolo's Chigi Chapel.

art, including some superb frescoes by Pinturicchio (in the first chapel of the right aisle and in the vault of the apse). The chapel to the left of the main altar contains two powerful and dramatic works by Caravaggio, the *Crucifixion of St Peter* and the *Conversion of St Paul,* as well as Annibale Carracci's *Assumption of the Virgin.*

The **Chigi Chapel**, in the left aisle, was designed for the fabulously wealthy Sienese banker Agostino Chigi by Raphael, who died, as did his patron, before the project could be completed. The chapel was finished by Bernini in 1652. It contains the striking pyramidal tombs of Agostino Chigi and his brother Sigismondo, as well as statues of four prophets. Two of these are by Bernini, the statues of *Habakkuk* and *Daniel and the lion.*

Three streets fan out from the south side of the Piazza del Popolo: Via del Babuino, on the left, which passes the Spanish Steps; Via del Corso, in the middle, leading to Piazza Venezia; and Via di Ripetta, on the right, which heads towards the medieval quarter of the city around Piazza Navona and the Pantheon. Framed by these streets are two Baroque churches, **Santa Maria in Montesanto** and **Santa Maria dei Miracoli**.

The **Corso** has been one of Rome's most important streets for millennia. In ancient times it was the *Via Lata,* the urban section of the *Via Flaminia,* the main road to northern Italy. The name by which it is known today comes from the celebrated carnival races, or *corse,* that were first held here under the pleasure-loving Venetian Pope Paul II in 1466. Today the Corso is lined with great Renaissance and

Baroque palaces, and crowded with shops and shoppers.

A short way down the Corso, Via dei Pontefici leads to the historic **Mausoleum of Augustus**. The Mausoleum or *Augusteum*, as it was known in classical times, was built by the Emperor as a tomb for himself and his family in 28 BC. A vast cylindrical drum, 87 m (286 ft) in diameter, constructed of travertine (the most widely-used building material in Rome), it was originally surmounted by a conical mound of earth planted with cypresses. The design owes much to the style of Etruscan tombs. The last emperor to be buried here was Nerva in AD 98. The later uses put to the mausoleum were distinctly secular: a fortress for the powerful Colonna family in the 12th century, a quarry, an amphitheatre for bullfighting, a site for fireworks displays, a circus and then a concert hall until 1936, after which considerable restoration took place under Mussolini. Il Duce is said to have intended the mausoleum to be used as his own tomb.

Between the Mausoleum of Augustus and the Tiber, a special glass-sided building houses the **Ara Pacis Augustae**. The Altar of Augustan Peace was erected in the Campus Martius and consecrated on 4 July, 13 BC to honour the peace brought to the Roman world by Augustus's victories in Spain and Gaul. The altar was discovered in 1568 beneath the Palazzo Farnese and some blocks from it were removed and dispersed, ending up in various displays in the Uffizi in Florence, the Louvre in Paris and the Vatican. The altar was reconstructed earlier this century (1937–38), using some of the original fragments and reproductions of the others.

The altar is enclosed by a screen of white Carrara marble decorated with reliefs. Some of the reliefs illustrate mythological and allegorical scenes but the most interesting section is the one showing the ceremony of consecration itself, a procession of officials, dignitaries and the imperial family, with Augustus at the head. The figures in the procession are caught in astonishingly lifelike poses, particularly the children, one of whom is the future emperor Claudius.

To the south, off Via di Ripetta, Via Borghese leads to the **Palazzo Borghese**, nicknamed the "harpsichord of Rome" on account of its shape. The palace was begun around 1560 and acquired by Cardinal Camillo Borghese, later to become Pope Paul V. The palace is now home to Rome's most exclusive club, the *Circolo della Caccia*, or Hunt Club. In the nearby Largo della Fontanella di Borghese an antiques market is held on weekday mornings, specializing in old books and prints. Via Fontanella di Borghese leads back to the Corso.

Just over halfway down the Corso, in Piazza Colonna, stands the **Column of Marcus Aurelius**. This imposing monument was built between AD 176 and 193 to celebrate the soldier-emperor's victories over barbarian tribes in Bohemia, the Ukraine and Germany. The column is 29.6 m (97 ft) high and is decorated with spiralling reliefs illustrating the Emperor's campaigns. Originally, a statue of the Emperor stood on top of the column but it was replaced by Pope Pius V with a bronze statue of St Paul in 1589.

Facing the column is **Palazzo Chigi**, built in the 16th and 17th centuries and now the official residence of Italy's Prime Minister. Just beyond, in Piazza di Montecitorio, is the **Palazzo di Montecitorio,** begun by Bernini in 1650 and completed by Carlo Fontana in 1694. It is now the seat of the Italian Chamber of Deputies. In the piazza stands the 6th-century BC **Obelisk of Psammeticus II,** brought to Rome by Augustus to celebrate his victory over Cleopatra. Rediscovered in 1748, it was placed here in 1792.

Further down the Corso, Via del Caravita leads to the magnificent Jesuit church of **Sant'Ignazio**, begun in 1626 by Cardinal Lodovico Ludovisi to celebrate the canonization of St Ignatius of Loyola, founder of the militant order. The church contains a spectacular *trompe l'oeil* ceiling by Andrea da Pozzo which rivals the famous ceiling of the Gesù.

Behind the church is the **Collegio Romano**, founded as a college for the Jesuits in 1585 by Gregory XIII. The main façade of the college is in Piazza del Collegio Romano, reached from the Corso by Via Lata. Facing the college on the opposite side of the piazza is the north wing of the huge **Palazzo Doria**. This façade (by Antonio del Grande) dates from the mid-17th century, that on the Corso is a Rococo masterpiece by Gabriele Valvassori from 1734. The south wing, on Via del Plebiscito, was created by Paolo Ameli in 1743.

The palace contains the **Galleria Doria Pamphili**, a splendid patrician art collection begun by Donna Olimpia Maidalchini, the notoriously rapacious sister-in-law of the Pamphili pope Innocent X. Its many fine works include Titian's *Spain succouring Religion* and *Salome with the head of St John the Baptist*, Alessandro Algardi's bust of the infamous Donna Olimpia and three superb paintings by Caravaggio, *St John the Baptist, Mary Magdalene* and *The Rest on the Flight into Egypt*. The highlight of the collection is Velazquez's searching, warts-and-all *Portrait of Innocent X*. When the Pope first saw the painting he is said to have remarked, "*Troppo vero*"—"too true". A more flattering depiction of the pope is provided by Bernini's portrait bust.

Another important patrician art collection is to be found nearby in Palazzo Colonna, just off the west side of Piazza Venezia. The palace (entered in Via della Pilotta) contains the **Galleria Colonna**, open on Saturday mornings only. Displayed in stately Baroque galleries are works by Van Dyck, Veronese, Bronzino and Tintoretto.

Four arches span Via della Pilotta, connecting the palace with the gardens of Villa Colonna. From Piazza della Pilotta it is but a short walk to one of Rome's most unforgettable sights, the **Fontana di Trevi**.

Reached through a maze of narrow streets, the fountain appears suddenly: an extravagant masterpiece of Rococo fantasy. It seems too big for the square in which it is set, but this only enhances its exaggerated air of theatricality. No wonder the fountain has proved a popular location for filmmakers, like Federico Fellini, for whom Anita Ekberg and Marcello Mastroianni frolicked in the waters in *La Dolce Vita*.

Nicola Salvi's 18th-century Rococo masterpiece, the Trevi fountain.

"In the design of the fountain," wrote the 19th-century American novelist Nathaniel Hawthorne, "some sculptor of Bernini's school has gone absolutely mad in marble." The artist in question is Nicola Salvi, who did, in fact, incorporate some of an earlier design by Bernini in his work. Salvi won the commission for the fountain in 1732 after impressing Pope Clement XII with his stage setting for a spectacular firework display in the Piazza di Spagna.

Salvi came up with an allegorical design centring on the colossal figure of the sea god Neptune, or Oceanus. The god stands astride a giant cockle-shell drawn by two winged sea horses, led by tritons. The triton on the left is straining to hold his rearing horse (representing a stormy sea), while his companion on the right, whose horse is under control (the calm sea), blows heartily on his conch to herald the sea god's coming.

The water for the fountain, reckoned to be the purest in Rome, comes from a source at Salone to the east of the city, called Acqua Vergine. The name comes from the story of a young virgin who first revealed the spring to a group of thirsty Roman soldiers. A panel over the statue of Health to the right of Neptune shows the scene in relief. On the other side of Neptune, over the statue of Abundance, a relief depicts the Emperor Agrippa approving designs for the aqueduct which brought the water to the city.

Musical Postcards from Rome

"Why should I use new techniques when there is still so much to say through the language of conventional music?" retorted the 20th-century Italian composer Ottorino Respighi when someone accused him of not being modern or progressive. His three symphonic poems inspired by Rome—Fountains of Rome, Pines of Rome and Festivals of Rome—have been dismissed as "musical picture postcards"; for others that's half their charm.

Fountains of Rome, the best-known of the three works, was suggested by "four of Rome's fountains contemplated at the hour in which their character is most in harmony with the surrounding landscape." It opens in pastoral mood with "The Valle Giulia Fountain at Daybreak", next, troops of naiads and tritons disport themselves in "The Triton Fountain in the Morning", then Neptune's chariot is drawn by sea-horses across "The Trevi Fountain at Midday", and, finally, rustling leaves and tolling bells are evoked in "The Villa Medici Fountain at Sunset".

One more curious detail is worth pointing out. It is said that the giant urn which emerges from the rock to the right of the fountain was set there by Salvi to obstruct the view from a nearby café, the haunt of a group of rival artists, who gathered there to mock the architect and his work in progress.

Before you leave, throw a coin over your shoulder into the fountain, a custom which has developed from the old tradition that drinking from the fountain would ensure a visitor's return to the city.

Opposite the fountain, the church of **Santi Vincenzo ed Anastasio** preserves the hearts and lungs of around 30 popes, who died between 1590 and 1903.

Via della Stamperia, to the north of the fountain, leads to Piazza dell' Accademia di San Luca, site of the Palazzo Carpegna. The palace houses the **Accademia di San Luca**, founded by the painter Girolamo Muziano in 1577. The academy's gallery holds over 1,000 paintings and sculptures, the bequests of past members of the academy. The collection includes works by Raphael, Rubens and Guercino. The *Sale Accademiche*, containing important works from the 15th century to the present day, is open on St Luke's Day (18 October).

A short distance away from the Accademia, is the busy shopping street of Via del Tritone. From Largo del Tritone, Via Due Macelli leads back towards the Piazza di Spagna. Just off this road, in Via Capo le Case, is the church of **Sant'Andrea delle Fratte**, which contains two of the angels Bernini sculpted for Ponte Sant'Angelo.

*T**he family arms of Pope Clement XII, patron of the Trevi fountain.*

VILLA BORGHESE

Fine Art and Fresh Air in a Park for Pleasure

Roller-skate, jog, cycle or stroll through Rome's finest public park—but take time to investigate the summer house of a pleasure-loving Renaissance cardinal, the showcase for his remarkable collection of paintings and sculptures. Explore too the enigmatic art of the Etruscans, housed in a papal villa.

Rome's finest public park, the **Villa Borghese**, was created in the 17th century by Cardinal Scipione Borghese, the nephew of Pope Paul V. In 1902 it was bought by Umberto I of Italy and presented by him to the city. The park contains lakes and fountains, galleries and museums, not to mention Rome's zoo, all criss-crossed with pleasant avenues and paths. **The Pincio**, at the south-west corner of the park, contains a formal park laid out in the early 19th

The Villa Borghese may be aristocratic in origin (it was created for a well-known cardinal) but now it's distinctly democratic: a park for pleasure.

century. Concerts by military and police bands are held here on Sunday mornings. The terrace of the Pincio overlooks Piazza del Popolo and offers a splendid vantage point to view the city. The Villa Borghese is a popular spot for walking, cycling and picnics.

The **Galleria Borghese** is housed in the Casino Borghese, in the east of the park. It was built as a summer house for the worldly, pleasure-loving Cardinal Scipione Borghese between 1613 and 1615. The cardinal was a great patron of the arts and laid the basis for the remarkable collection of paintings and sculptures on view today. He was an early patron of Bernini and the gallery contains an astonishing sequence of sculptures which the artist executed in his twenties. These include

his dramatic statue of *David*, caught just as he is about to release his slingshot (the face is said to be a self-portrait of the artist), *Apollo and Daphne* and the *Rape of Proserpine*. An even more precocious statue, of *Aeneas and Anchises*, was made, with help from his father, when Bernini was only 15. The gallery also contains the two remarkable busts of his patron, the Cardinal. A later masterpiece is Antonio Canova's seductive statue of Pauline Borghese, the sister of Napoleon. She married Camillo Borghese in 1803. The sculpture, executed the following year, portrays her as the *Conquering Venus*.

The gallery's superb collection of paintings includes Titian's beautiful and enigmatic *Sacred and Profane Love*, Raphael's celebrated *Deposition*, Correggio's sensual *Danae*, Dosso Dossi's *Circe*, a *Venus and Cupid* by

Antonio Canova's coolly erotic statue of Napoleon's femme fatale of a sister, Pauline Borghese.

Cranach and several fine works by Caravaggio.

The **Galleria Nazionale d'Arte Moderna** is found in the giant neoclassical Palazzo delle Belle Arti at the top of the Villa Borghese. It houses an important collection of 19th- and 20th-century art by Italian and foreign artists. Among the gallery's highlights are works by Cézanne, de Chirico, Degas, Monet, Klee, Kandinsky, Miro, Utrillo and Henry Moore. Look, too, for Klimt's *The Three Ages of Man* and sculptures by Rodin.

To the west lies the **Museo Nazionale di Villa Giulia**, Rome's museum of Etruscan art. It is housed in the Villa Giulia, a splendid late-Renaissance palace built as a summer villa for Julius III by Jacopo Barozzi da Vignola between 1551 and 1553. The museum gives a unique insight into the life and art of the enigmatic pre-Roman civilization of the Etruscans. Among the many outstanding exhibits are the dramatic fragments of a late-6th-century BC terracotta statuary group depicting *Apollo and Hercules*, thought to be the work of Vulca da Veio, the sculptor traditionally responsible for the statues of the Temple of Jupiter Capitolinus. Also dating from the 6th century BC is the *Sarcophagus of the Newlyweds*, a beautiful terracotta work showing a young husband and wife reclining on a couch.

Pauline Victrix
Given that her conquests in the bedroom matched her brother's on the battlefield, it's entirely appropriate that Napoleon's sister Pauline Borghese should have had herself sculpted as Venus Victrix. "Imperious" and "brazen" seem suitable adjectives to describe a woman who used ladies-in-waiting as footstools and had a giant negro carry her to her bath. One suspects that Pauline, like marble, never blushed. When asked how she could possibly have posed so scantly dressed, she replied "The studio was heated".

*E*truscan women dined alongside men—to the scandal of the chauvinist ancient Romans—as shown by the Sarcophagus of the Newlyweds.

Barberini Bees and a Taste of the Sweet Life

The Barberini pope, Urban VIII, stamped his mark on the Quirinal Hill—with the help of those Baroque rivals Bernini and Borromini. The Pope's name lives on in a palace, street and square; so does his family emblem: the Barberini bees. The international jet set who made the nearby Via Veneto their playground in the 1950s and 60s left only fleeting traces—unless you count the celluloid immortality Federico Fellini gave them in *La Dolce Vita*.

The **Quirinal** is the highest of the seven ancient hills of Rome. It is climbed from Largo Magnananapoli, at the beginning of the busy Via Nazionale, by Via Ventiquattro Maggio, named after the day on which Italy declared war on Austria in 1915. The street ascends between two palatial residences, the 15th-century Villa Colonna, on the left, and the early-17th-century Palazzo Pallavicini-Rospigliosi, on the right. In the garden of the latter palace stands the celebrated **Casino dell'Aurora,** a pavilion containing Guido Reni's Baroque ceiling **fresco** of the *Aurora* (1613–14). Reni's best work, it was immensely popular with 19th-century visitors to Rome. The palace itself houses the **Galleria Pallavicini**, a private collection of 15th–18th century art, including works by Botticelli, Carracci, Lotto and Rubens.

The summit of the hill is crowned by the vast **Piazza del Quirinale**. In the centre of the square are the colossal statues of the *Dioscuri*, the heavenly twins Castor and Pollux. The statues are Roman copies of Greek originals. Above the pair rises a tall **obelisk**, brought here in 1786 from the Mausoleum of Augustus.

*T*he statues of the demigods Castor and Pollux, with their horses Cyllaros and Harpagus, stand astride the summit of the Quirinal.

Dominating the piazza is the **Palazzo del Quirinale**, formerly the summer palace of the popes and now the official residence of the President of the Republic. The palace was begun in 1574 but not completed until 1740. In this time, Domenico Fontana, Carlo Maderno, Bernini and Ferdinando Fuga all had a hand in the palace's creation. Opposite the Quirinal Palace is the **Palazzo della Consulta,** designed by Ferdinando Fuga in 1734 for Clement XII and now the seat of Italy's supreme court.

*B*ernini used travertine *rather than the customary marble to create one of his finest fountains, the Fontana del Tritone.*

Via del Quirinale runs along the Quirinal palace's "*manica lunga*", its "long sleeve", and passes two Baroque churches by great architectural rivals of the 17th century: Bernini's **Sant' Andrea al Quirinale** and Borromini's **San Carlo alle Quattro Fontane**.

The **Quattro Fontane** are four Baroque fountains standing on the four corners of a busy crossroads. The fountains, designed by Domenico Fontana and Pietro da Cortona, personify the Tiber, the Nile, Diana and Juno. The crossroads offers views in four different directions: in the distance can be seen the obeslisks at Trinità dei Monti, the Quirinal and Santa Maria Maggiore, and Michelangelo's monumental gateway, the Porta Pia. These remarkable vistas are all part of the Baroque town planning of Sixtus V.

Via del Quattro Fontana leads to **Palazzo Barberini**, begun in 1624 by

Maderno for Urban VIII, with significant later contributions by Borromini and Bernini. The palace houses part of the **Galleria Nazionale d'Arte Antica**. The works of art include a *Madonna and Child* by Filippo Lippi (Room 2), Raphael's *La Fornarina*, the baker's daughter, thought to be a painting of the painter's mistress (Room 6), Titian's *Venus and Adonis* (Room 7), Caravaggio's *Narcissus* and also his *Judith with the head of Holofernes* (Room 14), a portrait of the 16th-century philosopher *Erasmus* by Quentin Massys, and a portrait of *Henry VIII* by Holbein (Room 20). The Salone, or Great Hall, is decorated with an allegorical ceiling fresco of *The Triumph of Divine Providence*, a Baroque masterpiece, by Pietro da Cortona painted between 1633 and 1639.

Piazza Barberini contains Bernini's celebrated **Fontana del Tritone**, created between 1642 and 1643. Four dolphins support a shell on which the triton sits, blowing a stream of water through a conch held above his head. The **Fontana delle Api**, on the north side of the piazza, was also designed by Bernini and is decorated with the ubiquitous bee symbol of the Barberini family.

The famous **Via Vittorio Veneto** ascends from Piazza Barberini to the Porta Pinciana and the Villa Borghese. In the 1960s, the Via Veneto was the setting for the legendary high-society life immortalized in Federico Fellini's film *La dolce vita*. The street still has its elegant hotels and fashionable bars but no longer boasts quite the same glamour.

Via Barberini leads from Piazza Barberini to Largo Santa Susanna and

> **Bone Idol**
> Visitors to the church of Santa Maria della Concezione in Via Veneto have a gruesome sight in store. Artfully arranged on the walls and vaults of the five chapels in the church's underground crypt are the bones and skulls of over 4,000 Capuchin monks. Most macabre of all are the defunct who've remained in one piece: full skeletons of monks still in their habits in niches along the walls.

the recently restored **Fontana dell' Acqua Felice** with its colossal statue of Moses.

The nearby church of **Santa Maria della Vittoria** contains one of the masterpieces of Baroque sculpture: Bernini's *Ecstasy of St Theresa*. The statue is the centrepiece of the Cornaro Chapel (in the left transept), which was built between 1645 and 1652 for the Venetian Cardinal Federigo Cornaro.

The statue is based on a mystical vision experienced by Theresa of Avila, one of the great saints of the Counter-Reformation. She described how an angel pierced her heart with a flaming golden arrow:

The pain was so great that I screamed aloud; but at the same time I felt such infinite sweetness that I wished the pain to last forever. It was not physical but psychic pain, although it affected the body as well to some degree. It was the sweetest caressing of the soul by God.

Bernini brilliantly fuses this pain and rapture. There is a sense that here divine love is bordering on the erotic. Is the winged figure who lightly holds an arrow over the saint an angel or perhaps Cupid?

Watching this scene from what appear to be theatre boxes on the sides of the chapel are members of the Cornaro family. The theatricality of the whole chapel, with its dramatic concealed lighting, reminds us that Bernini was a consummate stage designer as well as sculptor, painter and architect.

Via Venti Settembre (named after the date Rome joined the united Italy) runs north-east to **Porta Pia**, the impressive city gate designed by Michelangelo in 1561 but not completed until 1565, the year after his death. Beyond Porta Pia, the broad Via Nomentana leads out of the city. The road, a major bus route, is flanked by graceful aristocratic villas, including **Villa Torlonia**, Mussolini's private residence. The important early-Christian church of **Sant'Agnese Fuori le Mura** is reached after about 2 km (1¼ miles). The church was built over the site of the tomb of St Agnes (martyred in AD 304) in the mid-4th century by Princess Constantia, daughter of the Emperor Constantine. It was rebuilt by Pope Honorius I in the 7th century. The adjoining catacombs, discovered in around 1865, are remarkably well preserved. The nearby church of **Santa Costanza**, built as Constantia's own mausoleum, contains interesting 4th-century mosaics.

From Santa Maria della Vittoria, Via Orlando runs past Via Parigi, where Rome's EPT tourist offices are sited, to the Piazza della Repubblica. Here stand the vast **Baths of Diocletian**.

Built between AD 298 and 306 by the Emperors Diocletian and Maximian,

*P*ygmies hunting *crocodiles and hippopotamuses in a Nilotic mosaic.*

these Baths were the largest in Rome and could hold over 3,000 people at a time. Diocletian was an able administrator who put the Empire back on its feet after a period of decline. He was also a vigorous persecutor of Christians, 40,000 of whom are supposed to have been put to work on the construction of the Baths (some bricks marked with crosses were apparently found in the ruins). The Baths covered an area of around 380 m by 370 m (1,247 ft x 1,214 ft) and the complex contained libraries and exercise rooms, gardens and galleries, as well as the baths themselves. Visitors would change in the *apodyteria*, or dressing rooms, sit and sweat in one of the *sudatoria*, splash themselves with hot water in the *calidarium*, cool down in the *tepidarium*, before plunging finally into the cold waters of the *frigidarium*.

The Baths fell into decay after the Gothic invasion of AD 410 and the remains were plundered for building materials by successive popes. In 1561 Pius IV engaged Michelangelo to convert the great central hall of the Baths into the church of **Santa Maria degli Angeli**. Michelangelo incorporated much of the classical remains into his design, including eight massive columns of red granite, 13.8 m (45 ft) high and 1.5 m (5 ft) in diameter. These columns originally lined the nave, when Vanvitelli altered and reoriented the church in 1749 they became part of the vast transept.

Part of the Baths house the **Museo Nazionale Romano**, a superb museum of antiquities founded in 1889. For years much of the museum has been closed while a major programme of restoration takes place. A few rooms

A colossal horse's head in the Great Cloister of the Museo Nazionale Romano.

have been recently opened, including the one containing the celebrated **Ludovisi Throne**, which bears a 5th-century BC relief showing the goddess Aphrodite rising from the waves at the moment of her birth, attended by two nymphs.

The circular **Piazza della Repubblica** was formerly known as the Piazza dell'Esedra, after the *exedra*, or vestibule, of the Baths which once stood here. Some Romans even today still refer to the square by its old name. The square, opened by Pius IX in 1870, is dominated by the **Fountain of the Naiads**.

The voluptuous bronze nymphs, sculpted by Mario Rutelli (1901–11) and modelled, it is said, on two popular musical stars of the day, caused quite a stir when they were unveiled.

163

Midsummer Snow and the Garden of Paradise on the Esquiline Hill

Santa Maria Maggiore is one of Rome's four great patriarchal basilicas—but feminists needn't feel put out. The church stands on the site of a cult to a pagan goddess and is dedicated to the Mother of Christ. The Virgin even gets equal billing with her son in the glorious medieval mosaic in the apse.

Commanding the summit of the Esquiline Hill stands **Santa Maria Maggiore**, one of the four great patriarchal basilicas of Rome. According to legend the church was founded by Pope Liberius following a miraculous midsummer fall of snow on the night of the 4–5 August 352. Of Liberius's basilica, no trace remains. The church we see was built by Sixtus III (432–40) to celebrate the findings of the Council of Ephesus (431), which proclaimed

*A*ssociations with both the Mother of Christ and the pagan mother goddess Juno Lucina make Santa Maria Maggiore a propitious place to get married.

Mary as the Mother of God. Significantly, given early Christianity's practice of subsuming pagan beliefs, the church was built on the site of a cult to the mother godddess Juno Lucina.

The church's graceful 18th-century façade gives no indication of the building's true antiquity. But step inside and Santa Maria Maggiore's venerable origins become apparent. It may be the opulence of the magnificent coffered ceiling—gilded with what is said to be the first gold to reach Europe from the New World—or the beauty of the 12th-century Cosmatesque pavement which strikes the visitor first. But it is the serene harmony of the nave which will dwell in the memory.

Forty Ionic columns (36 of marble, four of granite) line this broad nave,

*B*aroque architects
*Flaminio Ponzio, Carlo Rainaldi
and Domenico Fontana worked
on the rear façade of Santa
Maria Maggiore.*

preserving the outlines of the early
Christian basilica. Surprisingly, the bal-
anced order and classical proportions
of these columns is largely the work of
Ferdinando Fuga's 18th-century
restoration.

Fuga, the architect of the façade,
was also responsible for the imposing
canopy over the high altar. An elegant
structure composed of four porphyry
columns entwined with gilt-bronze
vines, it was deliberately modelled on
Bernini's celebrated *baldacchino*
(canopy) in St Peter's.

Though the church is rich in artistic
treasures, perhaps the greatest are its
mosaics. The upper walls of the nave
are decorated with **5th-century mosaics**

illustrating scenes from the Old
Testament. More 5th-century mosaics
decorate the triumphal arch, depicting
the *Annunciation* and scenes from the
Infancy of Christ. The glorious mosaic
in the apse was created by the Franciscan monk Jacopo Torritiat the end
of the 13th century, but it is thought
to be based on a 5th-century classical
mosaic from the time of Sixtus III.

The mosaic depicts the *Coronation
of the Virgin* and shows Mary sitting
enthroned at the right-hand of Christ.
This scene takes place inside a roundel
set against a gold background patterned with beautiful decorative ara-
-besques featuring birds and small animals: peacocks, ducks; a snake in the
talons of an eagle, a crane striking at
a rat. Supporting the roundel are
groups of adoring angels with outstretched sweeping wings. On the left-
hand side, behind the angels, is the
small kneeling figure of Nicholas IV,
who built the apse and commissioned

the mosaic, together with Saints Peter, Paul and Francis. On the right-hand side is the kneeling figure of Cardinal Jacopo Colonna, whose largesse helped pay for the work, along with St John the Baptist, St John the Evangelist and St Anthony. The lower border of the apse contains scenes from the life of the Virgin by Torriti based on antique originals.

The whole mosaic, albeit incorporating classical elements, has been described as the finest medieval mosaic in Rome. Torriti, with some justification, has signed himself *"pictor"*, painter.

The *confessio* beneath the high altar houses a reliquary containing a fragment of the **Crib of the Infant Jesus**, purportedly brought to Rome in the 4th century by Helena, the mother of Constantine, the first Christian emperor. The massive kneeling statue before the reliquary is of Pius IX by Ignazio Jacometti (c. 1880).

The richly Baroque **Sistine Chapel**, the third chapel in the right aisle, was designed by Domenico Fontana (1585) for Sixtus V. In a grotto beneath the chapel lie the remains of the **Oratory of the Crib** containing late-13th-century statues by Arnolfo di Cambio. Set in the pavement outside the chapel is the tomb of the Bernini family; further up the right aisle is the tomb of Cardinal Consalvo Rodriguez (d. 1299) by Giovanni di Cosma containing a beautiful mosaic of the Virgin and Child.

In the left aisle, directly opposite the Sistine Chapel, is another richly decorated Baroque chapel, the **Cappella Paolina** or Borghese Chapel, commissioned by Paul V and designed by Flaminio Ponzio (1611). Enshrined on the altar is a venerated Byzantine-style picture of the Madonna. Now thought to date from the 12–13th centuries, it has been variously attributed down the years to Saint Luke and to an unknown 8th- or 9th-century Romano-Byzantine artist.

Above the altar is a relief in bronze and marble of the *Miracle of the Snow*. Each year on 5 August this legendary event is commemorated by a cascade of white rose petals from the dome of the chapel.

In Via Santa Prassede, just off Piazza Santa Maria Maggiore, stands the venerable church of **Santa Prassede**. The church was built by Pope St Paschal I in 822 and contains some of the most striking mosaics in Rome, the work of Byzantine artists. There are remarkable **mosaics** in the apse but even more impressive are those to be found in the tiny **Chapel of St Zeno**, built by Paschal as a mausoleum for his mother, Theodora. The walls and ceiling of the chapel, known in the Middle Ages as "the garden of paradise", are covered with glittering mosaics in gold, blue, and turquoise. In the vault, the head of Christ appears in a medallion held aloft by four angels. To the right of the chapel is an important relic: an oriental jasper column brought back from Jerusalem during the Crusades and reputed to be the one at which Jesus was scourged.

From Piazza dell Esquilino, which lies before the rear façade of Santa Maria Maggiore, the busy Via Cavour descends the Esquiline Hill towards the Roman Forum. Halfway down, a steep flight of steps, Via San Francesco di Paola, leads up to **San Pietro in Vincoli**.

The church of St Peter in Chains was founded in the 5th century by Eudoxia, the wife of the Emperor Valentinian III, as a shrine for the chains said to have bound St Peter during his imprisonment in Jerusalem. Over the centuries the church has been rebuilt and restored many times but the 20 ancient Doric columns lining the nave have remained. Francesco Fontana, early in the 18th century, was largely responsible for the Baroque look the church wears today.

St Peter's chains are preserved in a bronze and crystal reliquary beneath the high altar. It is not the presence of this venerated shrine, however, which draws the hordes of tourists who

M oses, the statue created for the tomb of Julius II, the accursed project which dogged Michelangelo's career.

descend on the church today. They come to see a monumental work of sculpture: Michelangelo's sublime **Moses**. The statue was executed for the tomb of Julius II, the accursed project which dogged Michelangelo throughout his career.

Only a portion of the tomb was ever completed: fragments are to be found today in Florence and the Louvre. San Pietro in Vincoli contains the most substantial parts, of which the statue of Moses is the centrepiece.

Michelangelo depicts the prophet as having descended from Mount Sinai with the tablets of the law to find the

---

Well Done

The grit and fortitude of the early Christian martyrs can be no better illustrated than by the tale of St Lawrence, grilled to death on a red-hot gridiron during the persecutions of the Emperor Valerian in 258.

Ordered by a Roman praetor to hand over the treasures of the church, St Lawrence produced the orphans and widows he had in his care, saying, "These are the church's treasures."

As he was being slowly roasted on the gridiron, the saint asked to be turned over, saying, "That side is done." His torturers failed to appreciate this rare piece of black humour: his Christian pluck was taken as a sign that he was too lazy even to wriggle, giving rise to the phrase 'Lazy as Lawrence'.

The church of San Lorenzo in Panisperna on the Viminal Hill marks the site of the saint's martyrdom; his body rests beneath the basilica of San Lorenzo fuori le Mura, a curious building consisting of two early-Christian churches joined together in the Middle Ages.

Israelites worshipping false gods. The colossal figure seems about to erupt with indignation. The statue has been described as a sort of spiritual self-portrait of the artist and it is not entirely fanciful to see elements of Michelangelo's tumultuous and belligerent personality, his anger and frustrations, in the righteous ire of the great lawgiver.

Another form of self-portrait is to be found in the majestic flowing locks of the prophet, which reveal, if you look closely, profiles of both Michelangelo and his patron. More readily apparent are the strange horns with which Michelangelo has endowed the prophet. This was a traditional feature in medieval iconography, based on a mistranslation of a Hebrew word for the beams of light upon Moses described in the Bible. Michelangelo was aware of this mistake but nevertheless still chose to follow the tradition and give the prophet his satyr-like horns.

On either side of the figure of Moses are niches containing statues of Leah and Rachel, also by Michelangelo and emblematic of the active and contemplative life. The remainder of the tomb is the indifferent work of Michelangelo's pupils.

South of San Pietro in Vincoli, Viale del Monte Oppio leads to the **Oppian Hill**, the site of Nero's legendary Golden House, the *Domus Aurea*. A popular tradition holds that Nero himself started Rome's great fire of AD 64 so that he would have room to build this vast new palace. When completed, the grandiose palace covered an area of 200 acres, including an immense lake, later drained to build the Colosseum. Nero's successors quickly began to demolish or build over the *Domus Aurea*. Trajan constructed here his great Baths, the most magnificent in the city. Their ruins can be seen on the hill today.

Parts of the *Domus Aurea* were rediscovered in the 15th century. The stucco reliefs on the walls of the underground chambers, or grottoes (the origin of the word "grotesque") were a great inspiration to the artists of the Renaissance, including Raphael, whose celebrated *Loggia* in the Vatican bear their influence.

At the bottom of the Oppian Hill, from outside the Colosseum, Via di San Giovanni in Laterano leads to one of Rome's most fascinating churches, **San Clemente**. Named after St Clement, the fourth pope, San Clemente is in fact two churches, one built on top of the other, beneath which there lie still earlier remains. The church has been in the charge of Irish Dominican monks since 1667. Its important archaeological heritage was first discovered by a Dominican prior, Father Mullooly, in 1861.

The church was originally built in the late 4th century over an ancient Roman apartment building, erected after Nero's famous fire of AD 64. Part of this building is thought to have been used for Christian worship from as early as the end of the 1st century. Also on the site is a 2nd-century AD *Mithraeum*, a Temple of Mithras, the Persian god whose cult spread to Rome in the 1st century BC. The cult, which offered some hope of an afterlife, and highly valued loyalty and fidelity, was extremely popular with the soldiers of the Roman legions. The worship of Mithras was at one stage a powerful rival to early Christianity and continued to be practised for some time after Christianity became the Roman state religion.

The original church was destroyed in 1084 during the sack of Rome by the Norman troops of Robert Guiscard. The new, or upper church was begun on the ruins of the old church in 1108. Some parts of the old building, like the beautiful 9th-century choir (*schola cantorum*) were incorporated in the new basilica.

Among the church's greatest artistic treasures are the superb frescoes which decorate the **Chapel of St Catherine** (at the beginning of the left aisle). The frescoes illustrate the life of St Catherine, the early-Christian martyr who was executed during the time of the Emperor Maxentius. The cruel form of torture devised for the saint was to tie her to a wheel—hence the Catherine-wheel firework. The life of St Ambrose is also depicted and there are frescoes of the *Annunciation* and the *Crucifixion*. The frescoes date from the first half of the 15th century and are the work of Masolino da Panicale, probably with the help of the great Florentine master Masaccio.

The lower church is entered by a staircase off the right aisle and contains frescoes dating from the 9th and 11th centuries. Unfortunately, they have deteriorated badly since they were uncovered last century. A staircase from the left aisle of the lower church takes the visitor even deeper and leads to the remains of the 1st-century **Roman House** and the 3rd-century **Temple of Mithras**. From beneath your feet comes the sound of rushing water, on its way to join the famous Cloaca

Maxima. Back in the open air, you will find, adjoining the church, a beautiful medieval courtyard, the occasional setting for alfresco opera and concert performances in the summer.

South of San Clemente on Via della Navicella is the 9th-century church of **Santa Maria in Domnica**, sometimes called Santa Maria della Navicella after the fountain of a boat which stands before it. The church's Renaissance façade is by Andrea Sansovino. Inside, the apse bears a fine 9th-century **mosaic of the Virgin and Child** enthroned in a luxuriant garden of paradise.

On the other side of Via della Navicella is **Santo Stefano Rotondo**, one of Rome's oldest churches, dating back to the 5th century. Its round design is thought to have been modelled on the church of the Holy Sepulchre in Jerusalem, giving rise to the tradition that this is the "New Jerusalem" of the Book of Revelation.

At the end of Via della Navicella, Via Druso leads to Piazzale Numa Pompilio and the towering remains of the Baths of Caracalla. (Bus 118 will make the journey shorter.)

The **Baths of Caracalla** were the most luxurious baths of ancient Rome and the city's largest until the completion of the Baths of Diocletian a century later. Begun in AD 206 by Septimius Severus, the baths were finished by his son, Caracalla, who opened them in 217. Additional work was carried out by the Emperors Heliogabulus and Alexander Severus, and the baths remained in use until the 6th century when the Gothic leader Vitiges cut off the water supply.

In their heyday these baths, which measured around 337 m x 328 m

(1,106 ft x 1,076 ft), could accommodate 1,600 people at a time. Visitors could enjoy the use of libraries and lecture rooms, a gymnasium and a stadium, gardens, shops and porticoes, quite apart from the complex of saunas and pools.

"The meanest Roman could purchase, with a small copper coin, the daily enjoyment of a scene of pomp and luxury which might excite the envy of the kings of Asia," wrote Edward Gibbon. For the 18th-century historian this was not exactly a point of commendation. Indeed, he attributed Rome's Decline and Fall, in part, to the decadent and slothful habits engendered by the baths.

Not only would most modern sports complexes be dwarfed by the ancient Roman baths, they would also seem distinctly Spartan. The interior of the Baths of Caracalla was richly decorated with works of art, the walls covered with coloured mosaics. Many magnificent statues have been unearthed here in recent centuries and scattered among various collections. The celebrated "mosaics of the athletes", discovered in 1824, are now in the Gregorian Museum of Profane Art in the Vatican.

Shelley's *Prometheus Unbound* "was chiefly written upon the mountainous ruins of the baths of Caracalla," he wrote in the poem's Preface, "among the flowery glades and thickets of odoriferous blossoming trees which are extended in ever-widening labyrinths upon its immense platforms and dizzy arches suspended in the air."

Since 1937 the ruins of the Baths of Caracalla have provided an evocative backdrop to Rome's summer season of operas in the open air.

Relics Survive the Ravages of Time in Rome's Cathedral

Sacked by Vandals, hit by an earthquake and twice destroyed by fire, San Giovanni in Laterano has certainly felt the ravages of time. But following each disaster the basilica has been patched up and rebuilt—in varying architectural styles. And through thick and thin the church has preserved a number of important relics, including the heads of Saints Peter and Paul, and the stairs Jesus ascended in the palace of Pontius Pilate.

Surprising though it may seem, Rome's cathedral isn't St Peter's but **San Giovanni in Laterano**. This is the Pope's official seat as the Bishop of Rome and hence the mother and head of all the churches of the city and of the world: "*Omnium urbis et orbis Ecclesiarum Mater et Caput*".

This importance is immediately proclaimed by the church's severely classical 18th-century façade, designed by Alessandro Galilei (1734–36). The façade is crowned by 15 huge statues,

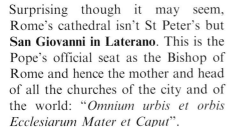

*T*he bronze statue of *St Francis shows the saint in the act of holding up the façade of San Giovanni in Laterano as dreamed by Pope Innocent III.*

visible from miles away, representing Christ, St John the Baptist and St John the Evangelist, and 12 doctors of the Church.

The basilica was founded in the 4th century by Constantine, the first Christian emperor, on land that had once belonged to the wealthy patrician family of Plautius Lateranus. The Laterani had forfeited the property following their involvement in an abortive conspiracy against Nero in AD 66. Two-and-a-half centuries later, the estate came into Constantine's possession as the dowry of his second wife Fausta (whom he was to have suffocated in the hot room of a bath). The Emperor presented the land to Pope Melchiades (311–14), along with that occupied by the barracks of the imperial horse guards, the *Equites Singulares*, who had fought on the wrong side during Constantine's war against his brother-in-law Maxentius. It's Constantine's statue, originally from his Baths on the Quirinal, that you see beneath the portico on your way into the church. The statue stands to the left of the antique bronze central doors, brought here from the *Curia Senatus* (Senate House) in the Forum.

The subsequent history of the church itself is every bit as chequered as the site's imperial past. It was sacked by the Vandals in the 5th century, hit by an earthquake in 896 and twice destroyed by fire in the 14th century, to be rebuilt and restored over and again. In the 17th century San Giovanni was in danger of collapsing and in 1646 Innocent X commissioned the temperamental but brilliant Baroque architect Borromini to rebuild the church. Borromini's brief was to conserve as much of the old edifice as possible and to finish the job in time for the Holy Year of 1650.

Borromini's nave, cool and spacious, does indeed preserve the basilican character of the ancient church. The splendid Cosmatesque pavement remains, as does the richly gilded wooden ceiling, dating from 1564. (Lack of funds prevented Borromini carrying through his ambitious plans to vault the nave.) Also impressive, though of later date, are the statues of the apostles which line the nave. Set in niches designed by Borromini, the sculptures are the work of pupils of the architect's arch rival, Bernini. But before you progress down the nave take a glance at the first pillar of the right-hand double aisle: it bears a

monument to Boniface VIII that incorporates a fragment of a *Trecento* fresco, thought to be by Giotto, showing the pope proclaiming the first Holy Year of 1300.

Only the Pope may celebrate Mass at the Papal Altar, which stands at the centre of the crossing and contains, so it's said, the wooden altar table of St Peter himself. Rising above the altar is Giovanni di Stefano's splendid Gothic canopy, made for Urban V in 1367, containing silver reliquaries purported to hold the heads of Saints Peter and Paul.

Before the altar, in the *confessio*, is the impressive bronze tomb slab of Martin V (d. 1431), upon which Romans customarily throw coins and banknotes to bring good luck. In the apse is a mosaic of *Christ the Redeemer* by Jacopo Torriti and Jacopo da Camerino, dating from the 13th century but based on an earlier classical work. In the Middle Ages it was believed that the head of Christ appeared miraculously in the apse. Sadly, what we see today is a lacklustre 19th-century copy of the work, made when Leo XIII had the apse rebuilt in 1885.

In the right transept is Luca Blasi's magnificent organ (1598), supported by two columns of red-veined yellow marble. Restored a few years ago, it now operates electrically. On the opposite side, in the left transept, is the Altar of the Holy Sacrament (a red light indicates the presence of the host), which incorporates four ancient gilt-bronze columns said to have come from the temple of Jupiter Capitolinus.

Pass from the transept into the left aisle and you will immediately find a small door leading to the **cloisters**, the

high spot of any tour of the basilica. Completed around 1230, the cloisters are the work of the father-and-son team of Jacopo and Pietro Vassalletto, supreme masters of the Cosmatesque school of mosaic work, which flourished in Rome in the 12th and 13th centuries. The columns, some plain and straight, others twisted in corkscrew-like spirals, are arranged in pairs and beautifully inlaid with chips of coloured glass and marble (plundered from ancient remains). The splendid frieze is similarly decorated. The cloisters also contain fragments preserved from the ancient basilica, including the late-13th-century tomb of Cardinal Riccardo Annibaldi by Arnolfo di Cambio.

The Lateran Palace

For almost 1,000 years, until the popes abandoned Rome for Avignon in 1308, the **Lateran Palace** was the official papal residence. Founded by Constantine in the 3rd century, the palace was severely damaged by fire in 1308.

*T*he serene cloisters of San Giovanni in Laterano.

When the popes returned from their "Babylonian Captivity", 68 years later, they moved into the Vatican, which was not only more comfortable and closer to the heart of the city but also more easily defended. This left the decaying old palace without a proper role and what remained was finally demolished in the course of Sixtus V's sweeping town planning of the 1580s, to be replaced by Domenico Fontana's Baroque palace. Originally intended as a papal summer residence the new building was never used as such. It now houses the offices of the Rome Diocese.

Scala Santa

Opposite the Lateran Palace, on the east side of Piazza di San Giovanni in Laterano, is one remnant of the ancient palace pulled down by Sixtus V: the **Scala Santa**, or Holy Stairs, once

175

the palace's main ceremonial staircase. According to legend these 28 marble steps (now protected by wood) were the stairs Jesus ascended in Pontius Pilate's palace in Jerusalem, brought to Rome by Helena, the mother of Constantine. The faithful ascend the stairs on their knees.

At the head of the stairs is the ancient **Chapel of San Lorenzo**, otherwise known as the *Sancta Sanctorum*. This was the private chapel of the popes in the old Lateran Palace, dating from the time of Constantine but remodelled by Nicholas III (1277–81). The chapel is not open to the public but may be viewed through the window gratings. Inside are many venerated relics and exquisite Cosmatesque mosaic decoration. Above the altar is the famous *acheiropoeton* painting, a portrait of Christ (on cedar wood and canvas) said to have been painted by St Luke, aided by an angel. More prosaically, it probably dates from the 6th or 7th century. Around the walls of the chapel are 28 Gothic tabernacles housing medieval paintings of saints and martyrs.

One further remnant of the ancient palace is the **Tribune**, built by Fuga for Benedict XIV in 1743, which houses all that remains of the *Triclinium* of Leo III (795–816), the vast and sumptuous banqueting hall of the old Papal Palace, which was destroyed in the fire of 1308. It is decorated with a faithful copy of the original mosaics (a fragment of which is preserved in the Vatican).

The **Piazza di San Giovanni in Laterano**, which opens on the north façade of the basilica, contains the tallest and most ancient **obelisk** in Rome. Dating from the 15th century BC, the red granite obelisk originally stood in front of the Temple of Ammon in Egyptian Thebes and was brought to Rome on a specially-built ship by Constantine in 357 to stand in the Circus Maximus. Discovered in 1587, the obelisk was set up in its present location by Domenico Fontana as part of Sixtus V's grandiose Baroque town planning.

The Baptistery

Historically and spiritually, the Lateran baptistery, **San Giovanni in Fonte**, is one of the most important buildings in Rome, not to mention the most ancient part of the basilica. The first baptistery in Christendom, it was built by Constantine in around 315–24, but is probably not the site of the Emperor's own legendary baptism. Sixtus III (432–40) converted the building to its present octagonal form, while Urban VIII carried out a radical restoration in 1637.

Inside, ringed by eight porphyry columns, is the giant font of green Egyptian basalt in which that 14th-century demagogue Cola di Rienzo, self-styled Tribune and would-be restorer of the ancient Roman Republic, took a ritual bath on the 1 August 1347 before being knighted. This grandly symbolic gesture would be used, when the tide turned against Cola, as one of the charges for his excommunication.

The Baptistery has four chapels (ask the sacristan to unlock them for you). The **Cappella del Battista** (St John the Baptist) has ancient bronze doors that emit a strange silvery musical sound when slowly opened. The doors are thought to have come from the Baths of Caracalla. The **Cappella di San Rufina**, originally the vestibule of the ancient basilica, contains a ravishingly beautiful 5th-century mosaic. There are other interesting mosaics (from the 7th and 5th centuries respectively) in the **Cappella di San Venanzio** (St Venantius) and the **Cappella di San Giovanni Evangelista** (St John the Evangelist). The latter chapel also boasts bronze doors dating from the 12th century.

Not far distant from San Giovanni in Laterano is Santa Croce in Gerusalemme, another of the seven pilgrimage churches of Rome, all of which pilgrims to Rome during Holy Years were required to visit in turn.

The church is reached from Piazza di Porta San Giovanni (named after the 16th-century gateway) by means of the tree-lined Viale Carlo Felice. In the piazza stands a statue of *St Francis of Assisi*, erected in 1927, which shows the saint in the act of holding up the façade of the basilica, as dreamed by Innocent III.

Santa Croce in Gerusalemme was traditionally founded by St Helena, the mother of Constantine, and takes its name from the relic of the True Cross which St Helena legendarily brought to Rome from Jerusalem early in the 3rd century. The original church was converted from a hall in St Helena's palace, the *Palatium Sessorianum.* The church was rebuilt in the 12th century and restored in the mid-18th century. It hence has a Romanesque bell tower, a Rococo façade and a Baroque interior. The pieces of the Cross collected by St Helena are displayed in the **Chapel of the Relics** at the end of the left aisle. St Helena also returned to Rome with earth from Mount Golgotha, the site of the Crucifixion. This patch of the Holy Land lies beneath the pavement of the **Chapel of St Helena** at the end of the right aisle.

In Piazza Santa Croce in Gerusalemme is the **Museum of Musical Instruments**, with over 800 instruments.

T he bustling street market in Via Sannio, just outside Porta San Giovanni.

Rome's Working-class Quarter "Across the Tiber"

A working-class quarter since the days of ancient Rome, Trastevere is fast becoming a trendy place to live. But give or take the odd spot of gentrification it has managed to hang on to its own special character.

Trastevere is Rome's traditional working-class district, a warren of narrow cobbled streets "across the Tiber" (*Tevere*). An artists' quarter for millennia, over the centuries its inhabitants have remained distinct from the rest of Rome. Proud and independent, they refer to themselves as "*Noiantri*", dialect for "we others" and the name of their age-old festival in July. Not until the 14th century was the district fully recognized as a part of Rome.

From his superb vantage point on top of the Janiculum Hill Giuseppe Garibaldi looks out over the city he called "the greatest theatre in the world".

But while indentifying themselves as a breed apart, the Trasteverini like to think of themselves as the only true Romans, the direct descendants of the city's ancient citizens. In actual fact, the district has a long history as the residence of outsiders. In classical times the area was inhabited by sailors from Ravenna who took part in the mock sea battles in the Colosseum. Trastevere has also been home to foreign merchants and to a sizeable Jewish colony.

In recent years Trastevere has become a trendy place in which to live, but despite the influx of wealthy non-Trasteverini (Italians and foreigners), not to mention the fashionable shops and clubs, restaurants and tea rooms that have sprung up of late, the district

*T*he elegant top-hatted and frock-coated figure of the 19th-century dialect poet, Gioacchino Belli.

A Poet of the People

Trastevere, some people have suggested, is an odd choice of location for a monument to the Roman dialect poet Gioacchino Belli (1791–1863). After all, it's probably the only district in the city in which the writer didn't live at one stage or other during his life. On reflection, though, this traditionally working-class district is the perfect spot for a writer who was, above all, a poet of the people.

The lives and voices of the ordinary citizens of mid-19th-century Rome live on in the 2,279 Roman sonnets which Belli composed between 1830 and 1849. The poems constitute a vivid document of the life of the age.

Outspokenly anti-clerical, Belli delighted in lampooning the reactionary Pope Gregory XVI (1831–46) (one of his poems was "Il Papa nun fa gnente?", Roman dialect for "The Pope does nothing?"). "I really liked Pope Gregory," he wrote, "because it gave me so much pleasure to speak ill of him."

has retained its special character and lively atmosphere.

Buses from the city centre approach Trastevere across the Ponte Garibaldi and pass through the Piazza Gioacchino Belli, named after the much-loved 19th-century Roman dialect poet. A monument to the writer, erected in 1913, stands in the square. Not far on, the buses decant their passengers in Piazza Sonnino, from which the busy Viale Trastevere runs through the quarter. Alternatively, visitors who have been exploring the Ghetto on the opposite bank of the Tiber may reach Trastevere on foot by means of the Isola Tiberina.

Off Via Genovesi, in a quiet and secluded part in the east of the quarter, Via di Santa Cecilia leads to the church of **Santa Cecilia in Trastevere**. The church is approached through an impressive Baroque gateway, by Ferdinando Fuga, which leads into a pretty rose garden arranged around a giant marble vase of ancient origin.

The church was built on the site of the house of one of the most celebrated of early Christian martyrs, St Cecilia, traditionally regarded as the inventor of the organ and the patron saint of music. St Cecilia was a woman from a wealthy patrician family who lived during the reign of the Emperor Alexander Severus (222–35). She converted her husband Valerian and his brother Tibertius to Christianity but was condemned to death for her faith in 230.

She was to have been executed by means of suffocation in her own *calidarium* (bath house). When this failed to kill her, an executioner was despatched to behead her in her own

home. But she survived three strokes of the axe, living for a further three days and converting 400 pagans by her preaching before she finally died.

Her tomb was opened in 1599 and her body was found to be in a state of perfect preservation. The artist Stefano Maderno was one of those who saw St Cecilia's body before it was re-interred and he made the beautiful statue of the saint which can be seen beneath the high altar. The work shows the saint in the attitude in which she was found when the tomb was opened: her touchingly fragile body lying on its right side, the hands crossed at the wrists and the neck showing the marks made by the executioner's axe.

The church is also notable for Cavallini's magnificent fresco of the **Last Judgement** (c. 1293), which is found in the choir of the adjoining Convent. The fresco can be seen on Tuesday and Thursday mornings

Stefano Maderno's beautiful statue of the 3rd-century Christian martyr, St Cecilia.

(10 a.m.–12 p.m.) and on Sundays (11.30 a.m.–12.30 p.m.).

San Francesco a Ripa, at the end of Via Anicia, contains a powerful late work by Bernini: a statue of Beata Lodovica Albertoni, noted benefactress of the Romans during the sack of Rome by German mercenary troops in 1527. The statue, sited in the Altieri chapel (the last on the left), was executed in 1674 when the artist was in his mid-seventies. Reminiscent of the more famous statue by Bernini of St Theresa in Santa Maria della Vittoria, the work shows the Blessed Lodovica at the point of death, rapt by a religious ecstasy which seems to border on the sensual. The marble is smooth, almost lubricious, while the contorted folds of the drapery only accentuate the mood of intermingled pain and rapture. The work is dramatically lit by two concealed side windows—not for nothing was Bernini hailed as the greatest stage designer of his day.

The church is not far from **Porta Portese**, a gateway built by Urban VIII (1623–44) on the site of the ancient Porta Portuensis. The Tiber is crossed here by the Ponte Sublicio (sometimes referred to as the Ponte Aventino), which stands on the site of the ancient Pons Sublicius, the first bridge to be built over the river. This is where Horatius "kept the bridge" and defended Rome against the Etruscan army of Lars Porsena (as described in Macaulay's *Lays of Ancient Rome*).

Rome's cheap and cheerful **flea market** is held near here on Sunday mornings. The stalls stretch south-west of the Porta Portese, along the Via Portuense towards Stazione Trastevere.

Via di San Francesco a Ripa leads back to the centre of Trastevere. **Piazza di Santa Maria in Trastevere** is the heart of the quarter and a popular meeting place for young Romans and foreigners.

Santa Maria in Trastevere is one of the oldest churches in Rome and the first to be dedicated to the Virgin. It was traditionally founded by Pope St Calixtus I (217–22) on the site of a hospice for old soldiers. A miraculous fountain of oil is supposed to have gushed forth here at the time of Christ's birth. (Incidentally, Calixtus was martyred nearby by being thrown down a well: the small church of **San Callisto** marks the spot.)

The church was completed by Julius I in the 4th century (352) and rebuilt in the 12th century by Innocent II (1130–43). Eugenio III added the Romanesque bell tower shortly after. Other additions and alterations were made to the church in the 16th and 17th centuries, with Carlo Fontana's Baroque portico added in 1702.

The splendid **mosaic** on the façade (dating from the 12th–13th centuries) shows the Virgin surrounded by ten female figures bearing lamps; two of the figures have unlit lamps and are veiled, the other eight are crowned. Much effort has gone into trying to interpret the meaning of this enigmatic scene. Some have suggested that the women on either side of the Madonna represent the Wise and Foolish Virgins – three of the lamps somehow having been mistakenly lit in the course of a restoration at one time or another.

There are more fine mosaics inside the church. The **12th-century mosaic** in the upper apse shows the *Coronation of the Virgin* and represents an important development in the iconography of the Madonna. The Virgin, crowned and robed in the manner of a Byzantine empress, is enthroned at the side of Christ—the first time a work of art had given her equal prominence. The lower apse contains a series of 13th-century mosaics by Pietro Cavallini showing scenes from the life of the Virgin. Also worthy of note inside the church are the 21 ancient granite columns which divide the nave from the aisles. The columns were taken from classical buildings including the Baths of Caracalla.

Just north of the church, Piazza Sant'Egidio contains Rome's **Museum**

The lovely, enigmatic medieval mosaic on the façade of Santa Maria in Trastevere.

of Folklore, housed in a former nunnery. The museum has copies of ancient sculptures, life-size tableaux of picturesque "Roman scenes" and exhibits devoted to Roman dialect poets, including Gioacchino Belli.

Beyond Piazza Santa'Egidio, Via della Scala leads into Via della Lungara. Here stands the **Palazzo Corsini**, an 18th-century palace designed for Cardinal Neri Maria Corsini by Ferdinando Fuga. The palace was built on the site of the 15th-century Riario Palace, home of Girolamo Riario, husband of the legendary beauty, Caterina Sforza, and the nephew of that infamously nepotistic pope, Sixtus IV. Queen Christina of Sweden was resident in the palace during the latter part of her exile in Rome and died here in 1689. Her bedroom was one part of the old palace to survive.

The palace houses part of the **Galleria Nazionale d'Arte Antica**. Among the gallery's works are paintings by Guido Reni (a portrait of *Beatrice Cenci*), Murillo (a fine *Madonna and Child*), Rubens, Titian and Caravaggio (a youthful and louche-looking *St John the Baptist*).

Opposite Palazzo Corsini lies the **Villa Farnesina**, built for the fabulously wealthy banker Agostino Chigi by Baldassare Peruzzi between 1508 and 1511. It was here, in a loggia overlooking the Tiber, that Chigi gave a celebrated banquet for Pope Leo X at which the guests were served on silver plates and dishes. After each course the servants were instructed to cast the plates and dishes into the river as a sign of their master's prodigal wealth and extravagance. Unbeknown to the astonished guests, a net had been laid beneath the surface of the water to catch the seemingly discarded dinnerware.

Chigi was also a noted patron of the arts and had his villa decorated with a series of beautiful frescoes. The **Loggia of Cupid and Psyche** has a fresco cycle designed by Raphael but executed by his assistants. The loggia next door contains a masterpiece of the High Renaissance: Raphael's **Galatea**, painted in 1514. The fresco shows the goddess of the sea, attended by sea-nymphs and tritons, borne over the waves in her shell. Other frescoes in this room include Peruzzi's *Constellations* on the ceiling and Sebastiano del Piombo's *Metamorphoses* (scenes from Ovid) in the lunettes.

Upstairs, the cunning **Sala delle Prospettive**, decorated by Peruzzi, offers *trompe l'oeil* views of Rome. The room next door, Agostino Chigi's own bedroom, contains superb frescoes by Sodoma illustrating scenes from the life of Alexander the Great. The second floor of the villa also houses the **Gabinetto Nazionale delle Stampe,** an extensive collection of prints and drawings from the 19th century to the present day.

The **Janiculum Hill** is climbed from Trastevere by the long and winding Via Garibaldi. On a terrace overlooking the district is the church of **San Pietro in Montorio**, built by Ferdinand and Isabella of Spain after 1481 on what was then believed to be the site of St Peter's crucifixion. The interior contains a number of interesting works, including the *Scourging of*

Christ by Sebastiano del Piombo (based on designs by Michelangelo), Baldassare Peruzzi's *Coronation of the Virgin* and a relief depicting the *Ecstasy of St Francis* designed by Bernini. Beatrice Cenci, the "beautiful parricide", is buried beneath the high altar.

The cloister to the right of the church contains Bramante's **Tempietto**, a beautifully proportioned circular building ringed by 16 Doric columns. This enormously influential work of High Renaissance architecture was built in 1502, soon after Bramante's arrival in Rome.

The **Janiculum Hill** was the scene of fierce fighting during the defence of the Roman Republic against French troops in 1849. Garibaldi played a leading role in the city's defence and farther up the hill, beyond the 17th-century **Acqua Paola** fountain, the Passeggiata del Gianicolo leads to a giant equestrian statue to the hero of the Risorgimento, erected in 1895. From this vantage point there are splendid views of Rome, both in the direction of St Peter's to the north and over the city's historic centre to the east. The Passeggiata continues through the Janiculum Park, past a

*T*he Dome of St Peter's, seen from the Janiculum Hill.

strange lighthouse, presented to Rome by the Italians of Argentina, and ends near the Renaissance church of **Sant'Onofrio**. Walkers who begin to flag can wait for bus 41 which passes along the Passeggiata and arrives in Piazza della Rovere, a short step from St Peter's. Those still on foot can reach the piazza by the steep Salita di Sant'Onofrio or by taking the looping Via del Gianicolo.

The Mouth of Truth and a Man-made Hill

Piazza Bocca della Verita boasts two classical temples, a Baroque fountain and a medieval church but it takes its name from a stone drain covering known as the Mouth of Truth. In ancient times the Aventine Hill was called the Sacred Mount; aptly enough, it's the site of pagan temples and early Christian churches. Today, its beautiful trees and gardens make it a popular residential district for the well-to-do. Nearby Testaccio has been working class from the year dot, as is evidenced by its outstanding landmark—a hill made up of six centuries of accumulated potsherds.

Piazza Bocca della Verita

This piazza occupies the heart of what was ancient Rome's mercantile quarter and is consequently an area rich in historic remains. Here stood the *Forum Boarium*, an open-air market for oxen that dates back to the earliest days of ancient Rome. Directly around the square are two well-preserved classical temples, an 18th-century fountain and a medieval church.

The Romanesque bell-tower of Santa Maria in Cosmedin rises over the Baroque fountain in Piazza Bocca della Verita.

Santa Maria in Cosmedin is a beautiful medieval church with a tall and elegant Romanesque campanile, erected in the 12th century. The Baroque façade which formerly disfigured the church's medieval aspect was fortunately removed at the end of the last century. The church was originally built in the 6th century with materials taken from older buildings. Enlarged by Hadrian I in the 8th century, it was given to a colony of Greek exiles from Constantinople who had settled in the area.

In the portico of the church is the celebrated **Bocca della Verita** (the Mouth of Truth), a cracked and weathered round stone slab with the rather mournful features of a man's face (they are supposed to represent

*T*he Mouth of Truth
was once a humble drain cover.

either Oceanus or the Tiber). This curious slab was originally used as a drain covering, but in the Middle Ages a legend grew up that if a witness put his hand through the mouth it would be bitten off if he told a lie. The custom is light-heartedly preserved today by the church's many visitors. (Gregory Peck demonstrated the efficacy of the myth to Audrey Hepburn in the film *Roman Holiday*.)

The church's interior has retained its medieval character. It contains much fine work of the Cosmati school of mosaic workers, which flourished in Rome in the 12th and 13th centuries. These works include an elaborately patterned Cosmatesque pavement, an impressive *schola cantorum*, or raised choir, and a beautiful paschal candlestick encrusted with glittering mosaic and glass.

Over the high altar (which contains the skull of none other than St Valentine) is a late-13th-century Gothic canopy by Cosma Deodatus (another skilful member of the Cosmati family). Behind the altar is the Bishop's marble throne, the arms of which are supported by two quaint lions, the back topped with a halo-like disc inlaid with Cosmatesque mosaic.

188

In the sacristy is preserved a beautifully simple **8th-century mosaic** showing the Virgin and Child receiving a gift from one of the Magi.

Opposite the church is a delightful **Baroque fountain**, built by Carlo Bizzaccheri in 1717. In a small garden behind the fountain stand two ancient temples, both dating from the end of the 2nd century BC: the rectangular **Temple of Fortuna Virilis** and the circular **Temple of Vesta**, the oldest marble temple to survive in Rome. Like so many other pagan monuments in the city, the temples owe their survival to their conversion into Christian churches in the Middle Ages.

On the far side of the Temple of Fortuna Virilis stands another example of medieval Rome's appropriation of its classical past: the **Casa dei Crescenzi**, a curious building which incorporates fragments from classical monuments. It was built by the powerful Crescenzi family around 1100.

The area immediately to the north of Santa Maria in Cosmedin is also rich in interesting remains. In Via del Velabro stands the sturdy **Arch of Janus**, thought to date from the time of Constantine. The arch was used by the merchants of the Forum Boarium as a shelter and meeting place.

The pretty church of **San Giorgio in Velabro**, which dates back to the 6th century, has a striking Romanesque tower and portico. Inside, the Cosmatesque altar contains part of the skull of dragon-slaying St George himself.

Next to the church is the **Arco degli Argentari**, a small classical arch built in AD 204 by the money changers of the Forum Boarium in honour of the Emperor Septimius Severus, his wife Julia Domna and their children Geta and Caracalla. When Geta was murdered by his brother, his name and effigy were obliterated—a fate which also befell his memorial on the Arch of Septimius Severus in the Roman Forum.

A street nearby leads to the church of **San Giovanni Decollato** (in English, St John Beheaded). This church was built (1488–1504) by the Arciconfraternita della Misericordia, a Florentine fraternity which gave spiritual succour to condemned criminals. The painting of the beheading of St John over the altar is by another Florentine, the painter Giorgio Vasari, better-known today as the biographer of his fellow artists.

From the southern end of Piazza Bocca della Verita, Via di Greca runs to the Circus Maximus, the largest and oldest circus in Rome (*see* THE PALATINE). To the south-west of the circus rises the Aventine Hill.

The Aventine Hill

The hill is a tranquil oasis in the heart of Rome, a place of trees and gardens rising peacefully above the hurtling traffic of the Circo Massimo. Considered the "Sacred Mount" in ancient times, it is the site of pagan temples and of some of Rome's earliest Christian churches.

Though one of the seven ancient hills of Rome, the Aventine remained for centuries outside the city walls. It was here, in 494 BC, that the revolting plebeians withdrew in protest at patrician rule. Their threat to found a separate community, the so-called

Aventine Secession, brought the patricians to the bargaining table and led to the election of two plebeian Tribunes as representatives of the people.

From these humble beginnings, the Aventine has moved up the social scale. The residence of foreign merchants and *nouveau riche* plebeians during the latter years of the Republic, the hill became an aristocratic district in the imperial era. Today it remains a well-to-do, highly desirable neighbourhood.

From Via del Circo Massimo, the Aventine is reached by the Clivo dei Publici—the ancient **Clivus Publicus**, paved by two brothers named Publici as reparation for having embezzled public money—or by the Via di Valle Murcia, bordered by a rose garden, the site of an international flower show each spring.

Up the hill, Via Santa Sabina leads to the **Parco Savallo**, a beautiful park planted with orange trees. The parapet at the end of the garden affords splendid views of Rome. From the adjoining Piazza Pietro d'Illiria, which has a wall fountain in the shape of a grotesque mask, you can enter the church of Santa Sabina.

Santa Sabina is a beautiful example of an early-Christian basilica. It was built in the 5th century by a priest from Dalmatia, Peter of Illyria, on the site of a house belonging to a Roman matron called Sabina, who was later confused with a saint of the same name.

A skilful restoration this century removed Domenico Fontana's 16th-century Baroque decorations and returned the church to its original classical aspect. The broad nave is lined with 24 white marble Corinthian columns, relics of the temple of Juno Regina which once stood here. In the middle of the nave is the curious **mosaic tomb stone** of the Dominican General Munoz di Zamora (d. 1300), thought to be the work of Jacopo Torriti, the artist responsible for the famous apse mosaics in San Giovanni in Laterano and Santa Maria Maggiore.

If you have entered the church from Piazza Pietro d'Illiria, make sure you leave by the **west door**. This ancient door, made of cypress wood, is as old as the church itself and dates back to the 5th century. The 18 panels (out of an original 28) depict scenes from the Old and New Testaments, illustrating the lives of Moses and Christ. The top-left panel contains one of the earliest representations of the crucifixion.

Past the nearby church of **Sant' Alessio**, with its pretty Romanesque bell tower, Via Santa Sabina leads into the **Piazza dei Cavalieri di Malta**, named after the Knights of Malta.

This ancient chivalric order was founded in 1080 as the Hospitallers of St John to run a hospital for pilgrims in Jerusalem. Over the centuries the Hospitallers developed into a powerful military order, based first on Rhodes and then, after their expulsion by the Turks in 1522, on the island of Malta. The Knights were expelled from this stronghold by Napoleon in 1798 and have been based in Rome since the middle of the 19th century.

The square, which pre-dates the fall of Malta, was designed by the 18th-century engraver Piranesi and has heraldic symbols containing allusions to the military and naval prowess of the Knights.

Piranesi was also responsible for the monumental gate in the square, beyond which lies the **Priorato di Malta**, the residence of the Grand Master of the order. Look through the keyhole in the doorway leading to the priory gardens and you will be rewarded with an unusual view of the dome of St Peter's, framed by an avenue of trees.

Also worthy of note on the Aventine is the 4th-century church of **Santa Prisca**, beneath which lies a 3rd-century **mithraeum**, a grotto sacred to the ancient Persian god Mithras, whose cult spread through the Roman Empire around the beginning of the Christian era. Discovered in 1958 by Dutch archaeologists, the grotto contains frescoes and stucco statues illustrating aspects of the cult. Further ancient religious activity is evidenced by the nearby Piazza del Tempio di Diana, whose name records the existence on the site of an ancient temple to the goddess.

An exotic touch of Egypt in the heart of Rome, the Pyramid of Caius Cestius.

From Piazza del Tempio di Diana, Via Santa Melania leads down to the busy Via della Marmorata and Porta San Paolo.

Porta San Paolo

Originally the *Porta Ostiensis*, it is one of the best preserved of the ancient city gates in the Aurelian Wall (the inner façade dates back to the 3rd century, the outer face was restored by Honorius in 402). Impressive though the gateway may be, it is overshadowed by an unusual monument nearby: the **Pyramid of Caius Cestius**. The pyramid, undoubtedly one of Rome's most curious sights, is the tomb of a wealthy and vainglorious Roman *praetor* who

The graves of the English poet John Keats and his friend, the painter Joseph Severn.

died in 12 BC. Built of brick and faced with marble, it is 27 m high (90 ft) and 22 m square at its base (70 ft).

Adjoining the pyramid is Rome's **Protestant Cemetery**, more commonly known as the English Cemetery (*Cimitero degli Inglesi*). The entrance is in Via Caio Cestio. Shaded by cypresses and set apart from the bustle and hubbub of the city, this is one of the most beautiful and tranquil spots in Rome. The cemetery is divided into Old and New sections, both of which contain the graves of notable figures from the worlds of art and letters. The English poet John Keats, who died in a house overlooking the Spanish Steps in 1821, is buried in the Old Cemetery. The moving inscription on his tomb reads:

"This grave contains all that was mortal of a young English poet, who, on his death-bed, in the bitterness of his heart at the malicious power of his enemies, desired these words to be engraven on his tombstone: 'Here lies one whose name was writ in water.'" The ashes of Keats' fellow romantic poet, Percy Bysshe Shelley, are buried in the New Cemetery. Shelley drowned off the coast of Viareggio and his body was cremated on the shore in the presence of Lord Byron and the piratical-looking adventurer Edward Trelawny, who cast oil and spices on the flames in pagan fashion. The ashes were interred here after being stored for several months in a mahogany chest in the wine cellar of the British Consul. (The flames of the funeral pyre did not consume the poet's heart; it lies alongside Mary Shelley in an English churchyard in Bournemouth.)

Trelawny himself is buried here, as are the 19th-century art historian, John

Addington Symonds, the Victorian writer of boys' adventure stories, R.M. Ballantyne, and Goethe's only son, Julius.

The cemetery is perhaps more properly regarded as the burial place of non-Catholics rather than just foreigners and it also contains the graves of a number of prominent Italians, including Antonio Gramsci, the founder of the Italian Communist Party. Beyond the cemetery, on the other side of the Via Zabaglia, is the **British Military Cemetery**, with the graves of over 400 servicemen who died during the liberation of Italy.

Testaccio

The nearby district of Testaccio is rather off the beaten track and not on the itineraries of most tourists. Nevertheless, this traditional working-class district is rich in character and history, and well worth a visit.

The quarter is dominated by Rome's strangest hill, the man-made **Monte Testaccio**, 45 m (150 ft) high and almost 914 m (3,000 ft) round, and composed of the broken shards of amphorae used to transport wine, oil and grain in ancient Rome. The amphorae were brought to Rome by ship and unloaded at the nearby river port to be stored in the many warehouses of the ancient Emporio (which lives on in the name of the present-day Piazza dell'Emporio). It is estimated that six centuries of discarded amphorae went into creating the hill.

Climb the hill and you will be rewarded with a unique vantage point from which to view Rome (begin your ascent at the corner of Via Galvani and Via Zabaglia).

Between Mount Testaccio and the Tiber are the remains of the **Mattatoio**, the disused 19th-century slaughterhouse (which moved out of town in 1975, like so many old city-centre markets in European capitals). Now it is home to the *carrozzelle*, the horse-drawn carriages which serve the tourist trade in Rome's historic centre.

The Mattatoio has been intermittently used as a site for exhibitions and other cultural events. City politicians have been wrangling for years over what should become of it, whether to pull it down or convert the buildings into a permanent cultural centre.

Testaccio has a number of good restaurants specializing, as befits the area's history, in offal and other innards, dishes like *trippa alla Romana* (Roman-style tripe) and *animelle alla griglia* (grilled sweetbreads), for those who have the stomach for such fare.

As well as being an area where over the centuries Rome has rolled up its sleeves to work, Testaccio has traditionally been a place where the city has let down its hair. In medieval times, when the surrounding area was known as the *Prati del Popolo Romano* (Fields of the Roman People), it was the site for the *Giochi di Testaccio*, riotous games that took place at carnival time. Each October the district was host to the "*Ottobrate*" wine festival.

Several of the wine cellars that were excavated beneath Monte Testaccio now house trendy jazz clubs; a sign that Testaccio may be already undergoing the creeping gentrification that has been a recent feature of that other old working-class district, Trastevere.

The Sad Fate of Rome's Golden Cathedral

Built on the site of St Paul's tomb, San Paolo fuori le Mura was once the most glorious church in Rome. Sacked by Saracens and gutted by fire, the basilica may have lost much of its ancient splendour but it still boasts the most beautiful cloisters in the city.

From Porta San Paolo, the Via Ostiense leads to the basilica of **San Paolo fuori le Mura**. (The church can be reached by buses 23, 318 and 673, or by Metro line B to the San Paolo stop.)

The Victorian writer Augustus Hare found the exterior of the basilica of St Paul outside the Walls "beneath contempt", likening it to "a very ugly railway station". If anything the church is even more ill-favoured today. When

*T*he statue of St Paul, *flanked by the giant columns of the four-sided portico to the basilica of San Paolo Fuori le Mura*

Hare visited St Paul it at least stood alone in open countryside, on the edge of the Roman Campagna. Today it is surrounded by factories, gasworks and dreary blocks of flats. Hardly a fitting setting for one of the most important religious sites in Rome and what was also once the largest church in Christendom.

The church stands on the supposed burial place of St Paul, who was martyred in AD 67 at Aquae Salviae about 3 km (2 miles) away (the Abbazia delle Tre Fontane in EUR marks the site). Constantine erected a small basilica over the saint's tomb and this was enlarged around 386 by the Emperors Valentinian II and Theodosius the Great during the confident papacy of St Damasus.

Over the centuries the church was further enlarged and enriched until it became the biggest and most splendid church in Rome: the "Golden Cathedral" in the words of the 5th-century poet Prudentius. But St Paul's site, outside the city walls, left it vulnerable to attack. In 846 maurauding Saracens sailed up the Tiber and sacked the basilica. Later in the 9th century, John VIII fortified the church against further raids, creating what was in effect a separate walled city called Giovannipoli. For a while San Paolo flourished but it fell into decline as pestilential malaria made the surrounding Campagna increasingly uninhabitable.

San Paolo's isolation and relative neglect did mean that it escaped the decorative additions and improvements that were imposed on those other ancient patriarchal basilicas, Santa Maria Maggiore and San Giovanni in Laterano. But, in 1823, this venerable building was almost totally gutted by a great fire. The church was rebuilt almost immediately under Pius IX to the original basilican plan (completed 1854) but in the reconstruction even more of the ancient structure was destroyed, unnecessarily, than had been lost in the fire.

The church is approached across a massive atrium, or *quadriporticus*, bounded by 146 columns of pink and grey granite. In the centre stands a **statue of St Paul**, who holds a sword, the symbol of his martyrdom, and a book, representative of the new law he brought to the Gentiles. Legend relates that when St Paul was beheaded, after having converted one of Nero's favourite concubines, milk instead of blood flowed from his veins.

There is a cold grandeur about the church's interior, with its vast nave and double aisles, but it does give a fair impression of the character of the old basilica. Fortunately, not all the church's artistic treasures perished in the fire. Visible from inside the basilica on the **Porta Santa** (the Holy Door, facing the right aisle) are the great bronze doors that were made in Constantinople in 1070 and presented to the abbot of the adjoining monastery, Hildebrand (afterwards Gregory VII) by Panteleone Castelli. The doors, severely damaged in the fire, are inlaid with silver and illustrate scenes from the Old and New Testaments. They have recently been skilfully restored.

Running in a frieze along the walls of the nave (and continuing in the aisles) are **mosaic portraits of the Popes** from St Peter onwards. A popular superstition holds that the end of the world will come when there is no room in the basilica for another papal portrait. These mosaic roundels are modern reconstructions—the few originals to survive the 1823 fire are housed in the basilica's museum.

Stendhal relates the story that as Pius VII lay mortally ill, the Roman people realized with disquiet that there was no room in the basilica for a portrait of the Pope's successor. On the night of the great fire on 15 July 1823, the dying pope was disturbed by a dream presaging some great disaster to the Church of Rome. News of the conflagration was kept from the Pope, who died shortly afterwards on 20 August without knowing of the basilica's fate.

The **Triumphal Arch** has striking mosaics dating from the 5th century, albeit much restored. The apse contains a 13th-century mosaic depicting Christ (blessing in the Byzantine, or Greek, manner) with Saints Peter, Paul, Andrew and Luke, the work of Venetian craftsmen sent to Rome by the Doge during the papacy of Honorius II (who can be seen in miniature at the foot of Christ).

Arnolfo di Cambio's elaborate **Gothic tabernacle** rises over the high altar, beneath which is traditionally held to be the tomb of St Paul. To the right of the altar is a magnificent 12th-century paschal candlestick by Nicolo di Angelo and Pietro Vassalletto. Vassalletto's majestic handiwork is also visible in the **cloisters** (entrance from the right transept), generally reckoned to

be the most beautiful in Rome, even surpassing those of San Giovanni in Laterano, on which Vassalletto also worked. The paired columns, whether spiralling or straight, smooth or richly encrusted with mosaics, give evidence of tireless artistic invention and of exquisite workmanship.

T he beautiful medieval cloisters of San Paolo fuori le Mura, miraculous survivors of the great fire which destroyed much of the basilica in 1823.

Bernini's Breezy Maniacs and the Bloody Story of a Papal Fortress

Originally built as an imperial tomb, the Castel Sant'Angelo has spent most of its history as a fortress. Several popes took refuge here, scurrying to safety along a special corridor from the Vatican. But, even if beleagured, the popes lived here in comfort, as is testified by their lavishly decorated apartments. Less fortunate were the castle's prisoners, languishing below in gloomy dungeons.

The **Castel Sant'Angelo**, tomb of emperors and fortress of popes, is approached across the Tiber by means of the **Ponte Sant'Angelo**, the ancient *Pons Aelius* of Hadrian, built in AD 134. The three central arches are original. The bridge today is adorned with statues of Saints Peter and Paul (placed here by Clement VII in 1530) and ten statues of angels designed by Bernini and executed by his pupils. Bernini's "breezy maniacs", the statues have been called. The two angels

One of Bernini's Breezy Maniacs, the angels designed by the great Baroque master for the Ponte Sant'Angelo.

Bernini himself sculpted have been replaced by copies, the originals long since removed to the church of Sant' Andrea delle Fratte.

The Castel Sant'Angelo began its history as the Mausoleum of Hadrian, a giant tomb for the Emperor and his family. Even more magnificent than the tomb of Augustus on the opposite bank of the Tiber, the mausoleum consisted of a circular tower rising from a square base and surmounted by a tree-covered earth tumulus. This mighty sepulchre was originally clad in marble and topped by a bronze statue of Hadrian, in the guise of the sun-god Apollo, driving a four-horse chariot. Inside the building, a spiral ramp (still in use today) led to the chamber in which the imperial ashes were kept.

*P*onte Sant'Angelo, the majestic approach to Hadrian's imperial mausoleum.

Begun in AD 130, the mausoleum had not been completed at Hadrian's death in 138 and was finished a year later by his adopted heir, Antoninus Pius. Successive emperors and their families were interred here, the last being Septimius Severus, who died in 211.

The building's later history has been bellicose and bloody. The Emperor Aurelian converted the mausoleum into a fortress in 271 as part of his efforts to strengthen the city's defences. When Rome was beseiged by the Goths in the 6th century (537) the castle's defenders resorted to smashing the magnificent statues which decorated the cornice and hurling the fragments at their attackers.

The name by which the building is known today dates from the end of the 6th century. Rome was then suffering from a terrible plague and its citizens were dying in droves. In 590 Pope Gregory I was leading a penitential procession to St Peter's to pray for deliverance when over the castle he saw the figure of an angel sheathing a bloody sword—a sign that the plague would soon be over. The pestilence did indeed come to an end and in remembrance of this miracle Gregory built a chapel and erected a statue of the Archangel Michael on top of the castle.

The *Sant'Angelo*, Holy Angel, that we see on top of the building today is a bronze statue placed there in the 18th century. Its immediate predecessor, a marble angel by Raffaello da Montelupo and erected in 1544, can be seen in a courtyard within the castle, the Cortile dell'Angelo, or the Court of the Angel.

The Castel Sant'Angelo is perhaps best remembered as a place of refuge for a succession of beleaguered popes. For centuries popes and anti-popes strove for possession of the castle. The anti-pope John XXIII (1410–15) began to construct the **Passetto di Borgo**, a covered passage running from the Vatican to the castle. Alexander VI completed the passage and had recourse to it in 1494 when seeking a haven from the army of Charles VIII of France.

Clement VII was twice driven to seek shelter in the castle in 1527—the second time during the terrible sack of Rome by troops of the Holy Roman Emperor Charles V. Benvenuto Cellini, the Florentine sculptor, goldsmith and celebrated autobiographer, played, by his own account, a heroic part in the castle's defence and purportedly shot the Constable of Bourbon, commander of the Emperor's forces.

This was by no means the end of the castle's sanguinary history. Since then, in addition to its use as a fortress, the Castel Sant'Angelo has been a barracks and political prison. Opera-goers will recall the conclusion of Puccini's *Tosca* (set in 1800) in which the heroine flings herself from the battlements after killing the evil Chief of Police, Scarpia.

Today the castle houses a museum, the **Museo Nazionale di Castel Sant' Angelo**. It contains an extensive collection of arms and armour down the ages, from prehistoric times to the 19th century, and many fine works of sculpture, paintings and frescoes. There are excellent views of the city from a terrace on top of the castle. Visitors may visit the lavish papal apartments and also the cells in which prisoners have been kept down the centuries. The castle's most notable inmates include the 16th-century heretical philosopher Giordano Bruno (burned at the stake in the Campo dei Fiori in 1600), the "Beautiful Parricide" Beatrice Cenci (immortalized in Shelley's play *The Cenci*) and Benvenuto Cellini, many years after his valorous exploits during the seige. Cellini, of course, managed to escape, taking the door to his cell off its hinges with a stolen pair of pincers, descending from the roof by means of a rope made from his bedsheets. But not even the ever-resourceful Cellini could pull off this daring jail-break without meeting some disaster. He broke his leg as he climbed the final wall.

The Castel Sant'Angelo, a tomb with a turbulent history.

The Grandeur and Grace of the World's Greatest Church

It is the most famous church in Christendom, a magnet for pilgrims from all over the world. Art lovers too are drawn here ineluctably, attracted by Michelangelo's sublime Pietà or Bernini's grandiose *baldacchino*. But whether one's impulses are sacred or profane, the sheer size of the basilica overwhelms everybody. For many, though, it's an ascent of the dome which is the real high spot of a visit to St Peter's.

History

The history of St Peter's traditionally begins with the building of a simple oratory, in around AD 90, on the purported site of St Peter's tomb, not far from the scene of his martyrdom during the persecutions of Nero.

It was here that Constantine erected a basilica in the 4th century (consecrated in 326). Lavishly adorned over the centuries, the church was one of the glories of medieval Rome. But by

*V*isitors to St Peter's cannot help but feel dwarfed by the basilica's immense size and grandeur.

the 15th century the edifice was in danger of collapse and in 1452 Pope Nicholas V decided on the dramatic step of constructing a brand new basilica. Work on the project didn't really get underway, however, until the time of Pope Julius II. In 1506 Bramante began the enterprise with a vengeance, earning the title "*il ruinante*" for the cavalier way he destroyed so much of the old structure. Money for the work came from (among other sources) the papacy's share in the wealth coming from the New World and from the vigorous sale of indulgences—sowing seeds of discontent across Europe that were to sprout in the Reformation.

After Bramante's death in 1514, the baton was taken up by a series of architects, such as Raphael, Baldassare

Peruzzi and Antonio da Sangallo the Younger. The new basilica's overall design meanwhile alternated between Bramante's Greek-cross plan (in which the arms are of equal length) and the Latin cross (longer lengthways than across) favoured by some of his successors. In 1546 Pope Paul III sent for the 72-year-old Michelangelo. He unwillingly took up the task, protesting that architecture was not his vocation (just as, almost half a century earlier, he had grudgingly complied with the commission to paint the Sistine Chapel ceiling, saying he was a sculptor not a painter). Michelangelo returned to Bramante's Greek-cross design but took it a stage further, radically developing his predecessor's plan for the basilica's great central dome. After his death, Michelangelo's conception—a relatively shallow dome—was in turn modified by Giacomo della Porta, producing the cupola we see

today—an unmistakable shape that is one of the enduring symbols of Rome.

Not that St Peter's architectural drama was yet over. In 1605, under Pope Paul V, the Greek cross was finally abandoned—on liturgical grounds. The basilica was transformed into a Latin cross with the addition of Carlo Maderno's nave and façade. The façade has been much criticized: it obscures the view of the dome as you approach the church and appears too wide in proportion to its height.

Piazza San Pietro

Bernini's majestic **oval piazza** echoes the shape of an ancient Roman amphitheatre and embodies the embrace of the Church—the arms symbolized by the two sweeping colonnades. Built for Alexander VII between 1657 and 1667, the square was then reached

through narrow, twisting medieval streets. Now it is approached along the broad Via della Conciliazione (begun by Mussolini in 1936, completed by the Holy Year of 1950) but even this grandiose boulevard cannot diminish the piazza's overwhelming impact.

In the centre of the piazza is an immense red granite **obelisk**, 25½ m (84 ft) high. Caligula brought the obelisk to Rome from Heliopolis in AD 37 and set it up on the circus on the Vatican hill which, as the Circus of Nero, was to become the site of many Christian martyrdoms. Fifteen centuries later, Pope Sixtus V decided to have the giant stone monument erected before St Peter's and engaged Domenico Fontana to undertake the almost superhuman task.

On 30 April 1586, with 900 men, 150 horses and 47 cranes, the enterprise began. The raising of the obelisk was carried out solemnly and in silence, the Pope having issued the command that none of the workers or onlookers should speak during the operation on pain of death. Five hundred tons in weight, the obelisk slowly rose until suddenly it appeared that the ever-tautening ropes were about to give way. A man cried out in a Genoese voice: "*Aigua ae corde*", "throw water on the ropes". The advice was heeded and disaster averted.

The obelisk's saviour was a sailor called Bresca from the village of Bordighera, and in reward his hometown, near San Remo in Liguria, was granted the privilege of supplying each year the Easter palms for St Peter's.

Before entering the basilica itself, look for two dark stone slabs set into the paving between the obelisk and each of the two fountains that flank it on either side. Stand on one of these stones and you will notice a clever optical trick: the four rows of columns in Bernini's colonnades will appear to become a single file.

The Basilica

As you climb the steps to the basilica, look up at the central balcony of the façade, the **Benediction Loggia**, from which the election of a new pope is proclaimed. Here the Pope appears on Easter Sunday to give the blessing "*urbi et orbi*", to the city and world.

Inside the **Portico** five doors lead into the church. The one on the extreme right is the **Porta Santa**, only opened during Holy Years. The central bronze doors are relics of the old basilica and were made by Antonio Filarete in 1439–45. The scenes shown in the reliefs include the martyrdoms of Saints Peter and Paul but, curiously, these Christian subjects are contained within a mythological framework depicting such figures as Ganymede and Leda and the Swan. (When you enter the church, look for the amusing self-portrait Filarete has left on the inner face of the right-hand door.)

Looking back for a moment, over the central doors you will see the remains of Giotto's celebrated **Navicella**, a mosaic from 1298 showing Christ walking upon the waters—another relic from Old St Peter's.

A curve of Bernini's colonnade in Piazza San Pietro.

205

Looking up into the dome of St Peter's.

At the right-hand end of the Portico is Bernini's highly theatrical **equestrian statue** of **Constantine**. Set against an enormous swirl of stone drapery, the statue shows Constantine, mounted on a rearing horse, at the moment during the Battle of Milvian Bridge (312) when he saw the vision of the cross and heard the words "in this sign thou shalt conquer".

Stepping inside the basilica for the first time, the visitor cannot help but be overawed by its size and grandeur. The church is 186 m (614 ft) long and 137 m (452 ft) wide across the transepts; the nave alone is 60 m (198 ft) across and 44 m (145 ft) high. It comes as no surprise to learn that there is room here for 60,000 worshippers. Along the nave, brass inscriptions in the pavement give the length of the world's other great cathedrals, showing how they all fall short of St Peter's.

The decoration of the basilica is largely monumental and magnificent, but in the first chapel on the right is a work of art on a much more human and intimate scale—Michelangelo's *Pietà*. The sculpture, executed in 1499 when Michelangelo was only 24, shows the Virgin cradling the broken body of the crucified Christ. Michelangelo was criticized for making the Virgin look too young. His friend and biographer Vasari retorted: "those who keep their virginity unspotted stay for a long time fresh and youthful".

This was the only work Michelangelo ever signed. Vasari relates how Michelangelo overheard a crowd of Lombards attribute the work to the Milanese artist Il Gobbo ("the hunchback", nickname of Cristoforo Solari). This prompted him to return at night and carve his name on the diagonal band across the Virgin's breast.

The work is now protected by a screen after being attacked in May 1972 by a deranged man with a hammer, who badly damaged the Virgin's face and left underarm. Fortunately, the sculpture has been perfectly restored. Even seen at a distance and from behind glass it remains a profoundly moving work of religious art.

At the end of the nave, before the last pillar on the right, is the famous bronze statue of **St Peter Enthroned** (attributed to Arnolfo di Cambio, c. 1296), the foot worn smooth and shiny by the kisses of the faithful.

In the niches of the four piers supporting the dome are a quartet of statues associated with famous relics: the lance of **St Longinus** (by Bernini), said to be the Roman centurion at the Crucifixion who pierced the side of Christ; the head of **St Andrew** (recently returned to the Greek Orthodox Church); a portion of the true cross, brought to Rome by **St Helena**; and the napkin **St Veronica** used to mop the brow of Christ on the way to Calvary, which, like the Turin Shroud, is supposed to bear the miraculous impression of Christ's face.

Bernini's **Baldacchino** (1624–33) is a Baroque extravaganza, an audacious fusion of sculpture and architecture. Cast of bronze looted from the Pantheon, this great canopy is as tall as the Palazzo Farnese, its four twisted columns rising exultantly over the high altar and the site of St Peter's tomb. The *Baldacchino*'s vast size symbolizes the triumph of Christianity over paganism. Even more emphatically, it

*T**he tomb of Alexander VIII: a grotesque* memento mori.

expresses the resurgent splendour of the Counter-Reformation church. (Look out for the Barberini bees amongst the decoration—symbols of Bernini's patron, Urban VIII.)

Beyond the *Baldacchino*, in the Tribune, is the **Chair of St Peter** (the **Cathedral Petri**), again the work of Bernini and hailed as the supreme example of Baroque sacred theatre. The gilt-bronze throne is raised high in the air, supported by four Fathers of the Church (Saints Ambrose, Augustine, Athanasius and John Chrysostrom). Above is a dazzling glory of angels and, still higher, an oval window of golden yellow glass with the dove of the Holy Spirit at its centre.

After such a dose of Berninian Baroque, you may long for the pure simplicity of *Quattrocento* Florence. The hardened addict may care to note two ornate funerary monuments by Bernini (complete with ghoulish bronze skeleton figures of Death): the tombs of *Urban VIII* (to the right of the *Cathedra Petri*) and *Alexander VII* (in the passage to the left of the transept). More restrained is Canova's *Monument to the Last Stuarts* (on a pier towards the end of the left aisle before you reach the Portico again) with its busts of the Old and Young Pretenders (1817–19).

Treasury

Over the years the Treasury has been subject to the depredations of a series of looters, from the Saracens in 846 to Napoleon in 1797 (after the Treaty of Tolentino) but much remains to admire. Entrance is by a door under the monument to *Pius VIII* in the left aisle. The Treasury now houses the **Museo Storico-Artistico di San Pietro** and among the items in its collection are the 9th-century bronze cockerel that stood on top of Old St Peter's, the 15th-century bronze monument of *Sixtus IV* by Antonio Pollaiuolo (also from the old basilica), and the *Colonna Santa*, a twisted column against which Christ is believed to have leaned when disputing in the Temple.

Vatican Grottoes and Necropolis

Entrance is by the pier of St Andrew (the SE pier), but entrances at the other piers are sometimes used. The exit takes you outside of the church, to the right of the Portico.

When St Peter's was rebuilt, the grottoes were created in the 3 m (10 ft) of space left between the pavement of the new basilica and the old one. The grottoes, or crypts, contain relics and funerary monuments from the old basilica, as well as the tombs of newer popes and such illustrious friends of the Church as Queen Christina of Sweden, who lived in Rome after renouncing her throne from 1655 until her death in 1689. Perhaps the most venerated tomb is that of Pope John XXIII, who died in 1963.

The ancient Roman **Necropolis** lies beneath the grottoes and contains pagan and early-Christian tombs dating from the 1st century AD, including what is believed to be the burial place of St Peter himself. The necropolis contains highly interesting paintings and mosaics, including a mosaic depicting Christ as the sun-god Helios. Admission is only by advance application (in writing or in person) to the Ufficio Scavi of the Vatican, reached through the Arco della Campana to the left of the basilica. Guided tours lasting around 1½ hours are conducted in groups of 15 people at a time.

Ascent of the Dome

For many people, the high spot of a visit to St Peter's is an ascent of the dome. Entrance is outside the basilica, to the right of the Portico. There are two types of ticket: the cheaper lets you make the climb to the top of the dome all the way on foot; for another 1,000 lire you can take a lift to the roof but must walk the remainder of the way: be prepared, the climb is very steep (last admission an hour before the basilica closes). The roof affords a fine outlook on the Piazza San Pietro and an unusual close-up rear view of the statues of Christ, St John the Baptist and apostles that line the attic of the church's façade. (A perspective that prompts the irreverent thought that the statues are members of a rock stadium supergroup.)

From the roof mount a staircase to the gallery that runs around the inside of the dome, and gives you a dizzying view of the inside of the basilica. The lantern of the dome is reached by a staircase that is extremely winding (in both pronunciations of the word) but the climb is well worth the effort. The **loggia** of the lantern offers splendid views of the Vatican, with its palaces and gardens, and of Rome and the surrounding countryside.

A curious view on the roof of St Peter's.

Painting and Sculpture in Rome

For a city so stuffed with artistic treasures, it's surprising how often Rome has looked to outsiders to provide the skill and inspiration to create its works of art. You can see this trait as far back as the 6th century BC when King Tarquinius Priscus summoned the Etruscan master sculptor Vulca from the city of Veio, north of Rome, to make terracotta images for the temple of Jupiter on the Capitoline.

Tradition holds that Vulca was also responsible for the Capitoline Wolf, the impressive bronze statue of a she-wolf now housed in the Palazzo dei Conservatori. Certainly it was from their Etruscan neighbours that the Romans learned the art of casting statues in bronze. Etruscan civilization, at its height in the 7th and 6th centuries BC, was eventually absorbed by Rome; it was from the Greeks that the Romans would next learn.

The first real impact of Greek art on Rome came in 212 BC when the glorious treasures looted by Marcus Marcellus in his conquest of Syracuse were paraded in triumph through the city. Marcellus, refined Romans felt, "had enriched the city with a spectacle of pleasure, Hellenic grace, and the varied aspects of art." But not everyone in Rome was so impressed. "Believe me, these statues from Syracuse are pernicious for our city," declared that stern upholder of republican Roman virtues, Marcus Porcius Cato. He feared that "these riches may have conquered us instead of our conquering them".

But while many Romans continued to feel that making art was somehow *infra dig*, the demand for Greek works in Rome rose and rose, outstripping even the massive quantities of plunder brought home by the city's victorious generals. Greek artists were imported,

The Capitoline wolf, *an Etruscan bronze from the late 6th or early 5th century BC (Capitoline museums).*

210

as were their materials and methods. Huge numbers of statues, for the decoration of houses, gardens and fountains, were provided through the wholesale copying of Greek works by the mechanical "pointing' process", itself a Greek invention. A typical work of this period is the Apollo Belvedere, a 2nd-century AD marble copy of a Greek bronze, made in around 330–320 BC, which once stood in the Agora in Athens.

The Ludovisi Throne, *a Greek relief of the goddess Aphrodite from the 5th century BC (Museo Nazionale Romano).*

Under the empire, the arts flourished in both domestic and public spheres. The Roman mania for interior decoration is evidenced in the beautiful wall paintings in the House of Livia on the Palatine and in the delicate murals created in Nero's Golden House by Fabullus, one of the few Roman artists whose name has come down to us.

The Esquiline Venus, *1st century BC (Capitoline Museums).*

Official Roman art served as imperial propaganda, as is demonstrated by the Ara Pacis Augustae, the marble altar consecrated in 13 BC to honour the peace achieved in the empire by Augustus through his victories in Spain and Gaul. The sculptural reliefs on the columns of Trajan (erected in AD 113) and Marcus Aurelius (built AD 176–193) are fine examples of later public art created to promote the achievements of the emperors. They also provide splendid insights into the military tactics of the times.

Classical traditions were preserved in Rome by Early Christian art, as shown by the 5th-century mosaics decorating the triumphal arch in the basilica of Santa Maria Maggiore. Commissioned by Sixtus III to celebrate the Virgin Mary's now official status as the Mother of Christ (proclaimed by the Council of Ephesus in 431), the mosaics illustrate the Annunciation and scenes from the Infancy of Christ.

The next outside influence to make its mark on Rome came from Byzantium,

Mosaic of Christ in the Chapel of St Zeno, Santa Prassede (9th century).

which in 330 had been made the capital of the Empire by Constantine, the first Christian emperor. The most important Byzantine works in Rome are the glorious mosaics of the Chapel of St Zeno in the church of Santa Prassede, built by Pope Paschal I in the early 9th century. In medieval Rome the glittering beauty of these mosaics earned the chapel the name "the Garden of Paradise".

In the 12th and 13th centuries the masters of the Cosmatesque school of mosaic work found a new way to recycle Rome's imperial past. The distinctive inlays of coloured glass and marble which are the hallmark of their work were plundered from the city's ancient ruins. The school's handiwork is seen to best advantage in the cloisters of San Giovanni in Laterano and San Paolo fuori le Mura.

The end of the 13th century saw a revolution in art: a departure from the stiff and stereotyped manner of Byzantine art and a return to classical forms. Signs of a new solidity and naturalism are apparent in Pietro Cavallini's fresco of The Last Judgement in Santa Cecilia in Trastevere (c 1293) but it was the Florentine painter Giotto who, according to the 16th-century art historian, Vasari, "banished completely" the crude traditional Byzantine style.

Giotto's celebrated mosaic of the Navicella, created for the old basilica of St Peter's in around 1298, has been restored so many times that it is now a shadow of its former self. The new spirituality and humanity Giotto brought to art is more clearly apparent in the Stefaneschi Altarpiece, also painted for Old St Peter's and now in the Vatican Picture Gallery.

The 15th century saw artists increasingly exploit the new figurative language established by Giotto. There is a powerful, sculptural quality apparent in the frescoes painted by the Florentines

Giotto's Stefaneschi Triptych
(c. 1330–35). (Vatican Picture Gallery.)

Masaccio and Masolino for the chapel of St Catherine in San Clemente (c 1428-30). The paintings of Fra Angelico, the Dominican friar from Fiesole who was summoned to Rome to decorate the chapel of Nicholas V in the Vatican (c 1447-51), are marked by a purity of form and an intense spirituality.

The patronage of the papacy continued to draw the best artists in Italy to Rome. Tuscan and Umbrian artists, including Botticelli, Ghirlandaio, Perugino and Signorelli, painted the walls of the Sistine Chapel in the Vatican (1481-83). A decade later, the Borgia pope, Alexander VI, commissioned Pinturicchio to decorate his private apartments in the palace (1492-95).

Under the papacy of Julius II (1503-13), Rome's status as the undisputed artistic capital of Europe was confirmed. Shortly after his election, Julius sent to Florence for the twenty-nine year old Michelangelo and commissioned him to create a monumental tomb. According to Vasari, Michelangelo's design for the tomb surpassed every ancient or imperial tomb ever made. Though Michelangelo was to work on the tomb, off and on, for nearly forty years, it was destined never to be completed—the statue of Moses in San Pietro in Vincoli, the most substantial figure finished,

gives us some idea of its heroic conception.

Three years later Michelangelo was ordered to abandon work on the Pope's giant mausoleum and undertake an ever greater project—painting the ceiling of the Sistine Chapel. Also in the Vatican at this time was Raphael, who was working on a commission to paint the Pope's suite of apartments, rooms that have come to be known as the Raphael Stanze. The work of both artists, the supreme achievements of the High Renaissance, shows a complete mastery of technique accompanied by a heightened idealization of nature.

Between them, Michelangelo and Raphael effected a profound shift in the

Raphael's Transfiguration, *his last work (1519–20). (Vatican Picture Gallery.)*

concept and status of the artist. Suppressing the fact of his early training, Michelangelo created the idea of the great artist as an untutored, divinely-inspired genius. Raphael, meanwhile, was reckoned to live more like a prince than a painter. At his death in 1520 it was rumoured that the Pope had intended to make him a cardinal.

The serene confidence of the High Renaissance ended in 1527 with the Sack of Rome. The terrible grandeur of Michelangelo's Last Judgement (1535–41) gives an indication of the darker mood which followed. During this time, in the hands of artists like Parmigianino and Giulio Romano, the clarity and harmony of the High Renaissance had given way to an exaggerated virtuosity known as Mannerism.

Towards the end of the 16th century the renewed spiritual confidence ushered in by the Counter Reformation found artistic expression in the vigorous theatricality of the Baroque. In painting, Caravaggio invested religious art with a new and vital sense of drama. His almost brutal realism, achieved by means of bold foreshortening and startling chiaroscuro, is clearly seen in the three paintings illustrating the life and martyrdom of St Matthew in the church of San Luigi dei Francesi.

In sculpture, the dynamism and energy of the Baroque is apparent in the astonishing sculptures which the young Bernini executed in the early 1620s for his patron, Cardinal Borghese: the Rape of Proserpine, David, and Apollo and Daphne (all in the Galleria Borghese). Later works, such as his statues of St Theresa (Santa Maria della Vittoria) and the Blessed Lodovica (San Francesco a Ripa), create a moving expression of the ecstasy of faith.

The Baroque love of illusionism is evident in the great *trompe l'oeil* ceiling frescoes painted in Roman churches and palaces throughout the 17th century. Annibale Carracci's magnificent

Bernini's Fountain of the Four Rivers *(1648–51). (Piazza Navona.)*

TRONVS·MEVS
IN·COLVMNA

One of Bernini's "breezy angels" on the Ponte Sant'Angelo.

decorative scheme for the Galleria of the Palazzo Farnese (now the French Embassy) was the model for subsequent works by artists such as Pietro da Cortona (Palazzo Barberini and Chiesa Nuova) and Giovanni Battista Gaulli (the Gesù). The style reached a peak with Padre Andrea Pozzo's masterpiece for the Jesuit church of Sant'Ignazio. Seen standing on a small disk in the middle of the nave, *sotto in sù* (from below upwards), the ceiling appears to be open to the sky, the painted figures seemingly floating in space above the spectator.

In the middle of the 18th century there was a reaction from the excessive emotionalism of the Baroque and its successor, Rococo. Artists turned once again to the art of the ancients. Neoclassicism, exemplified by the sculptures of Canova, was born in Rome and soon spread throughout Europe. It was the last time Rome would hold centre stage in the world of art.

Artistic Treasures in the World's Smallest State

The Vatican is the smallest state in the world, covering an area of less than half a square kilometre. But its sovereign is the Pope, Bishop of Rome, Vicar of Christ and spiritual leader of millions of Roman Catholics worldwide. The Vatican is also home to one of the world's richest collections of art.

The Vatican City is an independent sovereign state, established by the Lateran Treaty of 1929, signed between the Italian Government and the Pope. The Vatican City includes the Basilica of St Peter's, the Vatican Palace and Museums, and extensive gardens. It covers an area of 108 acres and is surrounded by high walls, except at Piazza San Pietro. Around 1,000 people are resident behind the

Giuseppe Momo's magnificent spiral ramp, built in 1932, leads to the world's largest treasure trove: the Vatican Museums.

walls and the Vatican has its own post office, banks, supermarket, radio station, railway station and garages. It prints its own newspaper, *L'Osservatore Romano*, issues stamps and strikes commemorative coins.

Tours of the Vatican Gardens, starting at 10 a.m., are bookable, at least a day in advance, from the Vatican Information Office in St Peter's Square. To attend a papal audience, visitors should apply in writing to the Prefetto della Casa Pontificia (Prefect of the Pontifical Household), Citta del Vaticano, 00120 Rome, or in person, one or two days in advance, to the offices of the Prefettura, reached through the bronze door in the right-hand colonnade in Piazza San Pietro (the main entrance to the Vatican).

VATICAN MUSEUMS

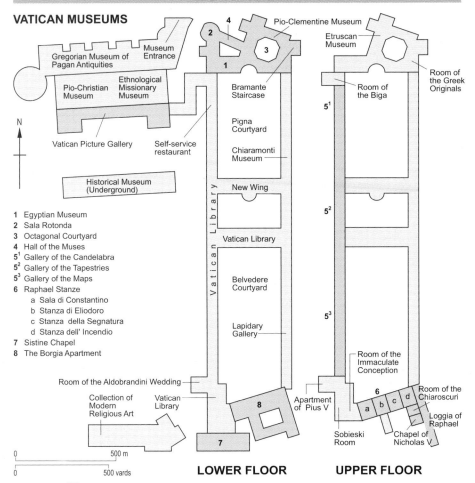

Gregorian Museum of Pagan Antiquities

Museum Entrance

Pio-Christian Museum

Ethnological Missionary Museum

Vatican Picture Gallery

Self-service restaurant

N

Historical Museum (Underground)

4

2

Pio-Clementine Museum

3

1

Etruscan Museum

Room of the Greek Originals

Bramante Staircase

Room of the Biga

5¹

Pigna Courtyard

Chiaramonti Museum

New Wing

Vatican Library

5²

Vatican Library

Belvedere Courtyard

5³

Lapidary Gallery

Room of the Immaculate Conception

Room of the Aldobrandini Wedding

Collection of Modern Religious Art

Vatican Library

8

Apartment of Pius V

6

a b c d

Room of the Chiaroscuri

Loggia of Raphael

7

Sobieski Room

Chapel of Nicholas V

1 Egyptian Museum
2 Sala Rotonda
3 Octagonal Courtyard
4 Hall of the Muses
5¹ Gallery of the Candelabra
5² Gallery of the Tapestries
5³ Gallery of the Maps
6 Raphael Stanze
  a Sala di Constantino
  b Stanza di Eliodoro
  c Stanza della Segnatura
  d Stanza dell' Incendio
7 Sistine Chapel
8 The Borgia Apartment

0   500 m

0   500 vards

LOWER FLOOR   **UPPER FLOOR**

Layout of the Vatican museums.

Vatican Museums

The entrance to the Vatican Museums is at the beginning of Viale Vaticano, a lengthy walk from the Basilica. The Vatican operates a bus service between Piazza San Pietro and the Museums. Alternatively, take Metro line A to Ottaviano, or one of a number of buses from the city centre to the nearby Piazza del Risorgimento.

One of the greatest museums in the world, the Vatican contains artistic treasures filling around 7 km (4½ miles) of halls, rooms, chapels and galleries. A single visit cannot possibly do them justice, but to help visitors make the most of their time, there are four colour-coded itineraries: A (violet); B (beige); C (green); and D (yellow). Violet, at around an hour and a half, is the shortest; yellow, which requires five hours, the longest. Each itinerary includes the Sistine Chapel. A one-way system operates in the Museums.

The Head of Medusa, taken from the Temple of Venus and Rome.

Octagonal Court contains the celebrated *Laocoön*, found near Nero's Golden House in 1506; the *Apollo Belvedere*, a beautiful 2nd-century Roman copy of a Greek original; this work was a great influence on Canova's *Perseus triumphant with the head of Medusa* (1800), which also stands in the court. The Hall of the Muses houses the *Belvedere Torso*, the remains of a 1st-century BC statue that was much admired by Michelangelo. The Sala Rotonda (round room) has a gilded bronze colossus of *Hercules* (2nd C AD).

The Apollo Belvedere, a Roman copy of a Greek bronze.

The following description can only touch the surface of what the Vatican Museums have to offer:

Egyptian Museum: includes a re-creation of an underground room of a tomb of the Valley of the Kings.

Chiaramonti Museum: a gallery of almost 1,000 pieces of ancient sculpture. In the **Braccio Nouvo**, or New Wing, of the gallery is the *Colossus of the Nile*, a reclining statue of the river god with accompanying sphinxes and crocodiles.

Pio-Clementine Museum: some of the greatest sculptures of antiquity. The

*T*he statuette of a
*Persian soldier in the Gallery of
the Candelabra.*

Gregorian-Etruscan Museum: painted
vases, sarcophagi, terracotta statues,
gold and bronze ornaments from the
mysterious pre-Roman civilization.
Founded by Gregory XVI in 1837.

Gallery of the Candelabra: named after the pairs of ancient marble candelabra which divide the gallery into
six sections; contains more ancient
sculpture.

Gallery of the Tapestries: tapestries woven in the Brussels workshop of
Pieter van Aelst from cartoons by
pupils of Raphael.

Gallery of the Maps: decorated with
16th-century maps of Italy.

Apartment of Pius V: collection of
tapestries from different periods.

Sobieski Room: named after the huge
painting by Jan Matejko depicting
the victory by which John III Sobieski, King of Poland, saved Vienna
from the Turks in 1683.

Room of the Immaculate Conception:
contains manuscripts in different
languages of the papal bull by which
Pius IX proclaimed the dogma of
the Immaculate Conception in 1854.

Raphael Stanze: a series of small rooms
decorated by Raphael and his assistants for Julius II and Leo X.
Raphael worked on the frescoes
from shortly after his arrival in
Rome in 1508 until his early death
in 1520. He was thus working on the
frescoes at the same time that
Michelangelo was executing the Sistine Chapel ceiling.

Stanza dell'Incendio: this, the pope's
dining room, was decorated by
Raphael's pupils in 1517. The main
fresco, the *Fire in the Borgo*, shows

how Leo IV miraculously extinguished the fire that broke out in Rome in 847 by making the sign of the Cross.

Stanza della Segnatura: the theme of the room is human intellect in four different spheres: Theology, Philosophy, Poetry and Justice. The famous *School of Athens*, illustrating Philosophy, is set in the halls of a great classical basilica. The central figures are Plato (thought to be a portrait of Leonardo da Vinci) and Aristotle, representatives of Moral and Natural Philosophy respectively. The solitary figure on the steps in the foreground has been taken to be a portrait of Michelangelo as Heraclitus. One of the masterpieces of High Renaissance painting. The *Disputa*, or *Disputation Concerning the Blessed Sacrament*, on the opposite wall, illustrates Theology.

Stanza di Eliodoro: the second room to be decorated, it illustrates Divine intervention on behalf of the Church. The influence of Michelangelo's then recently unveiled Sistine ceiling is apparent.

Sala di Constantino: four frescoes illustrating the life of Constantine, the first Christian emperor. The frescoes are thought to have been largely executed by Raphael's assistants both before and after his death.

Loggia of Raphael: the decorative scheme of the *loggia* was masterminded by Raphael; the "grotesques" here were inspired by the

*T*he Expulsion of Heliodorus from the Temple, by Raphael. Julius II, the painter's patron, is shown on the left.

stucco reliefs on the walls of the underground chambers in Nero's Golden House, which had been discovered in the previous century.

Room of the Chiaroscuri: contains a model of the dome of St Peter's, a copy of the model made by Michelangelo in 1558–61.

Chapel of Nicholas V: (also known as the *Cappella del Beato Angelico*) decorated with frescoes of a beautiful simplicity by the *Quattrocento* Florentine artist Fra Angelico, painted between 1447 and 1451.

Borgia Apartment: private rooms of the Borgia pope, Alexander VI, decorated with frescoes by Pinturicchio.

Collection of Modern Religious Art: includes works by Pietro Annigoni, Francis Bacon, Marc Chagall, Salvador Dali, Giorgio de Chirico, Max Ernst, Paul Gauguin, Paul Klee, Oskar Kokoschka, Henry Moore, Ben Nicholson, Graham Sutherland and many others.

The Collection comes immediately before the Sistine Chapel on the yellow and brown itineraries.

The Sistine Chapel

The Sistine Chapel was built by Sixtus IV in 1473–81 as the official private chapel of the popes. It was also used for the conclaves by which a new pope is elected, a function the chapel preserves today. It is Michelangelo's sublime frescoes, however, which have made the chapel universally famous.

Michelangelo was engaged to paint the chapel's ceiling by Pope Julius II in 1508. He did not welcome the appointment, trying every way he could to wriggle out of the commission (it meant abandoning work on the cherished project of the Pope's tomb). He protested that he was a sculptor not a painter, but to no avail. Michelangelo was convinced that his enemies had secretly plotted to burden him with this thankless task, hoping that, inexperienced as he was in fresco painting, he would make a botch of it.

At first Michelangelo worked with assistants but he soon decided to undertake all the work himself, dismissed his helpers and re-started from scratch. He continued, so his biographer Vasari relates, without even the aid of someone to grind his colours.

The task Michelangelo undertook upon himself—painting more than 300 human figures in an area of 305 m² (10,000 square ft)—was superhuman. It took him four years. He worked on scaffolding of his own devising, standing up and painting looking upwards. So habituated did he become to this position that when he came down from the scaffolding he was forced to hold letters above his head to read them.

The Pope was ever impatient for Michelangelo to finish the work, threatening at one point to throw the painter from the scaffolding.

When the work was finally thrown open, according to Vasari, "the whole world came running to see what Michelangelo had done; and certainly it was such as to make everyone speechless with astonishment." It set the seal on Michelangelo's reputation as the greatest living artist.

The dynamism of the figures, the wealth of invention, the mastery of colour, light and shade, all of these continue to astonish visitors to the chapel, as they did Michelangelo's contemporaries.

Along the centre of the vault, Michelangelo painted nine panels, depicting the stories of the Creation, the Fall and Noah. The panels (painted in reverse order) are as follows: (1) the *Separation of Light and Darkness*; (2) the *Creation of Sun, Moon and Planets*; (3) the *Separation of Land and Sea*; (4) the *Creation of Adam*; (5) the *Creation of Eve*; (6) the *Fall, and Expulsion from Paradise*; (7) the *Sacrifice of Noah*; (8) the *Flood*; (9) the *Drunkenness of Noah*.

The central panels are supported by a gigantic decorative framework: pairs of nude youths holding festoons and medallions, the enigmatic *ignudi*. On either side of the central panels, in the lower part of the vault, are 12 figures: 7 biblical prophets and 5 pagan sibyls, represented here as foretellers of the coming of Christ. In the lunettes between the prophets and sibyls are shown the *Ancestors of Christ*. The spandrels at the corners of the ceiling contain four violent scenes from the Old Testament: *Moses and the Brazen Serpent*; the *Punishment of Haman; Judith and Holofernes*; and *David and Goliath*.

The ceiling has recently emerged from a mammoth restoration, undertaken between June 1980 and March 1990 and sponsored by a Japanese television company. Centuries of grime—soot, dust, and candle smoke, plus the results of repainting and retouching—have been cleaned away to reveal what the restorers believe are the painter's original intentions. The colours that have emerged are remarkable: delicate pinks and pastels, peach, apricot, lime and lemon. Revealed too is the forcefulness of Michelangelo's brushstrokes, as if carved in the plaster, giving a sculptural quality to the painting.

The restoration has also provoked furious controversy in the art world. Critics of the project say that the restorers have not just removed centuries of grime but have actually effaced some of Michelangelo's original work. The restorers are meanwhile working on Michelangelo's painting of the *Last Judgement* on the altar wall of the chapel.

The Last Judgement

Two decades after completing the Sistine ceiling, Michelangelo was commissioned by Paul III to paint the chapel's altar wall. Again he tried to avoid the undertaking (he was still trying to complete the monumental tomb of Julius II). Once again he was unable to refuse. He began work on the *Last Judgement* in 1535, seven years after the calamitous Sack of Rome.

In the centre of the painting stands the figure of Christ as inexorable judge on the *dies irae*, the day of wrath. On the left, the saved are being raised by angels up to heaven, while on the right, the damned are being driven and dragged down to hell. The work contains all the awesome grandeur which Michelangelo's contemporaries called his *terribilità*.

The fresco aroused violent controversy, even before it was officially unveiled on All Hallows' Eve in 1541. Paul III's Master of Ceremonies, Biagio de Cesena, criticized the nudity of the figures as indecent. Michelangelo retaliated by portraying him as

*M*ichelangelo's Last Judgement, *a sombre and pessimistic work.*

Minos, the devil with ass's ears and a serpent coiled around his torso in the extreme bottom right-hand corner. When Biagio protested to the Pope to have the likeness removed, Paul III is said to have responded, "I might have obtained your release from purgatory, but over hell I have no power." Michelangelo included his own self-portrait in the features displayed on the flayed skin held up by St Bartholomew (the symbol of the saint's martyrdom).

Michelangelo's patron, Paul III, was overwhelmed by the work, truly appreciating its greatness. Some of his successors were not so enlightened. In 1564 Paul IV, in a fit of prudery, ordered drapery to be painted over some of the nude figures. This work was carried out by Daniele da Volterra who thus earned the nickname, *il braghettone*, the breeches maker.

The other paintings in the Sistine Chapel have been understandably overshadowed by Michelangelo's work. But the earlier frescoes painted on the chapel's lower walls are worthy of much of more than a passing glance. Illustrating scenes from the lives of Moses and of Christ, they include works by Pinturicchio, Botticelli, Perugino and Luca Signorelli.

Vatican Library: contains the **Room of the Aldobrandini Wedding**, a remarkably vivid fresco depicting a 1st-century AD wedding, found in

1605 and first owned by Cardinal Pietro Aldobrandini. In the same room are *Vetri d'Oro*, medallion-shaped discs of glass engraved with remarkably detailed faces, taken from Roman catacombs. Also there are frescoes depicting scenes from the Odyssey, dating from the 1st C BC.

Vatican Picture Gallery: this exceptionally fine collection of paintings is drawn from the 11th to 19th centuries. The Renaissance is particularly well represented. The gallery is arranged in chronological order; the rooms organised around schools of painting, periods and individual artists. Room II: Giotto's *Stefaneschi Triptych*, originally painted for the high altar of Old St Peter's (c. 1315); Room III: works by Fra Angelico, including *Scenes from the life of St Nicholas of Bari* (1437), and Fra Filippo Lippi, *Coronation of the Virgin*; Room VI: Carlo Crivelli's anguished *Pietà*; Room VII: 15th-century Umbrian School, including Perugino, *Madonna and child with saints*; Room VIII is devoted to Raphael and contains three of his most important works: the early *Coronation of the Virgin* (1505), the tender *Madonna of Foligno* (c. 1512) and the *Transfiguration*, the painter's last work. The room also contains ten *Tapestries* woven in Brussels by Pieter van Aelst from cartoons drawn by Raphael; Room IX: Leonardo da Vinci's unfinished *St Jerome* (c. 1480); Bellini, *Pietà* (c. 1470); Room X: works by Titian, Veronese, Fra Bartolommeo; Room XII: Caravaggio's *Descent from the Cross* (1604); Room XV: portraits, including *George IV* by Sir Thomas Lawrence.

Gregorian Museum of Pagan Antiquities: collection founded by Gregory XVI in 1844 and originally housed in the Lateran Palace.

Pio-Christian Museum: collection of Christian antiquities founded by Pius IX in 1854.

Ethnological Missionary Museum: artefacts from around the world illustrating the religions of non-European peoples.

The Carriage Museum: carriages of popes and cardinals, plus the first cars used by the popes.

Postal Museum of Stamps and Coins: stamps issued by the Vatican State from 1929.

*T*itian's Madonna of San Niccolò de' Frari, painted in 1528.

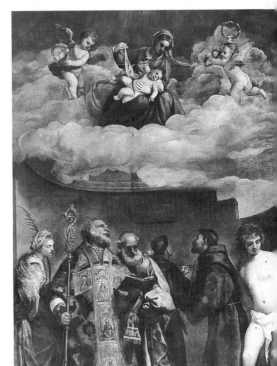

Roads, Ruins, Villas and Wine on the Outskirts of Rome

All roads may lead to Rome but the visitor to the Eternal City should spend some time travelling in the opposite direction. Near at hand are the Appian Way, the ancient road begun by a republican consul, and EUR, the satellite town started by a modern dictator. Destinations further afield include Ostia Antica, Rome's ancient seaport; Tivoli, site of the magnificent villas of a Roman emperor and a Renaissance cardinal; and the Castelli Romani, hilltop towns famous for their wines.

The Appian Way

The "Queen of Roads" was begun in 312 BC by the consul Appius Claudius and initially led from Rome to Capua, 200 km (124 miles) away. It was later extended to Benevento and Brindisi. As Roman law prohibited burial within the city walls, the Appian Way became lined with cemeteries and mausoleums. Later it became the site of the first catacombs built by the early Christians.

*W*ater cascades everywhere in the spectacular gardens of the Villa d'Este in Tivoli, built for a pleasure-loving Renaissance cardinal.

The Via Appia Antica, as the road is known today, can be reached by bus 118 from San Giovanni in Laterano. The bus passes the Colosseum and crosses Piazza di Porta Capena, the site of a gate in the ancient Servian Wall, once the limit of the city. This was the original starting point of the Appian Way. The bus route continues past the Baths of Caracalla and goes through **Porta San Sebastiano**, the best-preserved of the ancient gateways in the Aurelian Wall. The imposing fortified gateway now contains the **Museum of the Walls** (Museo delle Mura).

About 1 km (½ mile) from the gate stands the church of **Domine Quo Vadis**. This traditionally marks the spot where St Peter, fleeing Rome to

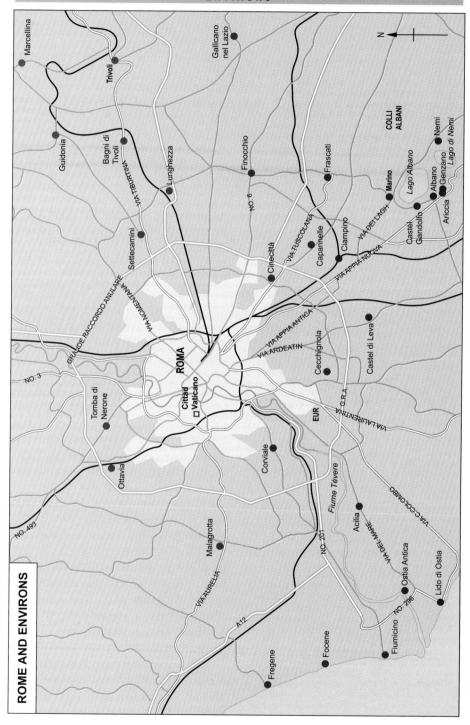

ROME AND ENVIRONS

escape Nero's persecutions, met Christ going the other way. "Domine, quo vadis?" (Lord, where are you going?) asked the Apostle, receiving the reply, "I am going to be crucified again." Chastened, St Peter returned to Rome to meet his own crucifixion.

The **Catacombs of San Sebastiano** (a bus stop is conveniently outside) date back to the 3rd century AD and are the ones which have given all the catacombs in Rome their name. They were built near the site of some stone quarries, or caves, *ad catacumbas.*

Contrary to popular belief, the catacombs were not places of hiding for the persecuted Christians but rather underground cemeteries quarried in the porous tufa stone. The early Christians buried their dead rather than follow the pagan custom of cremation because of their belief in the physical resurrection of the body. The catacombs were usually created on land belonging to wealthy Romans who had been converted to the new faith, as was the case here.

The Catacombs of San Sebastiano extend for miles underground and have been excavated on four levels. There are guided tours (in several languages) of the dank and gloomy subterranean galleries. As you pass the rows and rows of burial niches carved out of the soft rock, the guide will point out the Christian symbols and graffiti scratched on to the tombs.

The catacombs are named after St Sebastian, who was buried here

M *ap of Rome and the surrounding areas.*

towards the end of the 3rd century. St Sebastian was a soldier in Diocletian's bodyguard who was martyred for his faith in 288 by being bound to a tree and shot to death with arrows. He is consequently the patron saint of soldiers, archers and pin-makers (as the arrows in his body were as thick as pins in a pincushion). There is a statue of the saint, executed by Antonio Giorgetti from a design by Bernini, in the adjoining church.

One of the seven pilgrimage churches of Rome, **San Sebastiano** was built in the 4th century on the site of the temporary resting place of the bodies of Saints Peter and Paul, which had been placed here during the persecutions of Valerian during the previous century. The church was rebuilt in the early 17th century for Cardinal Scipione Borghese.

The nearby Via delle Sette Chiese leads to the **Mausoleo delle Fosse Ardeatine.** Here are the caves where 335 Italians were shot on 24 March 1944 in reprisal for the killing of 32 Germans by the Italian Resistance.

Via Appia Antica continues past the ruins of the **Circus of Maxentius**, built by the Emperor Maxentius in AD 309, and the remains of the **Mausoleum of Romulus**, which contains the tomb of the Emperor's son. The road then passes the **Tomb of Cecilia Metella**, built around 50 BC. Shortly after this point, bus 118 turns off the Appian Way into Via Cecilia Metella.

The following stretch of the Appian Way, which now moves through the Roman Campagna and is lined with pines and cypresses, is pleasant to explore on foot. The road is bordered by a number of classical tombs and sepulchres. However, the reliefs and sculptures which decorate them are mostly reconstructions.

EUR

Rome's modern satellite town, EUR, lies a few miles south-west of the city. The initials stand for Esposizione Universale di Roma, a great world fair planned by Mussolini as a showcase for the achievements of Fascism. EUR was to have opened in 1942, the 20th anniversary of the March on Rome, which had brought Mussolini to power. Work on the site began in 1938 but was suspended by the outbreak of the Second World War. The war and its aftermath reduced those buildings erected to a state of near ruin and work on the site did not begin again until 1952. The next year EUR's original architect, Virgilio Testa, was recalled to oversee the project.

Everything in EUR has been built on a massive scale, the buildings (mostly occupied by government offices and ministries) are huge and monolithic, while the roads are broad boulevards largely empty of traffic. EUR's most interesting building is the **Palazzotto dello Sport**, designed by Pier Luigi Nervi for the 1960 Olympic Games and a classic of modern architecture.

EUR is the location of four modern museums: the **Museo della Civiltà Romana**, a museum of ancient Roman civilization whose prize exhibit is a large scale model of Rome as it appeared in the time of Constantine; the **Museo Preistorico Etnografico "Luigi Pigorini"**, prehistoric remains found in Italy and an ethnographic collection drawn from Africa, the Americas and the Pacific; the **Museo dell'Alto Medioevo**, archaeological remains from the Middle Ages; and the **Museo Nazionale delle Arti e Tradizioni Popolari**, a museum of folk art and traditions.

EUR also has a giant permanent fun fair, **Luna Park**, to the left of Via Cristoforo Colombo in the north.

On the outskirts of EUR, to the east, is the **Abbazia delle Tre Fontane**, the legendary site of St Paul's martyrdom. Tradition holds that when the saint was executed, his decapitated head struck the ground three times, causing a fountain to spring up in each place.

EUR can be reached by Metro line B; by bus 93 from Stazione Termini or bus 97 from Piazza Sonnino; or by car along Via Cristoforo Colombo from Porte Ardeatina.

Ostia Antica

The evocative ruins of Rome's ancient seaport lie 23 km (14 miles) south-west of the city and are easily reached by train. Take Metro line B and change at the Magliana stop where a train will take you to **Ostia Antica** and to Lido di Ostia, Rome's less than inviting seaside resort. By car, take Via del Mare, just south of San Paolo fuori le Mura.

The port dates back to the 4th century BC and represents the oldest Roman colony. Following its foundation, Ostia soon grew in importance. It became the main base of the Roman fleet in around 300 BC and by the imperial era had become a major city with a population of 80,000.

*O*stia Antica, once the thriving sea port of ancient Rome. Only the ruins remain.

everyday urban life of ancient Rome. Among the umbrella pines and wild flowers of the site are the well-preserved remains of warehouses and shops, baths and barracks, temples and theatres.

On your way from the train station to the ruins you will pass the restaurant **Allo Sbarco di Enea**, the Roman equivalent of a theme restaurant. There are mock-ancient frescoes and chariots in the garden and the waiters even wear Roman costume (closed Mondays.)

Tivoli

Famous for two spectacular villas, one dating from the 3rd century AD, the other from the Renaissance, Tivoli lies 31 km (19 miles) east of Rome. It can be reached on ACOTRAL buses, which depart from Via Gaeta, near Stazione Termini. The journey takes around 75 minutes. The trains to Tivoli are slower and less frequent than the buses. By car, take Via Tiburtina from Porta San Lorenzo.

Tivoli (in ancient times, *Tibur*), was conquered by the Romans in 380 BC. By the time of Augustus it had become established as a summer retreat for Rome's wealthier citizens, who built here luxurious villas and temples.

By far the most notable of these imperial villas is **Hadrian's Villa** (Villa Adriana), which stands about 6 km (3½ miles) south-west of the town. (Local buses travel between Tivoli and the Villa.) This was the largest and most luxurious villa ever built in all the reaches of the Roman Empire and covers a site of around 180 acres.

The silting of the Tiber led the Emperor Claudius to build a new base for the imperial fleet at Portus Romae to the north. The port declined from around the time of Constantine (4th century AD), who favoured the new port. It remained a busy residential town for some time but eventually Barbarian invasions and malaria finished it off. The progressive silting of the Tiber has left Ostia 3 km inland.

The excavations, begun in the 19th century under the Popes Pius VII and Pius IX, give a good insight into the

*T*he water gardens of the Villa d'Este, built for Cardinal Ippolito d'Este, son of Lucrezia Borgia.

The villa was begun AD 118, the year after Hadrian had become emperor, and was completed ten years later. The Emperor was a skilled architect (he was the creator of the Pantheon) and he wished to build here reconstructions of buildings which had inspired him on his travels through the Empire. Among the buildings in the huge complex are copies of the *Stoa Poikile* in Athens, a colonnaded garden court, the *Canopus*, a renowned sanctuary at Serapis near Alexandria, and the *Vale of Tempe* in Thessaly.

Tivoli's other renowned villa is the **Villa d'Este**, which is sited in the town itself. Originally a Benedictine convent, the villa was rebuilt in the mid-16th century by Cardinal Ippolito d'Este, the grandson of the notorious Borgia pope, Alexander VI.

The villa's main attractions are its **gardens**, which contain a number of fantastic and ingenious fountains. They include the *Fontana del Bicchierone* (Fountain of Glass), designed by Bernini, the *Fontana dell'Organo Idraulico*, a water-operated organ (it sadly no longer works), the *Fontana dei Draghi* (Fountain of the Dragons) and the *Fontana della Civetta e degli Uccelli* (Fountain of the Owl and Birds), which once produced the screech of an owl and the song of birds by means of water power.

The Castelli Romani

South-east of Rome lie the Colli Albani, a group of volcanic hills which form a vast horseshoe-shaped crater, 60 km (37 miles) in circumference. Within this giant horseshoe are a number of smaller craters, two of which comprise the beautiful lakes of Nemi and Albano. Dotted among the Alban Hills are a number of picturesque towns, famous for their white wines and known collectively as the **Castelli Romani**.

The Castelli are best explored by car but they can also be reached by ACOTRAL buses, which depart from the car park at the Anagnina station at the end of Metro line A. Frascati is reached by car on Via Tuscolana; Castel Gandolfo, Albano and Ariccia by Via Appia Nuova. Lake Albano, Marino and Nemi are reached by Via dei Laghi, which leaves Via Appia Nuova just south of Ciampino Airport.

Frascati, famous for its white wine, is the nearest of the Castelli Romani, only 21 km (13 miles) away from Rome. In the Second World War the town was the headquarters of Field Marshal Kesselring, German commander of the Nazi defence of Rome. It suffered heavy damage from Allied bombing in 1943 and 1944, which left much of the town destroyed. Many of its historic buildings, including several churches, were rebuilt after the war.

Marino, another of the Castelli Romani noted for its wine, holds a celebrated *Sagra dell'uva*, or wine festival, each October. The town's fountains flow with wine and there is plenty of wine-tasting, as well as parades of musical bands and floats, decorated in allegorical themes, through the streets. The festival concludes with the proclamation of "Seven Kings of Rome", seven contemporary Roman personalities, chosen for their achievements in politics, the arts or the world of entertainment.

Castel Gandolfo, high up in the Alban Hills and overlooking Lake Albano, is thought to be the site of the legendary city of Alba Longa, the leading settlement in the Latin League, Rome's chief rivals during the 7th century BC. The town today contains the summer residence of the Pope.

Albano was founded in the late 2nd century AD as a legionary camp by Septimius Severus. The town contains a number of interesting Roman remains, including the **Porta Praetoria,** the gateway to the military camp, and a 3rd-century AD **amphitheatre**. Lake Albano, to the north-east of the town, was the site of mock sea battles in imperial times.

The nearby town of **Ariccia**, pleasantly sited on wooded slopes, contains a number of works by Bernini. He restored the **Palazzo Chigi** and designed the church of **Santa Maria dell' Assunzione** and the pilgrim sanctuary of **Santa Maria di Galloro**. The playwright Henrik Ibsen lived here for a while, writing the play *Brand* during his stay. The town is famous for its *porchetta*, sucking-pig roasted on a spit and flavoured with herbs and spices. *Porchetta* is sold in a number of small shops and kiosks around the town.

At **Nemi**, in imperial times, the goddess Diana was worshipped at a sacred shrine. The priest of the shrine was known as the *Rex Nemorensis*, the King of the Wood, and he was both priest and murderer. A candidate could only succeed to the priesthood if he first plucked a branch, the Golden Bough, from a sacred tree in the temple grove and then killed the existing priest. The new priest would remain in office until he himself was slain. This chilling ritual inspired Sir James Frazer to write his great work of comparative anthropology, *The Golden Bough*, first published in 1890. The Golden Bough is also the subject of a celebrated painting by Turner.

MUSEUMS, GALLERIES, MONUMENTS AND OTHER SITES

A Treasure House of Artistic Riches

The record of over two thousand years of social and artistic change is to be found in Rome today. Not only in the city's museums and galleries, but also in its many historic monuments and sites.

When it comes to art, Rome suffers from an embarrassment of riches. The city almost has more artistic treasures than it knows what to do with or can properly display. (UNESCO estimates that over two-thirds of the Western world's artistic heritage is in Italy.) As a consequence, many museums are closed clompletely for years on end or are only partially open. To make matters even more confusing for the visitor, opening times and entrance prices are liable to change at short notice. It is best to check with the city tourist office (EPT), which produces an updated leaflet on Rome's Museums and Monuments, or to phone ahead, before making a special trip.

EC citizens under 18 or over 60 are entitled to free admission to state-owned museums and monuments. But be warned, many museums are in private hands and the same concessions may not apply. Note also that the cost of admission has risen sharply in recent years—ticket prices for many of Rome's museums and monuments doubled, in some cases even tripled, in 1990 alone.

M arble comes alive in Bernini's dramatic Baroque statue of David in the Borghese Gallery. Bernini was twenty-five when he executed the work; the head is a self-portrait.

Art Galleries

Accademia di San Luca

77 Piazza dell'Accademia di San Luca. Tel. 6789243. Open Monday, Wednesday, Friday and last Sunday of the month 10 a.m.–1 p.m. Founded by the painter Girolamo Muziano in 1577, the gallery holds over 1,000 paintings and sculptures, the bequests of past members of the academy. Includes works by Raphael, Rubens and Guercino. The **Sale Accademiche**, containing important works from the 15th century to the present day, is open on St Luke's Day (18 October).

Galleria Aurora Pallavicini

Palazzo Pallavicini-Rospigliosi, 43 Via XXIV Maggio. Tel. 4827224. The **Casino dell'Aurora**, containing Guido Reni's Baroque ceiling fresco of the **Aurora**, is open on the first of every month: 10 a.m.–12 p.m. and 3– 5 p.m. Admission free. Visits to the private 15th–18th-century art collection, the **Galleria Pallavicini**, which includes works by Botticelli, Carracci, Lotto and Rubens, are only by special permission, obtainable from the Pallavicini Administration, 1b Via della Consulta. Tel. 4744019.

Galleria Nazionale d'Arte Antica

Italy's National Gallery is currently divided between two locations: the Palazzo Barberini and the Palazzo Corsini.

Palazzo Barberini, 13 Via Quattro Fontane. Tel. 4814591. Open 9 a.m.– 2 p.m.; Sunday (and Holidays) 9 a.m.–1 p.m. Includes works by Filippino Lippi, Raphael (*La Fornarina*), Titian, Caravaggio and Holbein. The *Salone*, or Great Hall, is decorated with an allegorical ceiling fresco of *The Triumph of Divine Providence* by Pietro da Cortona painted between 1633 and 1639.

Palazzo Corsini, 10 Via della Lungara. Tel. 6542323. Open 9 a.m.– 2 p.m., Sunday 9 a.m.–1 p.m. Eighteenth-century palace designed for Cardinal Neri Maria Corsini by Ferdinando Fuga. Includes works by Murillo, Rubens, Titian and Caravaggio.

Borghese Gallery

Villa Borghese. Tel. 858577. Open 9 a.m.–7 p.m.; Sunday and Holidays 9 a.m.–1 p.m. The Museum has been undergoing restoration for some years and remains partly closed. Admission free. The gallery is housed in the Casino Borghese, built as a summer house for Cardinal Scipione Borghese between 1613 and 1615. The rooms on the ground floor house an astonishing sequence of sculptures by Bernini, his celebrated *David, Apollo and Daphne*, the *Rape of Proserpine*, and *Aeneas and Anchises*. Other works include Canova's statue of Pauline Borghese, and paintings by Titian, Correggio, Cranach and Caravaggio.

Galleria Colonna

Palazzo Colonna, 17 Via della Pilotta. Tel. 6794362. Open 9 a.m.–1 p.m. Saturday only. Closed in August. An important patrician art collection, displayed in stately Baroque galleries. Includes works by Van Dyck, Veronese, Bronzino, Tintoretto and Annibale Carracci.

Galleria Communale d'Arte Moderna

Palazzo Braschi, 10 Piazza San Pantaleo. Tel. 655880. Rome's Municipal Gallery of Modern Art (formerly sited in the Palazzo dell' Esposizione on Via Nazionale) contains 20th-century works by Italian and foreign artists. Palazzo Braschi also houses the Museum of Rome. Both museums have been closed for repairs in recent years.

Galleria Doria Pamphili

Palazzo Doria Pamphili, Piazza del Collegio Romano. Tel 6794365. Open Tuesday, Friday, Saturday and Sunday 10 a.m.–1 p.m. Splendid patrician art collection begun by Donna Olimpia Maidalchini, the notoriously rapacious sister-in-law of the Pamphili pope Innocent X. Includes works by Titian, Caravaggio, Bernini and Velazquez's searching portrait of Innocent X.

Galleria Nazionale d'Arte Moderna

131 Viale delle Belle Arti. Tel. 8082751. Open 9 a.m.–2 p.m., Sunday 9 a.m.–1 p.m. Closed Monday. Important collection of 19th- and 20th-century Italian art housed in the giant neoclassical Palazzo delle Belle Arti. The museum also includes many outstanding works by foreign artists.

Galleria Spada

Palazzo Spada, 3 Via Capodiferro. Tel. 6861158. Open 9 a.m.–2 p.m.; Sunday 9 a.m.–1 p.m. Distinguished patrician collection begun by Cardinal Bernardino Spada (1594–1661), containing many fine 17th- and 18th-century paintings including works by Titian, Guercino and Rubens.

Museums

Antiquarium of the Forum

53 Piazza Santa Maria Nova. Tel. 6790333. Open Winter 9 a.m.–4 p.m.; Tuesday and Sunday 9 a.m.–1 p.m. Remains from excavations of the Forum, displayed in the Convent of Santa Maria Nova. Entrance included in ticket for Roman Forum.

Antiquarium of the Palatine

53 Piazza Santa Maria Nova. Tel. 6790333. (Times as for Antiquarium of the Forum.) Remains excavated from the Palatine. Currently closed for repairs.

Museo dell'Alto Medioevo

3 Viale Lincoln (EUR). Tel. 5925806. Open 9 a.m.–2 p.m.; Sunday 9 a.m.–1 p.m. Admission free. Collection of archaelogical remains from the end of the Roman Empire to the late Middle Ages.

Museo Barracco

Palazzo Piccola Farnesina, 168 Corso Vittorio Emanuele. Tel. 6540848. Museum composed of the personal collection of ancient sculpture gathered by Barone Giovanni Barracco and presented to the city in 1902. Currently closed.

Capitoline Museums (Musei Capitolini)

Piazza del Campidoglio. Tel. 6782862. Open 9 a.m.–1.30 p.m., Sunday

9 a.m.–1 p.m.; Winter: Tuesday and Saturday also 5–8 p.m.; Summer: Tuesday also 5–8 p.m., Saturday also 8–11 p.m. Closed Monday. Free admission last Sunday of the month. The oldest public collection of classical sculpture in the world, housed in two palaces on either side of Michelangelo's Piazza del Campidoglio. Its many famous works include the *Dying Gaul*, the *Capitoline Venus*, the *Capitoline Wolf* and the *Esquiline Venus*. The Capitoline Picture Gallery contains works by Titian, Veronese, Velazquez, Rubens and Caravaggio.

Museo della Civilta Romana

Piazza G. Agnelli (EUR). Tel. 5926041. Open 9 a.m.–1.30 p.m.; Tuesday and Thursday also 3–6 p.m.; Sunday 9 a.m.–1 p.m. Closed Monday. Museum illustrating the history of ancient Rome and the impact of Roman civilization on the world. Exhibits include plaster casts of statues and monuments, drawings, photographs and models. The most impressive exhibit is a large 1:250 scale model of Rome as it appeared in the time of Constantine (4th century AD).

Museo Nazionale delle Arti e Tradizioni Popolari

8 Piazza Marconi (EUR). Tel. 5926148. Open 9 a.m.–2 p.m.; Sunday 9 a.m.–1 p.m. Museum of Folk Art and Traditions.

Museum of Folklore (Museo del Folklore)

1b Piazza S Egidio. Tel 5816563. Open 9 a.m.–1.30 p.m; Thursday also 5–7.30 p.m.; Sunday 9 a.m.–12.30 p.m. Closed Monday. Museum housed in a former nunnery in Trastevere containing copies of ancient sculptures, life-size tableaux of picturesque "Roman scenes" and exhibits devoted to Roman dialect poets.

Museo Nazionale Romano

79 Viale E. de Nicola. Tel. 460530. Open 9 a.m.–2 p.m.; Sunday 9 a.m.–1 p.m. Closed Monday. Museum of ancient sculpture housed in the Baths of Diocletian. Most of the museum has been closed for many years with only the Great Cloister and a couple of rooms off the entrance hall currently open.

Museo Nazionale di Villa Giulia

9 Piazzale di Villa Giulia. Tel. 3601951. Open 9 a.m.–7 p.m; Sunday 9 a.m.–1 p.m. Closed Monday. Important collection of Etruscan art housed in the splendid late-Renaissance palace built as a summer villa for Julius III by Jacopo Barozzi da Vignola between 1551 and 1553. The museum gives a unique insight into the life and art of the enigmatic pre-Roman civilization of the Etruscans.

Museo del Palazzo Venezia

118 Via del Plebescito. Tel. 6798865. Open 9 a.m.–1.30 p.m.; Sunday 9 a.m.–12.30 p.m. Eclectic museum, housed in the first great Renaissance palace in Rome, containing a permanent collection of ceramics, jewellery,

Villa Giulia, the 16th-century Renaissance palace built as a summer villa for Pope Julius III.

German, Flemish and Italian tapestries, wood sculptures and bronze, the famous Odescalchi collection of arms and armour, and many fine paintings.

Museo Preistorico Etnografico "Luigi Pigorini"

1 Viale Lincoln (EUR). Tel. 5919132. Open 9 a.m.–2 p.m.; Sunday 9 a.m.–1 p.m. Prehistoric remains illustrating the growth of civilization in Italy through the Stone, Bronze and Iron Ages. The museum also includes an ethnographic collection with material drawn from Africa, the Americas and the Pacific.

Museo di Roma

Palazzo Braschi, 10 Piazza S Pantaleo. Tel. 6875880. Museum documenting the history of Rome from the Middle Ages to the present day, housed in a late-18th-century palace. It has been closed for repairs in recent years.

Museum of the Walls (Museo delle Mure)

18 Via di Porta San Sebastiano. Tel. 7575284. Open 9 a.m.–1.30 p.m.; Thursday also 4–7 p.m.; Sunday 9 a.m–1 p.m. Closed Monday. Museum illustrating the history of the city's walls, sited in the interior of one of Rome's ancient gateways.

Vatican Museums

Viale Vaticani. Tel. 6983333. Open 8.45 a.m.–1.45 p.m. Easter period and 1 July–30 September 8.45 a.m.–4.30 p.m. Closed Sunday (except last Sunday of the month, when admission is free), 6 January, 11 February, Easter Monday, 1 May, Ascension Day,

*B*utchered to make a Roman holiday: The Dying Gaul *(Capitoline Museums)*.

Corpus Christi, 29 June, 15 August, 1 November, 8 December, Christmas Day.

Specialist Museums

Burcardo Theatrical Collection (Raccolta Teatrale del Burcardo)

44 Via del Sudario. Tel. 6540755. Open 9 a.m.–1.30 p.m. Closed Sunday and entire month of August. Admission free. The museum has been closed in recent years.

Keats–Shelley Memorial House

26 Piazza di Spagna. Tel. 6784235. Open Winter 9 a.m.–1 p.m., 2.30 a.m.–5.30 p.m.; Summer 9 a.m.– 1 p.m., 3–6 p.m. Closed Saturday, Sunday. House overlooking the Spanish Steps in which the English poet John Keats died in 1821. Contains relics of the poet and his contemporaries Shelley, Byron and Leigh Hunt.

Museo Canonica

Viale Pietro Canonica, Villa Borghese. Tel. 8419533. Open 9 a.m.–2 p.m. Tuesday, Thursday also 4–7.30 p.m. Closed Monday. The house and studio of the Italian sculptor Pietro Canonica (1869–1959), containing a large collection of his works. The building was originally a 16th-century hunting lodge known as *La Fortezzuola*.

Museum of Musical Instruments (Museo degli Strumenti Musicali)

Piazza Santa Croce in Gerusalemme.

9a. Tel. 7014796. Open 9 a.m.–1.30 p.m. Closed Sunday. Collection of over 800 instruments from around the world, ranging in period from ancient Egypt, Greece and Rome up to the 19th century.

Napoleonic Museum

1 Via Zardinelli (off Piazza Ponte Umberto I). Tel. 6540286. Open 9 a.m.–2 p.m., Thursday also 5–8 p.m.; Sunday 9 a.m.–1 p.m. Closed Monday. Collection of works of art and relics of the Bonaparte family.

National Graphics Institute (Calcografia Nazionale)

6 Via della Stamperia. Tel. 6798958. Open 9 a.m.–1 p.m. Closed Sunday. Admission Free. Visitors may consult the impressive volumes of copper-plate engravings by artists such as Piranesi and Raimondi. To see the collection it is necessary to present some form of identification, such as a passport.

Gabinetto Nazionale delle Stampe

Villa Farnesina, 230 Via della Lungara. Tel. 6540565. Open 9 a.m. – 1 p.m. Closed Sunday. Admission free. Extensive collection of prints and drawings from the 19th century to the present day, housed on the second floor of the Villa Farnese.

Jewish Museum

Synagogue, Lungotevere Cenci. Tel. 6875051. Open 9.30 a.m.–2 p.m., 3– 5 p.m.; Friday 9.30 a.m.–2 p.m.; Sunday 9.30 a.m.–12.30 p.m. Closed Saturday. Museum illustrating the history of Rome's Jewish community through the ages.

Museo Nazionale d'Arte Orientale

248 Via Merulana. Tel. 735946. Open 9 a.m.–2 p.m.; Sunday 9 a.m.–1 p.m. Collection of Middle and Far Eastern works of art.

Waxworks Museum (Museo delle Cere)

67 Piazza Venezia (actually 67 Piazza Santi Apostoli, off Piazza Venezia). Tel. 6796482. Open 9 a.m.–8 p.m. Museum along the lines of Madame Tussaud's in London and the Musée Grevin in Paris.

Monuments

Ara Pacis Augustae (Altar of Augustan Peace)

Via Ripetta (between Mausoleum of Augustus and the Tiber). Open Winter 9 a.m.–1.30 p.m.; Sunday 9 a.m.–1 p.m. Summer 9 a.m.–1.30 p.m.; Tuesday, Thursday, Saturday also 4–7 p.m.; Sunday 9 a.m.–1 p.m. Closed Monday.

Castel Sant'Angelo

Lungotevere Castello. Tel. 6875036. Open 9 a.m.–2 p.m.; Monday 2–6 p.m.; Sunday 9 a.m.–1 p.m. Contains the Museo Nazionale di Castel Sant'Angelo.

Colosseum (Colosseo)

Piazzale del Colosseo. Tel. 735227. Open Winter 9 a.m.–3 p.m.; Summer 9 a.m.–7 p.m.; Sunday and Wednesday 9 a.m.–1 p.m. Free access to the ground floor; admission fee for access to first storey.

Mamertine Prison

Via del Foro Romano. Open 9 a.m. – 12.30 p.m., 2–5.30 p.m.

Roman Forum and Palatine (Foro Romano and Palatino)

Via dei Fori Imperiali. Tel. 6790333. Open Winter 9 a.m.–3 p.m.; Summer 9 a.m.–6 p.m.; Sunday and Tuesday 9 a.m.–1 p.m.

Markets of Trajan (Mercati Traianei)

94 Via IV Novembre. Tel. 67102070. Open Winter 9 a.m.–1.30 p.m.; Sunday 9 a.m.–1 p.m. Summer 9 a.m.–1.30 p.m.; Tuesday, Thursday, Saturday also 4–7 p.m.; Sunday 9 a.m.–1 p.m. Closed Monday.

Pantheon

Piazza della Rotonda. Tel. 369831. Open 9 a.m.–2 p.m.; Sunday 9 a.m.–1 p.m. Admission free.

Baths of Caracalla (Terme di Caracalla)

Via delle Terme di Caracalla. Tel. 5758626. Open Winter 9 a.m.–3 p.m. Summer 9 a.m.–6 p.m. Monday, Sunday 9 a.m.–1 p.m.

Tomb of Cecilia Metella (Tomba di Cecilia Metella)

Via Appia Antica. Open 9 a.m.–1.30 p.m. Closed Monday.

Tomb of the Scipios (Sepolcro degli Scipioni)

9 Via di Porta San Sebastiano. Open Winter 9 a.m.–1.30 p.m.; Summer 9 a.m.–1.30 p.m.; Tuesday, Thursday, Saturday also 4–7 p.m., Sunday 9 a.m.–1 p.m. Closed Monday.

Villa of Maxentius
153 Via Appia Antica. Open 9 a.m.–1.30 p.m.; Sunday 9 a.m.–12.30 p.m. Closed Monday.

Villa Farnesina
230 Via della Lungara. 9 a.m.–1 p.m. Closed Sunday. A beautiful Renaissance villa built for the wealthy Sienese banker Agostino Chigi by Baldassare Peruzzi between 1508 and 1511. The villa is decorated with a series of beautiful frescoes, including Raphael's *Galatea*. The villa houses the Gabinetto Nazionale delle Stampe.

Catacombs

Priscilla
430 Via Salaria. Tel. 838408. Open Winter 8.30 a.m.–12 p.m., 2.30–5 p.m.; Summer 8.30 a.m.–12 p.m., 2.30–5.30 p.m. Closed Monday.

The catacombs of San Callisto.

Sant'Agnese
349 Via Nomentana. Tel. 8320743. Open 9 a.m.–12 p.m., 4–6 p.m.; Sunday 4–6 p.m.

San Callisto
110 Via Appia Antica. Tel. 5136725. Open Winter 8.30 a.m.–12 p.m., 2.30–5 p.m.; Summer 8.30 a.m.–12 p.m., 2.30–5.30 p.m. Closed Wednesday.

Santa Domitilla
283 Via delle Sette Chiese. Tel. 5110342. Open 8.30 a.m.–12 p.m., 2.30–5.30 p.m. Closed Thursday.

San Sebastiano
136 Via Appia Antica. Tel. 7887035. Open 9 a.m.–12 p.m., 2.30–5 p.m. Closed Thursday.

Information to Help You Have a Good Trip

Emergency Telephone Numbers

Emergency Services: (Police/Fire/Ambulance) can be summoned throughout Italy by telephoning 113.

Other Useful Emergency: Numbers
Carabinieri, Tel. 112.
Polizia, Tel. 4686. Central Police Station, (Questura centrale) Via S Vitale 15.
Fire Brigade (*Vigili del Fuoco*), Tel. 115.
Ambulance (Red Cross), Tel. 5100.
24-hour Medical Service (operated by the Municipality of Rome, Via del Colosseo 20) Tel. 4756741.
ACI Breakdown Service, Tel. 116.

Hospitals with 24-hour emergency service:
Policlinico, Viale del Policlinico, Tel. 49971.
Sant'Eugenio, Viale Umanesimo 10 (EUR), Tel. 59041.
San Filippo, Via Martinotti 20, Tel. 33061.
San Giacomo, Via Canova 29, Tel. 67261.
San Giovanni, Via Amba Aradam, Tel. 77051.
Santo Spirito, Lungotevere in Sassia, Tel. 650901.
Dental emergencies, Tel. 8551312.

Other useful telephone numbers are to be found in the *Tuttocittà* section of the Rome Telephone Directory, which also includes city maps and a comprehensive A–Z of street names.

Alternative Accommodation

Perhaps neither Rome's five-star palaces nor humble *pensioni*, nor anything in between, will suit your accommodation needs. Here is a list of alternative accommodation, whether you're a backpacker on a near-zero budget or someone planning a lengthy stay in Rome.

Youth Hostels
Ostello del Foro Italico, Viale delle Olimpiadi 61 (Tel. 3964709)—advisable to book in advance.
Italian Youth Hostels Association (AIG), Regional office, Via Carlo Poma 2 (Tel. 385943/3599295) open 8 a.m.–2 p.m.
AIG, National HQ, Via Cavour 44 (Tel. 4741256/462342).
YWCA (for female students only), Via Balbo 4 (Tel. 463917/460460).

Out of term time, students can sometimes find low-cost accommodation in University lodgings. Contact EPT or AIG.
University Residence, Casa dello Studente, Via Cesare de Lollis 24b.
CIVIS International Students' Hostel, Viale del Ministero degli Affari Esteri 5 (Tel. 3962951).

Salvation Army, (Escerito della Salvezza) Via degli Apuli 39/41 (Tel. 490558).

Alberghi Diurni (Day Hotels)

Places for a wash and brush up, shoe shine or shave, but not to sleep.
Stazione Termini, Underground Halls
Allegrini, Via La Spezia 32.
Cobianchi, Via Cola di Rienzo 136.
Damiani, Via Castelfidaro 32.

Camping
Roma, Via Aurelia 831 (8.2 km [5 miles]) (Tel. 6223018).
Flaminio, Via Flaminia Nouvo (8 km [5 miles]) (Tel. 3332604).
Nomentano, Via della Cesarina 11, corner of Via Nomentana (11.5 km [7 miles]) (Tel. 6100296).
Capitol, Ostia Antica, Via di Castelfusano, 195 (Tel. 5662720).

Residence Hotels
Visitors planning a longer stay in Rome should consider one of the city's many apartment-style residence hotels. The EPT brochure on Rome's hotels also gives information on this type of accommodation. One such hotel is Palazzo al Velabro, which is located in a historic part of Rome (near Piazza Bocca della Verita) and has its own garage (Via del Velabro 16, Tel. 6792758). Some *pensioni* also offer reduced rates to longer-term residents.

The Right Place at the Right Price

Hotels

Rome offers every type of lodging from monastic to luxurious, including some of the world's most elegant hotels. Rates are about the same as London or Paris. Hotels are officially divided into five categories (from one to five stars) based on the amenities they offer, with a wide price range within each category. The hotels in the following list have been put into three price categories:

‖	less than L.150,000
‖‖	L.150,000–220,000
‖‖‖	over L.220,000

These prices refer to the cost of a double room with bath or shower and toilet. Rates are fixed by law and must be posted inside the door of your room. Breakfast is usually, but not always, included.

Aldrovandi Palace　　　‖‖‖
Via Aldrovandi 15 (Parioli)
Tel. 3223993
140 rooms. Old World style and service with many amenities.

Ambasciatori Palace　　‖‖‖
Via Veneto 70
Tel. 47493
150 rooms. Designed in 1927 by Marcello Piacentini. In the lobbby, great frescoed murals depict the beau monde of the 1920s. Still faithful to its pre-Depression grandeur in service and style.

Arenula　　　　　　　　　‖
Via Santa Maria dei Calderari 47 (Ghetto)
Tel. 6879454
45 rooms. Comfortable and in good location.

Atlante Star　　　　　　‖‖‖
Via Vitelleschi 34
(near St Peter's)
Tel. 6879558
80 rooms. Spectacular views from the roof garden, central for historical buildings.

Barrett　　　　　　　　　‖
Via di Torre Argentina 47
(near Largo Argentina)
Tel. 6868481
15 rooms. Tiny, central and comfortable for the price.

Brittania　　　　　　　　‖‖
Via Napoli 64
(near Termini Station)
Tel. 463153
32 rooms. Lots of amenities.

Campo Dei Fiori　　　　‖
Via del Biscione 6
(near Campo dei Fiori)
Tel. 6874886
27 rooms. Cheap but has charm.

Carriage　　　　　　　　‖‖
Via delle Carrozze 36
(Corso/Piazza di Spagna)
Tel. 6793152
27 rooms. Quiet with pleasant rooms simply furnished.

Cavalieri Hilton　　　　‖‖‖
Via Cadlolo 101 (Monte Mario)
Tel. 31511
374 rooms. A peaceful location away from the centre with splendid views from Monte Mario. Two swimming pools and jogging paths.

Cesari　　　　　　　　　‖
Via di Pietra 89A (near Corso)
Tel. 6792386
50 rooms. Pleasant, dating from the 18th century with high ceilings.

Columbus　　　　　　　‖‖
Via della Conciliazione 33
(near St Peter's)
Tel. 6864874
107 rooms. Close to the Vatican, a 15th Century palace with frescoes.

Colosseum　　　　　　　‖
Via Sforza 10
(near Santa Maria Maggiore)
Tel. 4743486
45 rooms. Good but has no air conditioning, 10 minutes from the Forum and Colosseum.

Condotti　　　　　　　　‖‖
Via Mario dei Fiori 37
(Corso/Piazza di Spagna)
Tel. 6794661
19 rooms. In centre of shopping district.

De'Borgognoni　　　　‖‖‖
Via del Bufalo 126
(Corso/Via del Tritone)
Tel. 6780041
50 rooms. Some rooms have a private garden or terrace.

Diana　　　　　　　　　‖‖
Via Principe Amedeo 4
(near Termini Station)
Tel. 484956
190 rooms. Simple, reasonably priced and near to the station.

Eden　　　　　　　　　‖‖‖
Via Ludovisi 49 (near Via Veneto)
Tel. 4743551
110 rooms. An established hotel with a good view from the 5th-floor restaurant and bar.

Excelsior　　　　　　　‖‖‖
Via Veneto 125
Tel. 4708
383 rooms. Recently renovated and extremely comfortable.

Fontana   ▌▌
Piazza di Trevi 96
(near Trevi Fountain)
Tel. 6786113
*28 rooms. A converted monastery
overlooking Trevi Fountain with a
roof garden.*

Forti's Guest House   ▌
Via Fornovo 7 (Prati)
Tel. 3212256
22 rooms. Friendly and quiet.

Della Lunetta   ▌
Via del Paradiso 68
(near Campo dei Fiori)
Tel. 6861080
35 rooms. Quiet and central.

Gerber   ▌
Via degli Scipioni 241 (Prati)
Tel. 3221001
*27 rooms. A quiet neighbourhood
A small garden and sun terrace
add to the comforts.*

Le Grand Hotel   ▌▌▌
Via V. E. Orlando 3
(near Termini Station)
Tel. 4709
*175 rooms. One of Rome's most
sophisticated hotels with
monumentally proportioned salons
and ornate decor. The vines in the
interior garden produce a real
urban wine.*

Gregoriana   ▌▌
Via Gregoriana 18
(near Spanish Steps)
Tel. 6794269
*19 rooms. A converted convent in a
pleasant location. Distinctive Deco
style and pretty, comfortable
rooms.*

Hassler Villa Medici   ▌▌▌
Piazza Trinità dei Monti 6
(above the Spanish Steps)
Tel. 6782651
*100 rooms. One of the world's
most romantic locations, above the
Spanish Steps, with furnishings,
service and a rooftop view to
match.*

**Holiday Inn Crowne Plaza
Minerva**   ▌▌▌
Piazza della Minerva 69
(Corso/Piazza Navona)
Tel. 6790650
*134 rooms. A 17th-century palazzo
that has been a lodging place since
Napoleonic times, now Rome's
newest luxury hotel.*

Holiday Inn St Peter's   ▌▌▌
Via Aurelia Antica 415
(west of the Vatican)
Tel. 5872
320 rooms
*American style in a semi-suburban
location.*

D'Inghilterra   ▌▌▌
Via Bocca di Leone 14
(Corso/Piazza di Spagna)
Tel. 672161
100 rooms. Period furniture.

Jolly Vittorio Veneto   ▌▌▌
Corso d'Italia 1 (Villa Borghese)
Tel. 8495
*200 rooms. Modern with air-
conditioning and soundproofing,
near the park.*

Locarno   ▌▌
Via della Penna 22
(near Piazza del Popolo)
Tel. 3610841
*38 rooms. Charming vine-covered
façade. Comfortable rooms;
complementary bicycles.*

Lord Byron   ▌▌▌
Via de Notaris 5 (Parioli)
Tel. 3609541
*50 rooms. The hotel hosts one of
Rome's most distinguished
restaurants, Relais le Jardin.*

Margutta   ▌
Via Laurina 34
(Piazza del Popolo/Corso)
Tel. 6798440
*26 rooms. Some rooms on upper
floors have terraces.*

Massimo D'Azeglio   ▌▌▌
Via Cavour 18
(near Termini Station)
Tel. 4880646
*207 rooms. Convenient for
transport.*

Mediterraneo   ▌▌▌
Via Cavour 15
(near Termini Station)
Tel. 4884051
*270 rooms. Classical style with
wonderful views from the 10th-
floor terrace.*

Milani   ▌▌
Via Magenta 12
(near Termini Station)
Tel. 4457051
*78 rooms. On the more sedate side
of Termini Station. Efficient
service.*

Mozart   ▌▌
Via dei Greci 23B
(Corso/Piazza del Popolo)
Tel. 6787422
*30 rooms. Air-conditioning, TV
and minibar, attractive and quiet.*

Navona   ▌
Via dei Sediari 8
(near Piazza Navona)
Tel. 6543802
25 rooms. Central.

Paisiello Parioli   ▌
Via Paisiello 47 (Parioli)
Tel. 864531
*50 rooms. A pleasant hotel close to
Rome's major park.*

Piccolo   ▌
Via dei Chiavari 32
(near Campo dei Fiori)
Tel. 6542560
A small place with a lot of charm.

Porta Maggiore   ▌▌
Piazza di Porta Maggiore 25
(track end of Termini
Station/Porta Maggiore)
Tel. 7004751
*200 rooms. Comfortable,
restaurant has terrace.*

Portoghesi   ▌
Via dei Portoghesi 1
(near Piazza Navona)
Tel. 6864231
*27 rooms. Well run, air-
conditioned and reasonably priced
with television and phones in every
room.*

Prati   ▌
Via Crescenzio 87 (Prati)
Tel. 6875357
*25 Rooms. Within reach of St
Peter's and Castel Sant'Angelo.*

Raphael   ▌▌▌
Largo Febo 2
(near Piazza Navona)
Tel. 650881
*85 rooms. This is the Rome
headquarters for Socialist Party
potentate Bettino Craxi, so you
may notice some not very discreet
plain-clothes police.*

Rinascimento   ▌
Via del Pellegrino 122
(Campo dei Fiori/Corso Vittorio
Emanuele)
Tel. 6874813
*13 rooms. Air-conditioned with
television and phones in all rooms.*

Restaurants

Sant'Anna
Via Borgo Pio 134
(near St Peter's)
Tel. 6541602
18 rooms. Very close to St Peter's.

Sant'Anselmo
Piazza di Sant'Anselmo 2
(Aventine)
Tel. 5743547
Very peaceful and pretty garden but not convenient for the centre.

Scalinata di Spagna
Piazza Trinità dei Monti 17
(above Piazza di Spagna)
Tel. 6793006
14 rooms. A fantastic view over the city and down the Spanish Steps.

Del Senato
Piazza della Rotonda 73
(near the Pantheon)
Tel. 6793231
51 rooms. Some rooms have a view of the Pantheon.

Sole
Via del Biscione 76
(near Campo dei Fiori)
Tel. 6540873
60 rooms. Large and in a convenient location.

Sole Al Pantheon
Piazza della Rotonda 63
(near the Pantheon)
Tel. 6780441
30 rooms. Has been an inn for 500 years and has recently been refurbished retaining its renaissance charm while adding modern comforts. Each room is named after an illustrious guest of the past.

Suisse
Via Gregoriana 56
(Piazza di Spagna/Piazza Barberini)
Tel. 6783649
28 rooms. Good location, very neat and clean.

Trevi
Vicolo del Babuccio 21
(near Trevi Fountain)
Tel. 6789563
21 rooms. Central and attractive.

Villa Delle Rose
Via Vicenza 5
(near Termini Station)
Tel. 4451788
29 rooms. An attractive former villa with a pretty garden and frescoed lounge.

Extravagant

Andrea
Via Sardegna 26
(near Via Veneto)
Tel. 4821891
Open noon to 3 p.m. and 8–11 p.m. Closed all day Sunday, Monday at lunch and 20 days in August. Reserve. Rich dishes. French and Italian wines.

Alberto Ciarla
Piazza di San Cosimato 40
(Trastevere)
Tel. 5816068
8.30 p.m.–1 a.m. Closed Sunday and 2 weeks in August and 2 weeks in December. Reserve. The city's top restaurant for seafood. The fish tank is worth a visit.

Il Pianeta Terra di Roberto e Patrizia
Via dell'Arco del Monte 94
(near Campo dei Fiori)
Tel. 6869893
8–11.30 p.m. Closed Monday and in August. Reserve. Creative food and fine wines.

Relais le Jardin
Via de Notaris 5 (Parioli)
Tel. 3220404
Noon–3 p.m. and 8–11 p.m. Closed Sundays and several weeks in August. Reserve. Very, very elegant.

Relais la Piscine
Via Aldrovandi 15 (Parioli)
Tel. 3216126
1–3 p.m. and 8 p.m.– midnight. Closed Sunday night. Reserve. Breton chef Jean-Luc Frenat does Italian-based creations with many French inspirations and ingredients.

Le Restaurant del Grand Hotel
Via V.E. Orlando 3
(near Termini Station)
Tel. 4709
Noon–3 p.m. and 8–11 p.m. Closed in August. Reserve. Luxurious dining rooms.

La Rosetta
Via della Rosetta 9
(Corso/Piazza Navona)
Tel. 6861002
Noon–3 p.m. and 8 p.m.–midnight. Closed Saturday at lunch and all day Sunday, and three weeks in August. Reserve. One of the original seafood restaurants.

Tentativo di Descrizione di un Banchetto a Roma
Via della Luce 5 (Trastevere)
Tel. 5895234
8 p.m.–midnight. Closed Sunday and 3 weeks in August. Reserve. Splendid seafood in summer, game in winter, lovely pastries.

El Toulà
Via della Lupa 29B
(Corso/Piazza Navona)
Tel. 6873498
Noon–3 p.m. and 8–11 p.m. Closed Saturday at lunch and Sunday all day and in August. Reserve. Notable wine list.

A Tre Scalini Rossana e Matteo
Via di Santi Quattro 30
(near Colosseum)
Tel. 7096309
Noon–3 p.m. and 8 p.m.–midnight, closed Monday. Reserve. An intimate, sophisticated restaurant that honours traditional recipes as well as inventing new variations.

With a Roman Accent

Checchino Dal 1887
Via di Monte Testaccio 30
(Testaccio)
Tel. 5746318
Noon–3 p.m. and 8–11 p.m. Closed Sunday night and all day Monday. Reserve for supper. A legendary place once the humblest of trattorie. A cuisine based on the cheap cuts and the offal from Testaccio's slaughterhouse.

Coriolano
Via Ancona 14 (Salario)
Tel. 8449501
Noon–3 p.m. and 8–11 p.m. Closed Sunday, weekends in July and in August. Reserve. An elegant place serving very nicely presented versions of hearty Roman fare and homemade pasta.

L'Eau Vive
Via Monterone 85 (near Largo Argentina)
Tel. 6541095
Noon–2 p.m. and 8–10 p.m. Reservations advised. French Colonial cooking. French wines.

Al Moro
Vicolo delle Bollette 13, between
Via dei Crociferi and Via delle
Muratte
(near Trevi Fountain)
Tel. 6783495
*12.30–3 p.m. and 8–11 p.m.
Closed Sunday and in August.
Reserve. Busy, crowded place with
excellent versions of salt cod and
vegetable dishes.*

Papa Giovanni
Via dei Sediari 4
(near Piazza Navona)
Tel. 6865308
*Noon–3 p.m. and 8–11 p.m.,
Closed Sunday and 10 days in
August. Reserve. One of the city's
top restaurants using seasonal
vegetables and has a good wine
list.*

Paris in Trastevere
Piazza di San Callisto 7A
(Trastevere)
Tel. 585378
*Noon–3 p.m. and 8–11 p.m.
Closed Sunday. Reserve. Baroque
dining room and a terrace for
summer suppers.*

Piperno
Via Monte dei Cenci 9 (Ghetto)
Tel. 6540629
*Reserve. Serves Jewish specialities
and other Roman dishes. Rich,
heavy food, good wines.*

Excellent Addresses

Apuleius
Piazza del Tempio di Diana 15
(Aventine)
Tel.5742160
*1–3 p.m. and 7.30–11 p.m. Closed
Sunday and in August. Reserve. In
a 1st century Roman house serving
seafood dishes and hearty fare. A
good midday stopping point for
Aventine sightseers.*

Artusiana
Via della Penitenza 7 (Trastevere)
Tel. 6547053
*8 p.m.–1.30 a.m. Closed Sunday
and Monday. A good place for
risotto and pasta.*

Camponeschi
Piazza Farnese 50
(Campo dei Fiori/Via Giulia)
Tel. 6874927

*8 p.m.–1am. Closed Sunday.
Reserve. Sophisticated menu,
elegant dining room, terrace with
view.*

Cannavota
Piazza di San Giovanni in
Laterano 20
(St John Lateran)
Tel. 775007
*12.30–3 p.m. and 8–11 p.m.
Closed Wednesday and 3 weeks in
August. Reserve. Charming, easy
trattoria offering big portions.*

La Canonica
Vicolo del Piede 13A (Trastevere)
Tel. 5803845
*12.30–3 p.m. and 7.30–11 p.m.
Closed Mondas. Outside table,
very good seafood at good prices.*

Il Cardinale
Via delle Carceri 6
(Corso Vittorio Emanuele/Via
Giulia)
Tel. 6869336
*1–2.30 p.m. and 8–11.30 p.m.
Closed Sunday and in August.
Reserve. Fresh versions of old
favourites.*

Carmina Burana
Via Luca della Robbia 15
(Testaccio)
Tel. 5742500
*Noon–3 p.m. and 8 p.m.–midnight.
Wine bar open until 2 a.m. Closed
Wednesday and several weeks in
August. Reservations advised.
Bright and fairly new with creative
cooking and a wine bar.*

Checco er Carrettiere
Via Benedetta 10 (Trastevere)
Tel. 5817018
*1–4 p.m. and 8–11.30 p.m. Closed
Sunday night, all day Monday and
in August. Reserve. Colourful old
Trastevere tavern offering Roman
menu. Outdoor tables in summer.*

Chez Albert
Vicolo della Vaccarella 11A
(Corso/Piazza Navona)
Tel. 6865549
*8 p.m.–midnight. Thursday to
Saturday also noon–3 p.m. Closed
Sunday. Reserve. A very
distinguished restaurant.*

Cicilardone
Via Merulana 77
(Santa Maria Maggiore/St John
Lateran)
Tel. 733806

*12.30–3 p.m. and 8–11 p.m.
Closed Sunday evening, all day
Monday and 3 weeks in
July/August. Reserve. Two
charming dining rooms, good
pasta.*

Il Drappo
Vicolo del Malpasso 9
(Corso Vittorio Emanuele/Via
Giulia)
Tel. 6877365
*8 p.m.–midnight. Closed Sunday
and 15 days in August. Reserve.
Small and attractive, serving
classic Sardinian dishes and wines.*

Giggetto al Portico D'Ottavia
Via del Portico d'Ottavia 21A
(Ghetto)
Tel. 6861105
*Noon to 3 p.m. and 8–11 p.m.
Closed Monday and several weeks
in July. Reservations advised. One
of the best known addresses for
Roman specialities in the heart of
the Ghetto.*

Giovanni
Via Marche 64 (near Via Veneto)
Tel. 4821834
*Noon–3 p.m. and 8–11 p.m.
Closed Friday evening, all day
Saturday and in August. Reserve.
Cuisine from the Marches.
Noteworthy vegetable dishes too.*

Girone VI
Vicolo Sinibaldi 2
(near Largo Argentina)
Tel. 6542831
*8 p.m.–midnight. Closed Sunday
and December 20th to January
10th. The name means the Sixth
Circle, the one in Dante's
Inferno devoted to gluttons.
Specialities from Provence and
Liguria.*

Margutta Vegetariano
Via Margutta 119
(near Piazza del Popolo)
Tel. 6786033
*1–3 p.m. and 8–11 p.m. Reserve.
Traditional vegetarian recipes
from south Italy served in pretty
surroundings.*

Mariano
Via Piemonte 79
(near Via Veneto)
Tel. 4745256
*12.30–3 p.m. and 7.30–11 p.m.
Closed Sunday. Reserve. Regional
cheeses and home-style cooking
from the Marches.*

Mario
Via della Vite 55
(Corso/Piazza di Spagna)
Tel. 6783818
*Noon–3 p.m. and 7–11 p.m.
Closed Sunday and August. Nicely
cooked food from Tuscany with
strong flavours, rich in meat and
game and filling pasta dishes.*

Il Matriciano
Via dei Gracchi 55 (Prati)
Tel. 3595247
*Noon–3 p.m. and 8 p.m.–midnight.
Closed Wednesday October to
April and Saturday May to
September. Reserve. Close to the
Vatican. Roman specialities served
in a comfortable atmosphere.*

Pino e Dino
Piazza di Montevecchio 22
(near Piazza Navona)
Tel. 6861319
*Noon–3 p.m. and 8–11 p.m. Closed
Monday, 1 week in August and 3
weeks in January. Reserve. 20
tables and a patio. Rich plates of
game in winter and delicate fish
dishes on Tuesday and Friday.*

Al Pompiere
Via di Santa Maria dei Calderari
  38 (near Largo Argentina)
Tel. 6868377
*12.30–3 p.m. and 7.30–11 p.m.
Closed Sunday. Reserve. Roman
cooking done with great finesse in
a tranquil and dignified spot in the
heart of a busy quarter.*

Porto di Ripetta
Via di Ripetta 250
(Corso/Piazza del Popolo)
Tel. 3612376
*1–3 p.m. and 8–11 p.m. Closed
Sundays and 15 days in August.
Reserve. Original unfussy cooking.*

Sabatini
Vicolo di Santa Maria in
  Trastevere 18 (Trastevere)
Tel. 5818307
*Noon–3 p.m. and 8–11 p.m. Closed
Tuesday and 2 weeks in August.
Reserve. Seafood and Roman
specialities.*

Sabatini
Piazza di Santa Maria in
  Trastevere 13 (Trastevere)
Tel. 582026
*Closed Wednesday and alternate 2
weeks in August to its sister
restaurant (see above). Seafood
and Roman specialities.*

Severino a Piazza Zama
Piazza Zama 5C
(east of Baths of Caracalla)
Tel. 7003901
*Noon–2.30 p.m. and 8.30–11 p.m.
Closed Sunday evening, all day
Monday and in August. Reserve.
Warm and friendly. Excellent
menu of Marches dishes.*

Taverna Giulia
Vicolo dell'Oro 23
(Corso Vittorio Emanuele/Tiber)
Tel. 6869768
*Noon–3 p.m. and 8 p.m.–midnight.
Closed Sunday and August.
Reserve. Ligurian food, much of it
green, the most famous dish being
pesto (basil sauce).*

Vecchia Roma
Piazza di Campitelli 18
(near Piazza Venezia)
Tel. 6864604
*Noon–3 p.m. and 8–11 p.m. Closed
Wednesday and 15 days in August.
Reserve. Tables on the square in
summer and cozy dining rooms in
winter, an excellent place to try a
long list of dishes based on local
ingredients, Polenta (savoury
pudding of maize or other flour)
with many sauces, salt cod stew
and game.*

Economical

Felice
Via Mastro Giorgio 29
(Testaccio)
Tel. 5746800
*12.30–2.00 p.m. and 8–9.30 p.m.
Closed Sunday and 15 days in
August. Wonderful food served in a
bustling, no-nonsense atmosphere.
The service may not be exquisite
but you will get huge portions.
There is no sign outside so take
note of the address.*

Er Filettaro Santa Barbara
Largo dei Librari 88
(near Campo dei Fiori)
Tel. 6564018
*5–10 p.m. Closed in August. Take-
away also. The king of fried salt-
cod joints. Rome's answer to fish
and chips, crisp and golden, eat on
the spot with a glass of wine.*

Da Lucia
Vicolo del Mattonato 2B
(Trastevere)
Tel. 5803601

*8 p.m.–midnight. Closed Monday
and the last two weeks in August.
Reserve at the weekend. A very
cosy family trattoria. Excellent
versions of Rome's popular cuisine.*

L'Orso 80
Via dell'Orso 33
(near Piazza Navona)
Tel. 6864904
*1–3 p.m. and 7.30–11 p.m. Closed
Monday and several weeks in
August. Reserve. Uncomplicated
meat and fish dishes cooked in the
style of the Abruzzo, a friendly
family-run restaurant.*

Al Piccolo Arancio
Vicolo di Scanderberg 112
(near Trevi Fountain)
Tel. 6786139
*12.30–3.30 p.m. and 7 p.m.
–midnight. Closed Monday and in
August. Attractive place near the
Trevi Fountain which takes food
seriously. Very good Roman food.*

Alla Rampa
Piazza Mignanelli 18
(near Piazza di Spagna)
Tel. 6782621
*Noon–3 p.m. and 6.30–11 p.m.
Closed Sunday and in August.
Good uncomplicated food, outdoor
tables, very central.*

Il Re Degli Amici
Via della Croce 33B
(Corso/Piazza di Spagna)
Tel. 6795380
*Noon–3 p.m. and 7.30–11 p.m.
Closed Monday and the last two
weeks in July. Roman cooking and
fish specials. A pleasant trattoria,
especially nice for lunch. Has been
in business since 1927.*

Scoglio di Frisio
Via Merulana 256
(near St John Lateran)
Tel. 7310205
*1–3 p.m. and 8 p.m.–midnight.
May to November, closed Sunday.
December to April. Closed
Monday. Reserve in the evening.*

La Taverna
Via del Banco di Santo Spirito 58
(Corso Vittorio Emanuele/Ponte
Sant'Angelo)
Tel. 6864116
*Noon–2.30 p.m. and 7.30–11 p.m.
Closed Monday and for several
weeks in the summer. A welcoming
trattoria. Very good value for
money.*

Trattoria Frascati
Via del Boschetto 28
(Piazza Venezia/Santa Maria
    Maggiore)
Tel. none
*Noon–3 p.m. and 8–11 p.m. Closed
Sunday and 3 weeks in August.
Roman menu with good food.
Wednesday and Friday, fish.
Thursday, gnocchi. Saturday, tripe
(trippa).*

Rooftop Dining: a View from the Terrace

Casina Valadier
Monte Pincio
(above Piazza del Popolo)
Tel. 6792083
*12.30–3 p.m. and 8–10.30 p.m.
Closed Monday, Reserve evenings
and weekends. A romantic place
with one of Rome's most splendid
views, dominated by the great
dome of St Peter's. Seafood is a
speciality. Romans come here more
for the atmosphere than for the
food.*

Les Etoiles dell'Hotel Atlante Star
Via Vitelleschi 34
(near Castel Sant'Angelo)
Tel. 6879558
*12.30–2.30 p.m. and 8–11 p.m.
Reserve. Elegant food and service.
A stunning close-up view of St
Peter's and of the city across the
Tiber is gained from the 7th-floor
terrace.*

George's
Via Marche 7 (near via Veneto)
Tel. 484575
*12.30–3 p.m. and 8–11 p.m. Closed
Sunday and in August. Reserve. An
international menu. Outdoor dining
on one of Rome's most beautiful
courtyard terraces.*

Hassler Roof Garden
Piazza della Trinità dei Monti 6
(above Piazza di Spagna)
Tel. 6792651
*12.30–2.30 p.m. and 8.30–11 p.m.
Reserve. An enclosed, air-
conditioned restaurant at the top of
the Hassler hotel with a romantic
view of the whole city. Excellent
service and food with dishes from
Veneto, Emilia-Romagna, Liguria
and Tuscany.*

La Pergola dell'Hotel Hilton
Via Cadlolo 101 (Monte Mario)
Tel. 3151
*7.30 p.m.–midnight. Closed Sunday
and the first three weeks in
January. Reserve. Classical dishes
are served by candlelight to soft
piano music and overlooking the
hills. It is one of the city's finest
restaurants.*

Ilcanto del Riso
Lungotevere dei Mellini 7
(near Pont Cavour)
Tel. 3610430
*Noon–3 p.m. and 8–11 p.m. Closed
Sunday evening and from
November to March. A barge
moored on the Tiber. First courses
are based on rice and mostly
seafood for the second course.*

Easy-going

Il Delfino
Corso Vittorio Emanuele 67
Tel. 6864053
*7.30 a.m.–9 p.m. Closed Monday
A central and convenience tavola
calda and take-away place. Pasta,
chicken, veal roast.*

Italy and Italy
Via Cola di Rienzo 204 (Prati)
Tel. 6874651
*8 a.m.–2 a.m. Closed Tuesday. A
fast food chain serving speedy
spaghetti and lasagna. Also salads.*

McDonald's
Piazza di Spagna 46
Tel. 6793382
*Also Piazza Luigi Sturzo 21 and
    Piazza della Repubblica
Daily 10 a.m. to midnight. It's
worth going to have a look at the
decor: faux marbre and mosaics
with lots of classical-looking
statuary and discreet golden arches
worked into the tiles. It was very
controversial when it opened but
Piazza di Spagna seems to have
survived more or less intact.*

Miss Italia
Via Barberini 14–16
(near Piazza Barberini)
Tel. 4826739
*Noon–1 a.m., Saturday until 2
a.m. October to April, closed
Tuesday. A cheap, easy, pleasant
place with a restaurant menu as
well as pizza and gelato.*

Pizzeria Baffetto
Via del Governo Vecchio 114
(near Piazza Navona)
Tel. 6861617
*5.30 p.m.–1.30 a.m. Closed
Monday. A student hangout since
the late 60s. The pizza is excellent.*

Pizzeria Panattoni
Viale de Trastevere 53
(Trastevere)
Tel. 5800919
*6.30 p.m.–2.30 a.m. Closed
Wednesday and 8–29 August. An
institution. The pavement tables
are always jammed. Good pizza
and other Roman fast food.*

Pizzeria Remo
Piazza di Santa Maria Liberatrice
    44 (Testaccio)
Tel. 574670
*Closed Monday. A bustling, noisy
pizzeria. Good bruschetta, pizza
and other simple fare.*

Vini e Porchetta
Via del Viminale 2
(near Termini Station)
Tel. 463031
*11 a.m.–3.30 p.m. Closed Sunday
and the last 3 weeks in August.
Perhaps the best lunch in the whole
of Rome. Crisp roast pig with an
aromatic stuffing, sliced and served
on a roll with a glass of wine.*

Late-night Places

Alla Villa Paganini
Vicolo della Fontana 28 (Salario)
Tel. 8840217
*Noon–4 p.m. and 8 p.m.–1 a.m.
Closed Sunday and 2 weeks in
August. Good steaks and pasta.
Terrace dining in a lovely park.*

Il Bistecchiere
Via dei Gigli d'Oro 3
(near Piazza Navona)
Tel. 6548104
*Open until 1 a.m. Closed Tuesday.
Chateaubriand on a splendid grill.
Fresh fish.*

Le Cabanon
Vicolo della Luce 5 (Trastevere)
Tel. 5818106
*10 p.m.–1 a.m. Closed Sunday and
1 week in August. Tunisian dishes
alternate with French. Cabaret
atmosphere with French songs from
the 30s and 40s.*

Il Carillon 19
Viale Aventino 39
(near Circus Maximus)
Tel. 576108
*Open until 2 a.m. Closed Sunday.
Italian regional specialities,
including game and a good wine
list.*

Club 56 La Zeppa
Via Basento 56 (Salario)
Tel. 8440196
*Open until 1 a.m. Closed Sunday
and in August. A creative menu
with dishes from Naples to Paris.*

Il Cortiletto
Piazza Capranica 77
(Corso/Piaza Navona)
Tel. 6793977
*Open until 1 a.m. Closed Tuesday
and August 15. Risotto, carpaccio
and many rich deserts.*

L'Eglise
Via di Monte Testaccio 40
(Testaccio)
Tel. 5743448
*Open until 3 a.m. Closed Monday.
International cuisine.*

Enoteca Spiriti
Via di Sant'Eustachio 5
(near Pantheon)
Tel. 6892499
*11 a.m.–3 p.m. and 6 p.m.–2 a.m.
Closed Sunday. Tasty appetizers
like* carbaccio *and* brushetta, *good
selection of Italian and French
wines and Spumanti.*

La Grapperia 12
Via della Lupa 17 (near Corso)
Tel. 6873604
*Open until 2 a.m. Closed Sunday.
Italian wines and 400 kinds of
grappa.*

Nel Regno di re Ferdinando
Via dei Banchi Nuovi 8
(near Piazza Navona)
Tel. 6541167
*Open until 1 a.m. Closed Sunday
and two weeks in August.
Wonderful pasta dishes, seafood
and pastries of Naples.*

L'Oca Bianca
Via di Santa Maria dell'Anima 8
(near Piazza Navona)
Tel. 6868100
*Open until 3 a.m. Closed Sunday.
Reserve.* Oca *means goose, this
restaurant's speciality. Other good
pasta and rice dishes.*

Il Piccolo 12
Via del Governo Vecchio 74
(near Piazza Navona)
Tel. 6541746
*Open until 2 a.m. Closed Tuesday.
Lively, central wine bar with a cold
buffet.*

Romolo a Porta Settimiana
Via di Porta Settimiana 8
(Trastevere)
Tel. 5818284
*Open until 1 a.m. Closed Monday
and in August. Classical and
creative pasta recipes. Terraced
garden in summer.*

Ropiè
Via di San Francesco a Ripa 104
(Trastevere)
Tel. 5800694
*Open until 1 a.m. Closed Sunday
and Monday. Italian with many
French accents. Candlelight
suppers.*

Vecchia Puglia
Via Principe Amedeo 325
(near Termini Station)
Tel. 7316919
*Open until 1 a.m. Closed Tuesday.
Outdoor tables. Food from Puglia.*

Santa Dorotea 18
Via di Santa Dorotea 9
(Trastevere)
Tel. 589530
*Open until 2 a.m. Closed Tuesday.
Champagne and* spumante, *cold
food, live music.*

Index

Bold page numbers refer to main entries.